DECOLONIZING FEMINISMS

Piya Chatterjee, *Series Editor*

DANCING TRANSNATIONAL FEMINISMS

Ananya Dance Theatre and the Art of Social Justice

EDITED BY

ANANYA CHATTERJEA

HUI NIU WILCOX

ALESSANDRA LEBEA WILLIAMS

FOREWORD BY

D. SOYINI MADISON

UNIVERSITY OF WASHINGTON PRESS
Seattle

Design by Katrina Noble
Composed in Minion Pro typeface designed by Robert Slimbach

26 25 24 23 22   5 4 3 2 1

Printed and bound in the United States of America

UNIVERSITY OF WASHINGTON PRESS
uwapress.uw.edu

LIBRARY OF CONGRESS CATALOGING-IN-PUBLICATION DATA
Names: Chatterjea, Ananya, editor. | Wilcox, Hui Niu, editor. |
    Williams, Alessandra Lebea, editor.
Title: Dancing transnational feminisms : Ananya Dance Theatre and the art of social
    justice / edited by Ananya Chatterjea, Hui Niu Wilcox, and Alessandra Lebea Williams.
Description: Seattle : University of Washington Press, 2022. | Series: Decolonizing
    feminisms | Includes bibliographical references and index.
Identifiers: LCCN 2021010546 (print) | LCCN 2021010547 (ebook) | ISBN 9780295749549
    (hardcover) | ISBN 9780295749556 (paperback) | ISBN 9780295749563 (ebook)
Subjects: LCSH: Feminism—Cross-cultural studies. | Social justice. | Art and dance. |
    Women artists. | Ananya Dance Theatre.
Classification: LCC HQ1155 .D36 2021 (print) | LCC HQ1155 (ebook) | DDC 305.42—dc23
LC record available at https://lccn.loc.gov/2021010546
LC ebook record available at https://lccn.loc.gov/2021010547

To all the artists, activists, and audiences

who have powered our dances of transformation

CONTENTS

ILLUSTRATIONS

FOREWORD

D. SOYINI MADISON

Love, justice, and beauty are our birthright and saving grace. They are three planetary and spiritual forces that manifest, for better or worse, in anything we imagine and in imagination itself. They have become the sempiternal forces that occupy my thinking, writing, and doing in this seventh decade of my life. Love, justice, and beauty are spiritually illumed, cast into motion and prayer, as both gift and call to action by Ananya Dance Theatre. This foreword is more a note of gratitude to ADT for their labor and their boundless offerings.

LOVE

Human interdependence, endurance, and desire constitute labor and love. This is embodied in the ensemble work of ADT and emerges in dance, poetry, sound, earthly interplays, and a visual feast of imagery and feminist power. A myriad of feminist stories, transnational and extraterrestrial, align in energy and sweat through the shared resonance of women belonging to each other. These women moving together depend on each other, trust each other, and in this togetherness conjure the Black spirit magic of one whole and separate parts, different bodies and the same body, and Black Indigenous women of color as a living species among other living species on this planet. ADT creates dialectics of storytelling that ignite alterity, dreams, and planetary stewardship. As the dance makers pay homage to the poetics of Black spirit magic, Audre Lorde's biomythography resonates in the ethnographic narrations of their dancing bodies and homeplace worlds. It is in these narrative moments that we see Ananya's footwork teaching as it rises up through Black and brown feminist heritages and everyday, local motions to remember the personal is political and the political is personal.

This carving of time and space is done through the organizing of love. I must be careful. I don't want to overdetermine love, turning it into a cliché or making it too precious. In this instance, I mean love as labor—realizing I just recalled the classic phrase "labor of love." What I mean to say is that ADT was founded and remains grounded in deep affection, intense concern, abiding care, and abundant gratitude for living beings—this living planet and its species. This is a sacred love that ADT puts into action. This action is hard labor, and it materializes into organizing the dance, the dancers, and their visions to build an institution and a praxis of transnational feminist performance in the service of global activism. ADT's method of organizing— that is, labors of love—is gorgeously illuminated through the deep, felt-sensing relationships the women have for one another as transnational women whose nation-states and homeplace worlds may be at distances far away from each other as they share the sweat, mission, and movement with such profound intimacy and connection. ADT makes war dances, intimate, relentless, with daring love, for decolonizing performance. Their footwork literally pushes past fire, walks on water, and catches the air like those time-less freedom fighters and art workers who called up death, named the guilty, and refused insipid peace empty of justice. All in the name of love. In one turn of the story, ADT foregrounds warrior women dancers hitting the floor with a loud and precise, unruly vengeance. In another story, place and time, the dancers are birds turning weightless through air, flying through the interstices of local and global flash points of hope and victories won. They dance multiple histories of recuperation, defeat, the senses and sensation accompanied by acts of hope grounded in love.

JUSTICE

One of ADT's many contributions is how the dancers both generate and embody what has been a fundamental principle of collective action since the beginning of time: organizing. ADT is a poetics of organizing. It is the power and intelligence of effective organizing that is foundational to making our hopes and dreams a reality. The alchemy of ADT's organizing is a triple layer-ing of organizational strategy: institution building that has grown and sus-tained for years as a company doing the business of social justice art and transnational performance; as innovative philosophers conceptualizing uncharted dialectics and discursive formations of decolonization, global justice, and feminist praxis; and as skilled movement artists committed to craft, technique, and improvisation that is outside, inside, and sideways to conventional modernist forms. Their art-making shows and tells us how dance making can be what is needed in the world in this very moment when we are witness to its rapture. Isn't this how art is supposed to make us feel? ADT carves out particular spaces and times armored with heart, mind, soul, and skill to gift us with temporal fragments of where we've never been before, deeper and differently. Conscious and/or dreaming.

Because ADT's labor of love is always and already global, and because the dancers are global and come from global places, ethnonationality, as a hermetically sealed group, is displaced by the biopolitics and transnational interventions generated by Black, Indigenous, and people of color. In an important essay by Zenzele Isoke with Naimah Petigny, titled "Dancing Black Militancies," the writers "envision Blackness as something that moves in, through, and across bodies and cultures, dancing its way through time/space and history in unpredictable yet unmistakably decipherable and familiar ways" (106). Reaching inside Blackness in its deepest reverberations and political histories requires not only an understanding of Blackness based on genotype or phenotypic appearance and African-descended people but, most importantly, defending Black spaces, defying Black death, propagating Black resilience, and having profound, consequential relationships with Blackened people. Blackness moves through phenotypically different bodies. The essay beautifully describes ADT's embodiment or *bodyspeak* as Blackness moves through the transnational and multicultural "Blackened" bodies of dancers performing networks and ecologies of Blackness. Black people are not a majority population everywhere, "but Black presences can be found in their circuits" (111). This is the brilliance and radical hope of ADT's feminist politics and ethics: the invention and spread of these circuits. And there is something more: Blackness is grounded in its original call and cry in the bodies of Black women. Therefore, it would follow that when, how, and who performs that call or cry remain open and contingent. As ADT performs diverse imaginaries of Blackness in its multiple forms with multiple bodies, it the black-skinned dancer who will most certainly take the lead. ADT is daring and bold in the intelligence and strategy of the both/and. Phenotype is unitary and multiple; ethnonationalism is both particular and universal. The intelligence and courage of an ADT performance is to witness how justice frames and determines a choice, must take a stand and honor the ethics and reality contingencies.

This book carries the reader into these contingencies and frames of justice as ADT travels the world to international festivals, thereby entering a panoply of performance spaces from opposite sides of global struggles: to grassland fields of water and rock to urban memorials of broken concrete and train track wreckage. We, as readers, are traveling with them because the writing is

honest, true, and poignant. We enter complexities of the everyday as international, quotidian moments because the dancer-ethnographer-writer unpacks
the undergirding profundity of political resonances that cross the map. As
somatic workers, ADT gathers the collective story, language, memory, and
sensation that transcend national and continental demarcations placed on
maps and land crossings. It is not that these demarcations become disap-
peared or ignored; instead ADT performs history and documents the present
and gifts the audiences with pieces of the world in both its particularities and
its shared resonances. Something is now differently realized about human
suffering and hope, the natural world, and my place inside or outside of it that
now, having seen this dance today, matters. What now and what more?

There is an inspiring conversation between Ananya and Thomas F.
DeFrantz where DeFrantz questions the material difference that dance can
make and the notion of its liberatory practice. It is a reminder that audiences
are echo chambers, and a magnificent performance can be the call that
enables the echo to resonate beyond the performance space into hearts and
minds beyond its reach—echoing the wonder and force of the artist's intentions for those who were not there. The performance becomes the grand possibility of enlivening activists from its audience members. Audience members
as witnesses become potential activists as they are now moved to spread the
performative vision. ADT's world-making is in the performances that spread
a truth and break open what we—as audience-witnesses—carry with us to
where we go, what more we can say and do, about a just world. Freedom and
justice sink deep with overbearing complexity in the new and ancient particularity of each instance. This is what ADT carves out and cracks open with the
prayer and possibility that audience-witnesses will begin to make that material difference, beyond the dance floor, and it will carry forth to make a ripple
or a riot for the good of all. This is the difference that difference makes.

BEAUTY

> Beauty awakens the soul to act.
>
> —DANTE ALIGHIERI

The artistry of transforming the demand for social justice into metaphor,
symbol, and embodied practice is the work of manifesting how "beauty
awakens the soul to act."

Much has been written about beauty: beauty as it calls and compels our
attention and focus, not wanting to look away or attend to anything but the

beautiful thing before us; beauty as it inspires us to replicate and interpret its elements, make something anew, or imagine something differently; beauty as it exceeds pain, not as disappearance or distraction but as more intensely felt, beauty as an invocation of goodness. This is the beauty ADT sets loose in the world with purposeful action and in the service of virtuous retribution. Beauty thrives in the dance, the dancers, their politics and vision. This labor of love that organizes and brings forth such beauty, without pause or exception, consistently captivates us toward feelings of pleasure now set loose beyond contemplation but more like marching orders. It has been said that only through affect can art be understood. ADT is among those artists who show us that it is only through affect that justice is truly felt and thereby understood beyond cognition. We interpret affect to be constituted by emotion, the senses, embodied responses, and connection. The affect that beauty invokes is inextricable from connection, and this is true for all living things on earth. As beauty, affect, and connection are reciprocally linked, generating life and pleasure, ADT shows us how this life and pleasure are profoundly shared, collaboratively made, and collectively experienced. We are witness and audience to the intimate politics of connection and sharing through narration, a feast of visual and cinematic design and the resplendence of textual brilliance. We are also experiencing the affects that beauty unleashes by attending to the ways these feelings and sensations honor embodied ways of engaging worlds of experience that sometimes exceed meaning, reason, and language. This is the power of felt sensory presence and the ways the body speaks through the mastery of beauty making as well as the hope for the good it produces. Beauty makes this hope for the good stick and become infectious; it is the alternative and antidote for complicity in the face of injustice

Beauty, in this instance, is not about glamour, nice-looking surfaces, or visually pleasing appearances. ADT shows us that it is about arresting the power of attention and emotion to unleash profound truths and radical goodness that must be brought to light, however ugly or troubling the path to that light may be. Watching the pain of humans gasping for breath or their life in a sealed glass box is not beautiful, yet it is beautifully symbolic and rendered in its truth and implications. The pleasure that beauty brings, even if the performance unleashes a disturbing beauty, invokes the generative pleasure of collaborative creation. ADT demonstrates throughout the pages of this book that the affect of being with, in relationship alongside, and in creative alliance for a purposeful act is a labor of love and a beautiful thing to behold.

ACKNOWLEDGMENTS

We offer our salutations to our Native sisters, Janice BadMoccasin and Sharon Day, whose vision and organizing have been vital guiding stars for our work over the years. Thanks also to inspiring BIPOC leaders in the Twin Cities community, whose work has often galvanized our artistic processes.

This anthology is inspired by the aesthetic and organizing labor of the many generations of artists who have danced these choreographies. To all of them, the artists who have been part of Ananya Dance Theatre in some way, our gratitude and appreciation. We are especially indebted to the founding members of ADT, who laid a solid foundation for our collective journey, and our current artist leaders, Kealoha Ferreira and Alexandra Eady, for their ongoing work in teaching Yorchhā to next generations of dancers through the Shawngrām Institute for Performance and Social Justice.

We thank our collaborating artists, whose brilliance has been crucial in the ways our artistry came to be chiseled. In particular, we hold up Laurie Carlos, who identified the choreographic process as being akin to the jazz aesthetic in which she was working. We are forever grateful for this legacy of her vision in our process, which is now being developed in a related yet different way through our work with Sharon Bridgforth.

We also hold up the foundational partnership with Dipankar Mukherjee, who directed our first work and established a strong base for our ensemble practice, and Meena Natarajan, whose role in helping us learn about organization-building has been invaluable.

Darren Johnson's brilliant filmic vision has lent a multimedia lens on our work, and resulted in beautiful recordings of all of ADT's productions, which grounded our theoretical reflections on our past dancing and choreographies. Thank you!

We also thank Marcus Young, whose directorial collaboration has been particularly important in shaping our Daak, the call to audiences to participate in our work.

Special thanks to Gary Peterson, who has been at the helm of the company, steering us through rough waters at times and navigating us toward an expansive vision. Thank you, Gary, also for your indispensable advice on the legalities in this manuscript.

We thank the many treasured community members who have served on the board of directors of the company, enabling us to work through the complications of a nonprofit structure and still remain accountable to our communities. And special thanks to our board president, Gina Kundan, formerly a founding artist of the company.

Our gratitude goes to Larin R. McLaughlin and Piya Chatterjee for their faith in the importance of our work and patient and insightful guidance as we shaped this anthology.

Special thanks to D. Soyini Madison for her detailed attention to each of our essays and her distinguished labor in forewording the collection.

We thank our teachers: those who taught us to dance and write with power and reminded us of the urgency of our own histories.

We are thankful for our audiences, who have been unwaveringly committed to witnessing the embodiment of Yorchhā and Black and brown women and femme stories in their live and screenic, performative form.

Finally, we owe deep gratitude to our families, who have supported us through our years of dancing, writing, and organizing.

DANCING TRANSNATIONAL FEMINISMS

DANCING AND WRITING TOGETHER

Feminist Embodiments, Transnational Solidarities

ANANYA CHATTERJEA, HUI NIU WILCOX,
AND ALESSANDRA LEBEA WILLIAMS

> Watching Ananya Dance Theater [*sic*] is like reading Sara Ahmed.
> You understand, feel, and remember that which made you feel
> fragility. But you know it was really endless assault. You remember
> and feel that moment of dissent, refusal. And ADT reminds you
> that it was never you alone. That self-care is not health and well-
> being purchased through neoliberal consumerism, but forged in
> intentional "squadcare," intimacies, breath, and bodies in dyads,
> triads, and those moments where we gather and reconnect across the
> space-time of capitalism.
>
> —JIGNA DESAI, FACEBOOK POST, SEPTEMBER 17, 2017

DANCING TRANSNATIONAL FEMINISMS ENTANGLES REFLECTIONS ON,
responses to, and critical analyses of the embodied creative practices that
have been part of the work of Ananya Dance Theatre (ADT) for over fifteen
years. ADT is a Twin Cities–based professional dance company of Black,
Indigenous, and women and femmes of color who work at the intersection
of artistic excellence and social justice.[1] We engage in the scholarly and
creative research that bolsters our artistic practices through the lens of radical, transnational feminisms with a focus on critiquing the dynamics that
overdetermine the dance field, such as global capitalism, white supremacist paradigms, and heteronormative patriarchies. We began envisioning
this anthology to mark the tenth anniversary of Ananya Dance Theatre's
mission to make "people powered dances of transformation." As in our
creative process and performance, our desire is to build alliances across

communities of color, raise awareness about the global issues that affect the lives of Black and brown women and femmes, invoke questions about the ways in which embodied artistic practice can make vital interventions in a neoliberal, and often hostile, cultural environment. We are also committed to carving spaces for audience responses that remind us about the dialectical work of meaning-making in and through dance and choreography.

Through documenting and reflecting on Ananya Dance Theatre's creative processes and organizational strategies, and through engaging with varied disciplinary and theoretical perspectives on ADT's work, this book aims to demonstrate how Black and brown women and femme artists, working with a marginalized movement aesthetic, claim the space of contemporary concert dance and transform it into a site of empowerment, resistance, and knowledge production. Through our own multilensed perspective—as artists within the work, as organizers within and outside the company, and as scholars—we study the ways in which the work circulates through spaces and communities. Specifically, we address the three core areas that are interwoven in our framework and practice: transnational feminisms refracted through frames of indigeneity and diaspora; intersectional analysis of power relations and the precarious exigencies of artistic survival; and our particular embodiments of intertwining aesthetic excellence, social justice, and solidarity.

Our processes of writing and editing have invited reflections on our practice: How can concert dance be reclaimed and transformed into a space of progressive politics/resistance and knowledge making? How can dance-making speak back to nation and systemic power and illuminate histories of migration? How does ADT remold dimensions of diaspora through its attention to queer and nonbinary bodies? What does it mean to do social justice work through a radical, transnational feminist lens in the context of contemporary dance? What is the significance of ensemble work as practice, as a metaphor for feminist collaboration, and as a methodology of solidarity? How does ADT's insistence on naming its practice "contemporary dance" rub up against the dichotomies between contemporaneity and tradition, globality and locality, and how does that descriptor chafe against claims of ethnonationalist belonging? We hope these questions resonate with scholars of many fields because many aspects of these questions go beyond the space of this anthology.

This book is grounded in more than fifteen years of shared practice and sustained intellectual dialogues, both within the company and between ADT and audiences around the world. We have intentionally designed this book as a confluence, a multivocal, multigenre volume, more accurately reflecting our artistic labor, which integrates academic research, poetic and metaphoric articulations, creative collaborations, and community-building practices. Through this structure, and by invigorating a dialectic between discourse and practice, we hope to highlight how dance-making and creative processes, imagined intersectionally, can generate new knowledges and shift perspectives in multiple fields beyond dance studies, such as performance studies; women, gender, and sexuality studies; critical race and ethnicity studies; cultural studies; and critical ethnography. Moreover, our choreographic methodology, emerging from investigations of our bodily histories and remappings, locates our work squarely in diverse fields, in epistemological questions about how we come to know the world through cellular and kinesthetic resonance. This theorization of embodied epistemologies makes crucial contributions to disciplines that center marginalized subjectivities.

In this, our project is aligned with dance studies scholar Brenda Dixon-Gottschild, whose seminal work uncovers the historic Africanist presences within American concert dance and wrestles with racial, sexist, and classist hierarchies that vitiate mainstream dance.[2] Although we share the conceptual frameworks about decolonizing dance exemplified in the anthology *Worlding Dance*, we specifically route our theorizing of the complex global circulation of dance in our embodied, creative practice of dance-making and world-making.[3] We are building on the scholarship about Black and brown women artists in contemporary choreography through an intersectional framework and through the prism of resistance and radical postcolonial aesthetics that undergirds *Butting Out: Reading Resistive Choreographies through Works by Jawole Willa Jo Zollar and Chandralekha*.[4] Our book also amplifies the theorization of alternative contemporaneities in the work of artists from resonant global South, diasporic, Black, Indigenous, and people of color (BIPOC) communities in *Heat and Alterity in Contemporary Dance: South-South Choreographies*.[5] Simultaneously, in our movement foundation, we bring forth a model of intralocalness—that is, a mosaic of overlapping tension and asymmetrical alliances—that allows us to think particularly about practices of "worlding" in dance studies. This enables us to push past inherited notions of "purity of line" and facile categories of "otherness" within official multiculturalisms while emphasizing aesthetic specificity and shared understandings of artistry. Our anthology offers a different perspective on contemporary dance in a global context through a multivocal approach with theoretical essays and reflections from scholars, artistic collaborators, and community activists to illustrate the social and political impact of contemporary dance theater.

This anthology stands on the shoulders of powerful dialogues in the field of women, gender, and sexuality studies, such as feminist scholar Chandra Talpade Mohanty's 1984 groundbreaking essay "Under Western Eyes."[6] We analyze our performance of and subjection to different kinds of "gaze": How are we looked at in different spaces? How can we look back at audiences, refusing to be contained by expectations of exotica and fear? How can we refract the white gaze, which holds us all as undifferentiated "Others" while simultaneously constructing a space where we can participate in each other's histories and recognize our mutual implication in hierarchical systems? Can we think of such intentional entanglements as a central practice of transnationality? We came to understand gendered violence through the global circulation of consumer goods and services so we can grapple with what women are enduring and resisting, particularly from impoverished and working-class communities across the globe. As we make dances about the work women and femmes do, we repeatedly remind our audiences that marginalized communities can and do challenge the inequitable ways in which multinational corporations are destroying ecosystems and livelihoods. In keeping with Mohanty's classic work *Feminism without Borders*, our choreographed juxtaposition of disparate story fragments stages a resistance to corporate globalism that elides the violences of neoliberalism.[7] Dancing overlapping and interstitial local and global stories allows us to recognize the resonances of our experiences with women and femmes who might be, in terms of geopolitical locations, far from us.

As we claim space and rhythm cycles to articulate our rage at the inequities that mark our histories, we are inspired by women and femmes' relentless struggles in multiple communities to search for poetry and spirit in the midst of resistance. In *Pedagogies of Crossing: Meditations on Feminism, Sexual Politics, Memory, and the Sacred*, M. Jacqui Alexander urges readers to develop a practical consciousness about how histories of colonization subjugate queer women of color and how supposedly democratic traditions of nation-states are firmly embedded in notions of heteronormativity.[8] We are inspired by Alexander's notion of crossing as metaphor as much as material practice: she reminds us that dismantling ideologies of empire must simultaneously work through collective self-determination and the spiritual labor of reimagining home and community. Aligning with Alexander's ideas, we ground our artistic and intellectual work in our understanding of how the exploitation of multiple communities of women and femmes is integral to the flourishing of global capital. And we resonate with Alexander's foregrounding of spiritual labor in transnational feminisms as we choose to engage dance as an embodied spiritual practice that critiques neoliberalism while reaching toward hope and healing.

With our essay "So Much to Remind Us We Are Dancing on Other People's Blood," we began a process of writing that paralleled our collective embodied work: four of the artists from Ananya Dance Theatre—Chatterjea and Wilcox with gender and sexuality studies scholar Omise'eke Natasha Tinsley, and literature and creative writing scholar Shannon Gibney—responded to an invitation from a group of scholars who came together to think through collaborative transnational feminism, recognizing that the three terms that constitute this formation live in contestation.[9] Our cowritten essay responded to this complexity from the embodied experiences that we brought together: "What does it mean to collaborate in physical and visceral ways, not sharing space in terms of discrete chapters of a book, but dancing on a floor drenched with all of our sweat, articulating shared rhythms, if with different accents. Our writing has followed that model/experience of working together in movement and performing, interwoven thoughts and ideas, moving together even as our feet rise and fall individually."[10] This model of moving together differently, articulating particular histories in community, has been the epistemological model of our dancing and thinking together.

We respirited and deepened that model of writing together as we dreamed up this anthology. The three of us met up outside of rehearsals and classes, worked through ideas and wrote simultaneously on shared documents, discussed the project with different generations of dancers and collaborators and invited their responses to the process, communicated with thinkers with whom we have connected over the years to request contributions, and interwove perspectives from our writing, dancing, and organizing experiences. All of these have been part of the cocreative and cotheorizing process. And while the collectivity-in-discursivity has made for the intersection—sometimes resonant, sometimes clashing—of different stories, histories, memories, and analyses, it has asked for the resources of time, listening, and patience. With no material resources and the complex demands that came with the expansion of the company's work, we were unable to meet our goal of publishing the project for ADT's tenth anniversary. Perhaps a collaborative, transnational, feminist process must take the time it needs: We truly understand the labor of such work and the value of strategies that keep us grounded and nimble.

Dancing Transnational Feminisms is dialogically engaged with the field of critical ethnography. We take to heart the work of D. Soyini Madison, who cautions that actual engagement with the lives of subjects in performance can only be achieved with responsible representation, a process transferred through the performer's body to audience imaginations, creating pathways for transformation.[11] Therefore, when dealing with experiences and voices different from ours, we must work mindfully, directed by a politics of remaking the linkages between self and other. We hold up Madison's argument that we redirect how such binaries are typically deployed when we enact "subversive stylized acts inherited by contested identities," that is, when we articulate actions that disrupt the repetition of hegemonic formations that would keep us compartmentalized.[12]

Our work is in conversation with theorists who investigate their own embodied practices in order to analyze, interpret, and document multivalent cultural experiences. As such, it is aligned with dance ethnographers such as Marta E. Savigliano and Cindy Garcia, whose scholarship has reimagined the participant-observer model through the lens of race, class, and gender.[13] This book expands such work by suggesting that dance making itself can be an ethnographic practice, revealing cultural formations, documenting women and femmes' work, and offering nuanced, material representations of the different ways in which they respond to and are affected by social issues.

Our dancerly ethnographic work, which manifests as story-ing practices in our creative process, is in the nature of Audre Lorde's biomythographies.[14] Here, stories of women and femmes' lives and work, both of which have slipped through the cracks of history, are refracted and interwoven through embodied practices. The body becomes the site of weaving together research, memory, and imagination to invoke and create new collective memories and stories. This is an intentional project of interdisciplinary cotheorizing, of interweaving our different writing rhythms, academic trainings, and schedules on the page, in the service of our shared ideas and politics. It mirrors the way in which our artistic practice privileges individuality-in-collectivity. This practice of story-ing, where the tensions and resonances between multiple stories reveal an emotional map of the physical choreography and trace connections, puts us in conversation with various communities and in alignment with our commitment to decolonized knowledge production. Moreover, because these stories are not compartmentalized, and because they catalyze each other through our conversations and dancing, they create complex discursive lines (figure 1.1).

FIGURE I.1. Alexandra Eady as Byengomi / Mythical Bird and Kealoha Ferreira as Ua / Rain-Spiritwoman in *Sutrajāl: Revelations of Gossamer* (2019). A great example of mythographic imagination and femme intimacy at work in Ananya Dance Theatre's choreography. Photo by Paul Virtucio. Courtesy of Ananya Dance Theatre.

Dancing Transnational Feminisms also invites scholars in performance studies to further investigate cultural archives that come to live within performing bodies. Diana Taylor's *The Archive and the Repertoire: Performing Cultural Memory in the Americas* demonstrates how performance work by some Latin American artists functions as a system of knowledge that activates and documents history.[15] Our anthology expands Taylor's premise as we claim performance as a mode of historical documentation but also of historical world-making, as we carve shared space, labor, and rhythm and balance histories of alliance-building among women and femmes from diverse Black and brown communities working through differences of sexuality, class, faith, profession, and age. Through this book, we welcome readers to reconsider dance as a way to create alternative cultural formations, deliberately not uniform in terms of social categories that govern checklisted understandings of identity. We invite contemplations on how performance becomes a way to embed these formations in the lives and memories of our communities.

Through our work, we came to understand transnational feminism as a disruption of traditional constructions of nation-states. Our connections across different communities are not accessed through individualized, self-willed mobility and visa-policed border crossings. Rather, they are grounded in partnerships with Indigenous peoples and made possible by conditions of diaspora and recognition of the violence of forced dislocation, immigration, and refugeeism. Our deep support of Indigenous sovereignty in the United States was forged through the relationships we built with local Dakota and Ojibwe leaders and organizations. Our practice begins and ends with a *pranām*, a salutation to the ground on which we dance, a tradition learned from Indian dance practices that are at the root of our training. In our reimagination of the traditional *pranām*, we layer it with our dedication to Minnesota as Native land, and particularly as Dakota land: Mni Sota Makoce. This daily practice inspired our dancing in productions such as *Daak: Call to Action* (2008). In the section "Finding Our Feet," for instance, lit from our knees down, our relationships with Native leaders softened our footfall, made our feet intentional about touching the floor, and led us to recognize the aliveness of the ground that supported our balance. This piece coincided with the sesquicentennial celebration of the founding of the state of Minnesota, which depended on the banishing of the Dakota peoples from their ancestral land. Our creative process, punctuated with collaborations with community organizers, aligned us in solidarity with Native leaders working toward acknowledgment and reparations.

Our relationship with Native communities has deepened over the years. We have partnered with Dream of Wild Health, a Native organic farm, in creating a piece about women and femmes' work with seeds (*Roktim: Nurture Incarnadine*, 2015). On the invitation of our longtime friend and collaborator Janice BadMoccasin, we have participated in the Dakota Commemorative March in 2014 to remember the history of the forced walk of Native communities to Fort Snelling. On her invitation, we have danced in 2016 on the grounds of the Standing Rock Sioux Reservation in support of the water protectors. All of these embodied experiences show up in our work through the details of choreographic and design decisions, larger strategies of community engagement, and the way we thematize the repertoire. Through our commitment to decolonizing dance, knowledge, and research, we position ourselves in dialogue with scholars of Indigenous studies such as Linda Tuhiwai Smith.[16] The life force of our Black- and brown-women-centered dance is vitalized through this alliance with Indigenous activism in our performance research and the epistemological and political dimensions of decolonization.

Concomitantly, we dance our solidarity through complex rhythmic and imagistic realizations, and we arrive at choreographic arcs that were never linear but always making visible the fault lines, even through an evening-length dance piece. For instance, in creating *Pipaashaa: Extreme Thirst* (2007), which inaugurated our trilogy on environmental justice, we juxtaposed many noncontiguous stories: Côte d'Ivoirian women devastated by the loss of their children to the toxic sludge dumped in Abidjan in 2006 by Trafigura, a transnational oil and commodity shipping company; working-class women in the "arsenic triangle" area of Minneapolis, specifically in the Phillips neighborhood, home to many low-income, Indigenous, Black and brown communities forced to endure high levels of toxins in the soil, as discovered by the investigations in 2001; and the outrage following the leaked 1991 World Bank memo on trade liberalization that advocated dumping industrial waste in global South countries for economic benefits.

Our transnational feminisms have also insisted that we balance the representation of devastation and oppression with the courage of resistance movements across the world and their repeated material invocations of hope. For instance, in creating *Mohona: Estuaries of Desire* (2013), the culminating piece in a quartet of works exploring women and femmes' struggles against systemic violence, we juxtaposed many stories about their work with water, cultural imaginations of this vital resource as goddess figures, and the desecration of women and femmes' livelihoods by monopolizing potable water sources in global South villages by the multinational bottled-water industry. Moreover, dancing *Mohona* supported our realization that gender oppression is immediately environmental violence because the concerns of Black and brown women and femmes about safety, survival, and joy are connected to their ability to access and nurture an ecosystem that has supported life for millennia.

In this way, the choreography then becomes a strategy of making adjacent stories that are connected not along linear narratives of causality but through thematic resonance, understood prismatically. This principle of thickening energy to amplify an investigation, juxtaposing different perspectives on it, is our choreographic mode of "Shawngrām," a Bengali word that means struggle and resistance. Shawngrām suggests that our dancing of story is about the crossing of differently lensed experiences that do not constitute one single story chain but rather connect rhizomatically, yearning toward and pulling away from each other, producing tension and coagulation. This dialectic then ignites the energy that ultimately propels change. Shawngrām's mode of visibilizing multiplicities becomes another way of shaping transnational feminist solidarities with nuance and an embodied ethics that is both granular and gritty.

An example of this might be how different grassroots revolutions against petroleum corporations inspire different sections in *Moreechika: Season of Mirage* (2012), simultaneously heightening the differences and coalescences among these histories. A floor section of flow and breath was inspired by the concept held by the U'wa people of Colombia that oil is *ruiria*, the blood of the earth, and must be left as found. This moves kaleidoscopically into another section inspired by the women of the Ecuadorian Kichwa community running through forests shouting "Anchuri!" (Get out!) as they protested against corporate oil drilling on their lands in 2003. Here, we danced with fast footwork, runs, quickly shifting configurations of bodies, and martial kicks and jumps. Dancing came to be a practice of critically understanding and participating in the world.

In building solidarity and connection with indigenous politics, we also grapple with our identity as diasporic Black, Indigenous, and artists of color. Such dance-making necessitates that we recognize the ways in which nation and diaspora are constituted through particular directional flows, always underscoring the legibility of belonging bestowed by state-sponsored citizenship. Our choreographic process asks that we then trace our transnational connections with complexity, such that relationships among different communities are woven not simply through linear narratives. In this mode of working, home is not coterminous with policed state borders, and location and identity must be imagined outside of the constrictive notions of nationalist identity politics. Rhizomatic, diasporic relationing asks that we connect our struggles with those of our sisters and relatives elsewhere, even as we recognize the different valences of these movements. It demands that we spark multiplicity and kineticness of consciousness, so we are able to imagine the consequences of actions here, there, and beyond the immediate context. In so doing, we aim not to resolve the tensions among different sites of knowing and experiencing but to grapple with the contestations.

Diaspora then need not immediately suggest dispersal from a point of origin, the "homeland," but can be about multinodal community building and renarrativizations of histories. Following the framework of diasporic studies scholars such as Vijay Agnew, we trace the intersectional layers of gender, culture, and embodiment to reconstruct understandings of diaspora as "deterritorialized or constructed across borders and boundaries of phenomena such as race, ethnicity, nationality, and citizenship."[17] This allows us to imagine dancing as embodying the potential to express histories of living between and across the lines of geography and social structures rather than within the very limited dimensions of nation, racial origins, and territory. Like Caribbean anthropologist Tina Ramnarine, who connects W. E. B. Du Bois's "double consciousness" with contemporary theorizing of multiple subjectivities that underscore process, practice, and experience, we go against the grain of nationalist ideologies and political terrains as we outline the particular positionalities of performative bodies.[18] Ramnarine reminds us that instead of theorizing diaspora only, or even primarily, in terms of "dispossession, disconnection, fragmentation, or fracture," we might think of diasporic spaces as creating opportunities for rehearsing multiple iterations of subjectivity.[19] Such plural lines of identity, belonging, and connection cross and influence each other in a politics of solidarity that is centered in our work and embodied crucially in the ensemble sections.

Moreover, our investment in the stories of Black and brown women and femmes as a radical and progressive politics becomes the groundwork for shifting ideas about nationalism, belonging, and identities. We see this not as a preexisting aspect of ourselves that we carry and bring into our shared space but as a process of becoming through working and dancing together; it is an ever-changing, spacious, and porous home that we have created in relation to each other and to the work we do. It is a precarious home that requires constant negotiating, improvising, and choreographing. The mixing of our bodily fluids—literally our sweat, blood, and tears—in dancing spaces continues to teach us something critical about the malleability of social categories, especially as artists of multiple diasporic experiences. Our home base in Twin Cities, Mni Sota Makoce, has always been a complex one. We locate our work in relation to local struggles such as the 2020 Uprising sparked by the murder of George Floyd, the devaluation of Black lives, and the crisis of affordable housing. Simultaneously we forge connections, through our artists, collaborators, and creative process, to many geographical, political, and social movements around the globe. Over the past fifteen years, artists' own histories have been rooted in India, China, Ethiopia, Kenya, Liberia, Mexico, Caribbean, Japan, Vietnam, Palestine, Laos, the United States, and the Pacific Islands.

Through the years, certain modalities of maneuvering our home and identities on shifting grounds have come to be more explicitly named and aligned with the company's working philosophy. One of the major sites of this might be how we came to the current alignment of our work with Black and brown queer politics. And while femme intimacy has always been part of the choreographic practice since *Bandh: Meditation on Dream* (2005), queerness as a crucial choreographic mode has come to be named and centered in our work. In part, this happened as a response to social and political realities of intensifying violence against Black and brown queer and trans communities. It was also an acknowledgment that our audiences did not always comprehend the place of sexualities within the spectrum of resistive practices. Thus, no matter how much femme intimacy was staged within the choreography, audiences and critics prioritized what they considered to be "serious" issues over articulations of desire. Our dances have repeatedly emphasized our conviction that our sexual politics were part of the continuum of revolution. For instance, Hui Wilcox and Ananya Chatterjea came together in long kisses in *Neel: Blutopias of Radical Dreaming* (2014); Leila Awadallah and Renée Copeland held sensual embraces in a love duet in *Shyamali: Sprouting Words* (2017); and Orlando Zane Hunter and Toan Thanh Doan danced passionate yearning in *Sutrajal: Revelations of Gossamer* (2019). This forced audiences to reckon with the claiming of queer politics as central to our practice of love and diasporic connection.

Our concomitant commitment to Black and brown women, femme, and queer frameworks also leads us to nonessential understandings of femininity. We lay claim to our platform as a BIPOC woman and femme company that engages in experiences of gender and sexuality without reiterating the social and political limitations associated with cisgender bodies. Dancers presenting as men but prioritizing femininity in their daily interactions and sexualities have often been part of the company. Ananya Dance Theatre has been a very rare space for queer masculine bodies to critically explore femininity that intersects with questions of race, ethnicity, class, caste, and nation. Orlando Zane Hunter's dancing of "Plastic Desire" in *Moreechika: Season of Mirage*, where Hunter manipulated a long sari made of black plastic on stage, created space both to deconstruct the "sari," intersect Black and brown cultural lineages, and critique the dominance of oil-based plastic production globally.

Our project is persistently transnational and resistive to formations of feminisms that circulate within and leave intact structures of whiteness, heteronormativity, cisgender, and Brahminical patriarchy. For us, decolonizing feminisms through dance has meant working with and through difference, via our understanding of feminist praxis and our engagement with embodied, collaborative modes of inquiry. It has meant challenging the old, yet ubiquitous, Cartesian body-mind binary and foregrounding artistic labor and embodied theorizing and learnings. Decolonizing has also meant constant negotiation and reflection on ideas of ensemble, community, social justice, resources, engagement, access, and dialogues about traditional versus contemporary dance, and social versus stage choreographies. Ananya Dance Theatre is the ground on which we have explored unlikely and uncanny confluences across these categories and have come to value the interstitial spaces between formations that are otherwise held as distinct, sometimes even oppositional. And we have come to recognize that these ideas and our attempts to materialize them in dance shape and reshape our work and how we imagine our community. Through this book, we attempt to share this praxis: the dialectical and indistinguishable processes of dancing, theorizing, dreaming, and organizing.

ADT's creative process reminds us that dance is a rare form of work that offers the possibility of freedom from alienating the process and products of labor. Reanimating and practicing feminisms as inflected through the prism of race, class, caste, sexuality, and accumulation of capital in our work have led us to articulate images of femininity, empowerment, and history in very particular and nuanced ways. As we share these images with broad and diverse publics during performances, we intersect and often collide sharply with civic debates on these issues. Because we make dance about politics that haunt our daily lives and, often, the experiences of the various communities who follow our work, the public space of performance becomes a vital forum of exchange and interface with diverse audiences.

As we tour and perform our work, we often find ourselves enmeshed in ripples of current conversations about nation and demographics, which often devolve into particular questions of representation: "What does an American company look like?" or "What's American about this work?" The insistent transnationalism in our ensemble pieces sometimes disrupts audiences' fixed notions of identity. "You are Chinese. Why are you doing Indian dance?" We try to work such questions to our advantage, instigating dialogues with different audiences about the trap of ethnonational belonging, while encouraging conversations about cultural specificity and mainstream appropriations. At other times, we recognize that in a context shaped by old legacies of multiculturalism, the cross-racial solidarities woven into the choreographic fabric of our lives slip us into a zone of invisibility. Our lived complexities and shifting formations of diaspora and hybridity lead us to actively contest the discrete, water-tight, racial, ethnic, gendered, sexual, and national groupings that we have inherited.

Importantly, as grassroots movements like Black Lives Matter, Missing and Murdered Indigenous Relatives, and Me Too swell and deliberately use embodied strategies such as "die-ins" to highlight their protest, our commitment to corporeal and performative articulations of resistance is further chiseled. Hearing Eric Garner's, and then again, George Floyd's, repeated plea "I can't breathe, I can't breathe, I can't breathe" has only heightened our intentional use of breath. We understand more than ever that the stakes in dancing for life and survival are high. We are even more dedicated to our philosophy of "people powered dances of transformation," where the transformation emerges from the repeated recommitment to hope, to the material and energetic conjuring of more just, compassionate, and joyous tomorrows.

This anthology is organized into five sections thematized broadly. Each section includes critical analyses, creative writings, and reflection narratives. The first section, *Multiple Identities: Shared Dreams of Collective Dancing*, looks back at our work from an internal perspective and reflects on the history of the company. The chapters here reinvigorate some of the questions that fueled our initial formations and practices and the emergence of ensemble dancing by a diverse group of Black and brown women and femmes.

A central tenet of Ananya Dance Theatre's work is to build coalitions among BIPOC communities with different histories and coalesce feminist undoings of hierarchical power. The second section, *Embodying Solidarities and Intersections: Black and Brown Dancing*, journeys through critiques of nation and empire and offers analyses of and reflections on ADT's work as solidarity practice among African American and Asian American artists and collectives, both in the context of daily creative processes and in the company's touring across national borders.

The third section, *Transgressing Space and Borders: Local Politics, Transnational Epistemes*, looks at the dialectical tensions between local and transnational histories and the crossing lines of different diasporic urgencies in Black and brown communities. The authors in this section remind us of the concurrent exchanges in our work: even as our choreographies are inspired by local and global social justice movements, they in turn play an active role in moving people to act and resist.

The fourth, *Against Categories of Time: History, Tradition, Contemporary Dance*, examines the choreographic methodologies of reworking linear temporal histories in order to access a constellation of stories and creative inspirations that together nudge open different spaces of cultural possibility. The authors in this section focus on the reshaping of tradition and particularly the Indian dance form of Odissi as it intersects with ethnography, Black cultural practices, and feminist ideas. They wrestle with how dance practices become a site for negotiating multiple identities and reinvestigating the historical meetings of Black and brown bodies.

The fifth, *Imagining Resistance and Hope*, reflects on ADT's sustained practice of generating hope through the vectors of struggle. The writers in this section ask: How do we keep hope alive in the work of resistance through dance? How does hope manifest in the world we live in and the world we conjure through dance? These offerings attest to the transformative power and multiple creativities generated by Black and brown women and femmes sweating together to create works grounded in our embodied histories. Our hope indeed lies in our will to imagine, to resist, and to dance.

Often the organizing questions in the sections overlap, but the different chapters approach and comment on them from the perspective of their specific thematic foci. The concerns we discuss in this introduction flow through many of the sections. Together, they address the different, related sections of our performances, foregrounding women and femmes' histories, intersectional resistances, environmental injustices, supercapitalization of communally shared resources, healing, and connectivities. Because our contributors come from different disciplines and approaches to writing, there are multiple tonalities in the engagement with our dance work. The collection is intentionally kaleidoscopic, highlighting different points of entry into critical thinking and discourse. We marvel at the beautiful ways in which our colleagues theorize transnational feminisms through our dancing and how movement becomes the critical beauty that holds together multiple ways of thinking through choreography.

We believe that the poetic offerings, the reflections on creative processes, and the critical analyses, emerging from very different relationships to the dance and located at different distances from the work, illuminate each other and allow for unresolved complexities to emerge. Moments of stickiness, refusing to dissolve into neat surfaces, truly reflect the nature of our process—rubbly, uneven, and escaping the consolidations of capitalist economies. They allow us to celebrate the nonmaterial and infinitely renewable nature of dance's work, where we must bring forth our bodies daily to realize ideas, histories, and dreams on empty stages, fill spaces energetically with rhythm, relationships, flow, color, and light, and witness these spaces' return to darkness. We are thankful for dance's endless rescriptings, which offer opportunities to recommit the everyday to a practice of Shawngrām, resistance, and a remaking of scapes of beauty and connection.

NOTES

1   At the time of the founding of the company in 2004 in Minneapolis, Minnesota, Ananya Dance Theatre was primarily using the descriptor "women of color"; however, we embrace the nuance articulated in more recent descriptors such as Black Indigenous people of color (BIPOC). In keeping with our practices, we will use "Black and brown women and femmes" or "BIPOC" interchangeably. Moreover, though at the time of its founding this was not articulated as such, we have come to embrace the multiplicitous understanding of the category of "women" to indicate all those who identify as women, including those assigned women at birth, trans, femmes, and noncisgender female bodies. In particular, we use the term "femmes" to indicate those who operate in the world with an embodiment of femininity.

2   Brenda Dixon-Gottschild, *Digging the Africanist Aesthetic in American Performance: Dance and Other Contexts* (Westport: Praeger, 1996).

3   Susan Leigh Foster, ed., *Worlding Dance* (New York: Palgrave Macmillan, 2009).

4   Ananya Chatterjea, *Butting Out: Reading Resistive Choreographies through Works by Jawole Willa Jo Zollar and Chandralekha* (Middletown, CT: Wesleyan University Press, 2004).

5   Ananya Chatterjea, *Heat and Alterity: South-South Choreographies* (Cham: Palgrave Macmillan, 2020).

6   Chandra Talpade Mohanty, "Under Western Eyes: Feminist Scholarship and Colonial Discourses," *Boundary 2* 12, no. 3 (Spring–Autumn 1984): 333–58.

7   Chandra Talpade Mohanty, *Feminist without Borders: Decolonizing Theory, Practicing Solidarity* (Durham: Duke University Press, 2003).

8   M. Jacqui Alexander, *Pedagogies of Crossing: Meditations on Feminism, Sexual Politics, Memory, and the Sacred* (Durham: Duke University Press, 2005).

9   Omise'eke Natasha Tinsley, Ananya Chatterjea, Hui Niu Wilcox, and Shannon Gibney, "So Much to Remind Us We Are Dancing on Other People's Blood: Moving toward Artistic Excellence, Moving from Silence to Speech, Moving in Water, with Ananya Dance Theatre," in *Critical Transnational Feminist Praxis*, ed. Amanda Lock Swarr and Richa Nagar (Albany: State University of New York, 2010).

10   Tinsley et al., "So Much to Remind Us," 164.

11   D. Soyini Madison, *Critical Ethnography: Method, Ethics, and Performance* (Thousand Oaks: Sage, 2005).

12   Madison, *Critical Ethnography*, 165.

13   Marta E. Savigliano, "Fragments for a Story of Tango Bodies on Choreocritics and the Memory of Power," in *Corporealities: Dancing Knowledge, Culture, and Power*, ed. Susan Leigh Foster (London: Routledge, 1996), interweaves sexuality, postcolonial thought, and ideas about female roles in tango. Cindy Garcia, *Salsa Crossings: Dancing Latinidad in Los Angeles* (Durham: Duke University Press, 2013), examines the performance of Latinidad in LA's diasporic communities.

14   Audre Lorde, *Zami, a New Spelling of My Name: A Biomythography* (Berkeley: Crossing Press, 1982).

15 Diana Taylor, *The Archive and the Repertoire: Performing Cultural Memory in the Americas* (Durham: Duke University Press, 2003).

16 Linda Tuhiwai Smith, *Decolonizing Methodologies: Research and Indigenous Peoples* (New York: Zed, 1999).

17 Vijay Agnew, "Introduction," in *Diaspora, Memory, and Identity: A Search for Home*, ed. Vijay Agnew (Toronto: University of Toronto Press, 2005), 15.

18 Tina K. Ramnarine, *Beautiful Cosmos: Performance and Belonging in the Caribbean Diaspora* (Ann Arbor: Pluto Press, 2007), 5–6.

19 Ramnarine, *Beautiful Cosmos*, 5–6.

I

MULTIPLE IDENTITIES

Shared Dreams of Collective Dancing

1

HISTORICAL RUMINATIONS

Breath, Heat, and Movement-Building

ANANYA CHATTERJEA

THE EVOLUTION OF ANANYA DANCE THEATRE (ADT) FROM AN informal ensemble of artists to a dance company, with dreams of developing an Institute of Performance and Social Justice and festival appearances, seems like a magical story. The reality is exactly the reverse. As with any organization, the tremendous labor and physical and emotional exhaustion of institution-building often begged questions about whether it was worth it. The magical moments, glimpsed briefly during the creative process, performances, and dialogues, often seemed to be overshadowed by the struggle for resources, failed grant applications, and the sheer volume of work. Yet the struggles of ADT had particular edges, largely stemming from its constitution as a "dance company of women and femmes of color creating and producing original dance works at the intersection of artistic excellence and social justice," its insistence on intersectional organizing as part of its cultural agenda, and its highlighting of an alternative dance aesthetic that fit neither within the frame of tradition nor as part of the fusion wave. These edges suggest certain trends that overdetermine the performing arts field in the United States and elsewhere, and tensions in the formation of the global stage. This essay is an opportunity for me to reflect on nearly two decades of work as the founder and artistic director of the dance company, and to think about what questions and inspirations have fueled our artistry. While the chronological linearity in parts of this chapter belies the layered growth of the work by a collective of artists, some of the time-based, anecdotal reflections reveal the conditions of possibility for our work, forces that we were sometimes able to harness to sustain our practices.

SHARING THE DREAM

I had arrived in New York City from Kolkata, India, in 1989, to study dance and dance education at Columbia University. As I listened eagerly to New York's African American mayor, David Dinkins, talk about the "gorgeous mosaic" of the city's demographic diversity, I was excited to explore the possibilities of multiculturalism.[1] Soon after, following the bruising battle over the grants to the "NEA Four," National Endowment for the Arts president John Frohnmayer announced in 1990 that the NEA's five new priorities would include "international arts programs, rural arts initiatives, arts-in-education, multicultural activities and so-called 'core institutions,' a term for the largest and most established cultural organizations."[2] Addressing fears of resulting inequities and lack of support for more controversial work, he also insisted that he was "very committed to access" and to support for some of "the smallest organizations."[3] Relatively new to this cultural scene, I imagined such policies as still leaving space for innovative artistic practices, like opportunities for artists from across the world, particularly the global South, to meet and inspire each other.

It turned out that I had totally missed the fine print. But for that moment I was excited to imagine what might become possible. I was, at that time, working part-time as an administrator at the Asian American Arts Center located in Chinatown in New York and dancing in the company associated with the organization, the Asian American Dance Theater. I did not understand when the founder and one-time choreographer of that company, Eleanor Yung, said that she became exhausted from battling the seemingly insurmountable barriers to presenting stories of Asian American identity and history and had turned away from concert dance. My years of dancing in that company and elsewhere in the city, where I inevitably had to preface my offerings of choreography in "contemporary" Indian dance with performances of "classical" Odissi repertoire, should have clued me in right away.[4] But I was slow to realize that multiculturalism in artistic policy was still based on cultural categories that themselves had been constructed on a set of convenient stereotypes that buttressed white centrality.[5]

These historical particularities, and the tensions with which they were fraught, while outside the history of ADT, are important in setting the context for the way the company came to be shaped and its mission. Through my years in New York and subsequently in Philadelphia, my expectation that I would connect with artists from different aesthetics and cultures, enthusiastic about working together to find resonances and create something new, slowly eroded. I had particularly hoped—since these cities had a reputation for being so culturally rich and diverse—for creative confluences with artists from different Black, brown, and global South communities, artists who did not belong to the mainstream, so we might together find ways to articulate our stories about our pathways. Little of this happened, and of what was dreamed up, even less found infrastructural and resource support.

I soon realized that despite the much-publicized rhetoric of multiculturalism, successful projects usually involved a white-and-other artist formula, and Black, brown, and global South artists were meant in fact to be culturally boundaried in particular ways. They were meant not to build solidarities across racial and cultural lines, nor to defy the cultural categories into which they had been cast. The few who created powerful innovative projects *in spite of* existing cultural formations had to be vigilant to not be scripted as fulfilling the true promise of the American dream or escaping the tyranny of their cultural traditions.

Excitement and disappointment dogged my steps over the next few years, yet I was slowly but surely gaining critical perspective and understanding of the field. But even as I was building a small body of work and an audience for my work on the East Coast, family and job circumstances forced me to relocate to Minneapolis in 1999, where I did not know a single person. Perhaps it was because of my circumstances of arriving here as a single parent in a society of strangers that made the search for community so urgent. I had already learned the pitfalls of defining community in limited ways, along lines of race, ethnicity, and culture only. I began to dream of relationality built through shared practices and values.

SMALL BEGINNINGS, HIGH ENERGY

Ananya Dance Theatre was conceived as a company of progressive women and femme artists from global Black and brown communities specifically in response to narrow definitions of multiculturalism and the fixities of cultural formations imposed upon us. It was imperative to frame dance-making as a possible framework for liberatory practices, entirely different from being "saved" by neoliberal cultural policies that remained first-worldist in the ultimate distribution of power and cultural capital. As with all big dreams, ADT's radical space-making started with small steps.

In Minneapolis, in 2004, the early dream that I could not make good on in New York was rebirthed—reimagined in a broader, community-based context, no longer the dream of several individual artists but rather of a community. By now, it had become clear to me that one of the most dangerous results of pervasive racism was the lack of conversation among Black, brown, and communities of color, fueling categorical separations among people, weakening possibilities of alliance-building, and ultimately preserving white power structures. The dialogues and alliances that were inaugurated in the early convenings of ADT, when a group of artists and activists got together in response to a call, opened up some critical perspectives that have been foundational in shaping the company's work.

About forty women responded to a call, circulated through listservs and word of mouth in the early months of 2004, to Black and brown dancers and activists who wanted to engage in an act of dreaming. As we gathered in a dance studio inside the University of Minnesota's Dance Program building, many reasons for coming together were articulated, as were concerns about sharing space. Shannon Gibney, a writer and activist, shared her experiences in a deeply divided women's movement: "When the shit hits the fan, I know that my Black and Latina sisters will stand for me, while the Asian women will go ahead and join the mainstream women's movement." In sharp contrast, Sophie Liu, a writer and actor, an immigrant from Hong Kong, said that in her experience "Asian women always get left behind because of their accents, while the others simply go ahead in their conversations with white women." While the vectors of race and nationality were not quite comparable in this exchange, and many places of implicit collision and conflation (Asian versus Asian American, for instance) remained unpacked, two things became clear: (1) a history of broken alliances among individual Black and brown women and a concomitant history of distrust; and (2) a recurring fear of co-optation by the white women's movement, stemming, again, from historic experiences. At the end of those sessions, the charge became unavoidable: the publication of *This Bridge Called My Back* in 1981 and of *All the Women Are White, All the Blacks Are Men, But Some of Us Are Brave* in 1982 had jolted many of us into action, but a lot of work remained to be done in terms of building intersectional, cross-cultural, cross-racial alliances. And the work began with training in dance together.

At that point, with almost no grant-writing experience and no contacts with funders, I had little monetary compensation to offer this brilliant group of artists. I offered to train them in dance: not a fusion technique with different elements from different styles thrown in, but the basics of Indian dance and movement forms I had studied, with the hope of building a shared contemporary, feminist dance vocabulary. Indeed, it was amazing how many women and femmes across ages, races, nationalities, sexualities, and professions came and stayed through the grueling hours of rehearsal and footwork training, as well as the difficult, if engaging, conversations. While people came in with different degrees of training in dance, some none at all, the specific training I led, with its focus on supportive alignment, lines of force, and footwork, inaugurated a culture of practice where we could all identify and aspire toward the technical hallmarks of this aesthetic.

The organic growth of a group of strangers into an ensemble, with aspirations of becoming a company, even though the process was not without its frustrations, was extraordinary to witness. The intensity of working continuously on rhythm and curvilinearity, workshopping ideas of dream, conducting dialogues that held multiplicity, rehearsing a piece repeatedly, and enduring the rigors of a professional engagement caused some dancers to withdraw their participation, while for others, there was often some friction, most often ideological. Several dancers left because they could not align with a space just for Black and brown women and femmes, feeling strongly about the "exclusion" of white artists. Many of us tried, unsuccessfully, to share that our focus within the company was on creating a space where some conversations regularly pushed under the rug in other areas were welcomed, and where particular alliances could flourish. On the other hand, a group of dancers emerged naturally as leaders, joining me in writing grants and organizing rehearsal and tech schedules. These women ultimately came to form the steering committee, the administrative core of the company, and wrote the first grants to support the work. Our model at that time was of a dancers' co-op of sorts, where dancers were in leadership and played a key role in decision-making. This steering committee also led the company toward the eventual incorporation of the company as a nonprofit in 2006, notwithstanding our hesitations about the nonprofit institutional structure, and set up the first board of directors, comprising prominent community members.

FIRST ARTICULATIONS

ADT's first work was produced at the historic Southern Theater in Minneapolis in 2005. *Bandh: Meditation on Dream*, was a coproduction with the Southern, which was to remain our home for eight years, hosting annual premieres of our work. The sold-out houses of *Bandh* and audience testimonies at conversations and postperformance talkbacks about the "new" aesthetic and ideas that the work brought to the Twin Cities cultural field provided the artists with a huge boost of confidence. We had just barely raised enough money for expenses and paid artists minimally, yet the collective decision was to move forward on this journey. And for the first two years, the work of the company remained inward-focused, delving into the stories of Black and brown communities who were represented in the company already, and building the culture and professional ethic of the company. Workshops led by the celebrated feminist organizer Shamita Das Dasgupta, theater activist Dora Arreola, and company members Shannon Gibney, activist, writer, and journalist, and Beverly Cottman, storyteller and performer, as well as movement improvisation responses to ideas and concepts discussed, were part of building the internal focus and commitment of the company to an agenda of antiracist, antisexist, and antihomophobic cultural production.

In this time, we deepened the consistent process of decolonizing our thinking about excellence and success, what characterized dancerly bodies, and how we might speak about aesthetic difference and embodiments of alternative senses of beauty. We embodied and practiced these articulations during our weekly training sessions, which grew in intensity and depth through the year. The increasing physical rigor was matched by conversations that provoked and confronted personal and cultural memories and painful realizations, necessitating that we arrive at collective understandings of what it meant to share space as Black and brown women and femmes with very different histories.

My body remembers/ stretching my right leg into the light/
pushed through by the heel/
A head appears behind me/ the forehead smeared with blue/
another leg by my side/ two hands gripping long wooden sticks/
So many/ pushing through into the space/ wielding these swords/
like instruments of destiny and balancing/
a reaching to create light
And space/
to dance.
—THE STICK SECTION FROM *BANDH*

2005–6: If *Bandh* had been created around the thematic focus of generating energy through friction, nudging open spaces that were closed, animating new grounds, *Duurbaar*, our 2006 work, was all about flow, materialized in a concluding dance on surfaces flooded with water. Almost as if it signified a principle activated by the play of young girls, dancers carried the water onstage in large pots and poured it on the stage, darkening the costumes of the dancers who then entered the flooded stage on their bellies.

> The Womb Section from *Duurbaar: Journeys into Horizon*: Women and femmes edging into stage on their forearms, knees, and chests, looking forward, into the light. Shannon reciting the *bol*, slow and measured. Artists taking their time to lie on their backs, crossing their ankles in the air.[6] Their hands travel through the opening between their prone chests and upturned legs, marking the yoni with a circling gesture of the hands. Finally coming to standing, gathering energy from the nerve centers, blessing the audience. There are some moments that, rehearsed to ripeness, performed with clarity and intention, remain historic in the self-defining of a community.

BUILDING DEPTH AND LOOKING OUT

By the end of the 2006 production, the company was ready to look outward at the world in which we were living and working. I had been noticing environmental shifts in my travels through Asia in the last couple of years, and a conversation with Shalini Gupta, who had performed in *Bandh* and was now leading her own environmental justice projects, revealed an urgent need to address these issues. Discussions with Shalini and her colleague and eventually a collaborator in our process, Cecilia Martinez, led us into the next phase of our work: the creation of multiyear projects.

We entered our exploration of environmental injustice and racism without realizing that this would transform our process. Our research revealed the depth and range of the issues we were seeking to investigate and the deep intersectionality of climate chaos with other systemic hierarchies engendered by capitalism. What began as an inspiration for one piece expanded into our environmental justice trilogy and forged a particular creative process for us, which made the company's commitment to social justice more palpable. Working with collaborators like Gupta and Martinez, and organizations such as Women's Environmental Institute, ADT artists persevered for three years, engaged in researching and embodying different aspects of environmental injustices, the impacts of proposed solutions, and the human and cultural costs of environmental destruction.

The first piece of the trilogy, *Pipaashaa: Extreme Thirst* (2007), juxtaposed stories of children dying from the toxic dumping in Abidjan by the Dutch multinational company Trafigura; women in the Philippines sitting on mounds of used, some corroded, wires from the global North, sorting them for recycling; and the contamination of land in South Minneapolis due to the improper management of materials in an arsenic factory, creating the "arsenic triangle," close by where I lived. Images of burning skin, madness as the external manifestation of toxic body burden, and dancing on a stage covered with ashes descending from the ceiling and occasionally plunged into darkness became important metaphors for exploring an upside-down world.

The willful contamination of the soil pushed us to ask questions about how to care for and live in respectful relationship with the land, leading to the next piece, *Daak: Call to Action*. 2008 was the sesquicentennial year of the state of Minnesota. Yet the struggles of the Dakota communities, the original peoples of this land, were eclipsed in celebrations that occluded the history of the state's establishment at the price of violent settler colonialism. This theme of robbing of Indigenous lands resonated through time and distinct histories: in the stories of damage to human, animal, and environmental ecosystems through the construction of the US-Mexico border wall, the related disappearance of many women and femmes who worked at the *maquiladoras*, and the allocation of Special Economic Zones all across India for use by multinational corporations, resulting in the theft of land from farmers who had lived on them for generations. *Daak* ended with a meditative section, "Finding Our Feet," where dancers, lit only from the feet to the knees, found different ways to connect the soles of their feet to the ground on which they danced.

By the time we premiered this piece, energy was already gathering for the Climate Change Conference to be held in December 2009 in Copenhagen. The last piece in this trilogy, *Ashesh Barsha: Unending Monsoon*, explored the chaos of a destabilized natural world: tsunamis followed by droughts, a nuclear winter adjacent to a scorching desert. This embodied exploration of extremes, often investigated through the juxtaposition of rapidly increasing and decreasing speeds and harshly distinct movement qualities, allowed us to signal a world rent with crises, where the panic around survival dissipated possibilities of community.

Two big shifts happened in our process from working on this trilogy. First, ADT established a tradition of creating multiyear projects dedicated to a single issue. Returning to the same theme explored from different perspectives, over longer periods of time, became an effective methodology to create urgency around an issue. Second, for three years, we wrestled with questions such as: How can Black and brown women and femmes come to know the world in ways that empower us to change it? How can we relate to global material inequities through the materiality of our own bodies? As a result, embodied exploration of intersectionally understood issues—how environmental injustices were in fact integrally connected to racial, gendered, and class- and caste-based injustices—became embedded in our creative process.

It was also through this project that a determination to always make space for hope—as an essential imaginative and scaffolding practice for our artistic practice—became integral to our work. We have come to frame hope as a fragile but urgent practice of conjure, linked to prophecy, revolution, and mindful labor, to share our process of wresting something out of nothing and to inspire audiences to action. This is how performance scholar Awam Amkpa talks about the hope he sees in postcolonial cultural production: "What hope affirms . . . is the impulse to find modes of articulating subjectivity and democratic citizenship regardless of the barricades cultural and political crises place in our way. Such affirmation is existentially imperative for producers of culture who must confront and use it to imagine and practice perpetual decolonization of our minds, places, and histories."[7]

FEMINIST HISTORIOGRAPHIES

The quartet that followed the trilogy deepened our investigation of ecosystemic relationships and capitalist violence. Each year's work emerged from juxtaposing stories of how women and femmes in global Black and brown communities grappled with the commodification of a naturally occurring element. Each of these elements—land, gold, oil, and water—offered particular paradigms to trace different phases in the history of capitalism, always laced with systemic violence against these global Black and brown communities and other marginalized groups. The structure of the pieces emerged organically from the stories we were articulating, reflecting the particular ways in which that element had been marked as capital, "discovered," mined, and trapped in exploitative, transactional economies. Because of the little-known, often deliberately hidden, nature of these stories, we came to think of our work as performed documentation. These stories and the burn caused by the particular embodiment of these histories remain archived in our bodies, and perhaps in the memories of audiences.

Research questions, of course, are self-perpetuating. Our work in the quartet in turn revealed the tremendous work that women and femmes do to sustain and evolve their communities, though this is seldom acknowledged as labor. In 2014, the tenth anniversary of the company, we launched another new multiyear project, a quintet of pieces exploring the theme "Work Women Do." The first piece, created in the time of Malala Yousafzai and her complicated rise in the minds of a global public, explored the power and possibilities in women and femmes dreaming, envisioning spaces where they could access their wholeness, hope, and joy. The themes for the coming years included women and femmes' work with seeds, earth, farming practices, food preparation, and acts of nurture; strategies of healing; dissent and talking back, even in dangerous circumstances; and women and femmes' insistence on world-making and weaving connections.

Transnational feminist historiographies: what does it mean to come to know, through imagined narratives, metaphoric choreographies, and embodied memories, the justice-bound journeys of women and femmes in various Black and brown global communities across space and time? As I think of the corporeal archives that, over the last sixteen years, have settled in our kinesthetic and somatic fibers, I am reminded of the way theater historian Joseph Roach connects performance to history and memory, even as he attends to the sometimes contested relationship between historicized and remembered accounts of the past: "Performance genealogies draw on the idea of expressive movements as mnemonic reserves, including patterned movements made and remembered by bodies, residual movements retained implicitly in images or words (or in the silences between them), and imaginary movements dreamed in minds not prior to language but constitutive of it."[8] I also find it useful to reflect on my choreography and our collective dancing in terms of the analytical tools Roach offers—"kinesthetic imagination, vortices of behavior, and displaced transmission," which I interpret as creative methodology for illuminating hidden dimensions of history, particularly at the intersections of racialized, gendered, classist, casteist, sexualized, homophobic, and other violences.[9]

I describe my choreography as juxtaposing stories that are "partly researched, partly remembered, and largely imagined." We gather little-known stories that in fact reveal huge social and political forces at work through researching community newspapers, blogs, and photographs;

through oral interviews; and through our #spinespin series, where we engage in dialogue, dance parties, story sharing, and organizing with members of our communities, all around particular themes. We respond to these sessions through movement explorations where collectively created stories resonate through our bodies and activate similar memories from our own genealogies. These are reshaped through an active imagining of new stories, not as a recuperation of history but as a way of embodying and aligning with the affect of events across multiple geographies and temporalities. Our unraveling of these choreographies in the heightened space of the stage, a magical yet hyperreal frame facilitated through design and production elements, witnessed by audiences, might be thought of as reimagined transmissions of the vortices of behavior, rife with the possibility of change.

Roach also invokes French historian Pierre Nora, who, in his 1989 essay *Les lieux de mémoire*, urges us to think about the sociality and urgency of considering memory as a way of knowing time. He reminds us that "the nation has become a given; history is now a social science, memory a purely private phenomenon."[10] This relegation of memory to the place of the private and individual serves modernity's imperative toward nation-states, consolidated through written histories. The embodied and performative public staging of remembered and imagined stories—stories of women and femmes from marginalized communities, stories that are seldom part of History though their historic impact is indubitable (through the modality of dance, which is defined in its dissolution-in-realization), where stories are archived cellularly and through shared memory—invokes Nora's concept of "milieux de mémoire," environments of memory, as opposed to material sites that are organized to memorialize History.[11] While, for Nora, these milieux are the oral and corporeal retentions of cultural traditions, I think of communally held performative memories as sites where knowledge and imagination are activated to hold space for difference and intersectional justice, not as discrete objects of knowledge but as the necessary condition of historic co-incidence. Such activation, experienced by both performers and audiences, might also seed change, little movements toward larger societal shifts toward justice.

QUESTIONS AND TENSIONS

In this last nearly two decades, we have grappled with many questions of identity and location, as well as the scope of our work. As dancers flowed in and out of the company, we have also gained clarity about ADT being a

company of women and femme artists of color. We responded thought-
fully to evolving descriptors, currently aligning the company as a BIPOC
organization, and always recognizing the flux within each descriptor. For
instance, the four male-presenting dance artists who have worked with the
company, three Black and one Asian, were clear about their desire to be part
of the work, about the technical and artistic challenges it offered, and about
their alignment with its politics. Though the journey was not always
smooth, their willingness to work through inherited power relations was
essential to participating in a Black-and-brown-feminist space, and their
presence, even as it altered the space, provoked generative tensions between
borders and boundaries. Both the materiality of the descriptor "Black and
brown women and femme artists" and its conceptual value remain urgent
to the formation of our space, but we are wary of essentialized notions of
race/gender and simple identity politics. Moreover, we have learned to stand
by our refusal to work with facile identitarian binaries, to insist on rigorous
practice and dialogue to understand location at deep cellular levels, and to
champion intersectional justice even as we understand the complications
of surviving within a capitalist system.

Responsive to growing understandings of cis-identities, we moved from
describing ourselves as "women" to "women and femmes" even as we recognize and believe in the "strategic essentialism" that remains inside that
descriptor.[12] One strategy to nuance this descriptor has been to emphasize
the company's inherent multiplicity—artists that are distinctly different in
race, sexuality, and overt gender identification, but also in terms of bodily
presentation, height, weight, and body type—by juxtaposing uniform
ensemble choreography with choreographic variations that offer different
interpretations of the basic phrase structure. We understand that simultaneity and precision do not automatically produce sameness, but can result
in unconventional adjacencies of bodies and aesthetics, and design asym-
metries, highlighting difference within shared formations. Sometimes such
choreography, juxtaposing a range of Black and brown skin tones in close
proximity, creates challenges for lighting design, but most often it reminds
us of the nuance necessary when reckoning with the many ways difference
circulates within marginalized communities. Such choreographies become
our methodology of troubling expectations of boutique multiculturalism
or even strong multiculturalism that are offered as convenient solutions to
address the needs of "diversity."[13] Dancing ensemble movement that indi-
cates a platform to accumulate agency for BIPOC women and femmes,

while ensuring that different bodies are able to interpret the choreography through the prism of their experience, holding the aesthetic frame of our particular dance language and encouraging audiences to engage with us even as we insist on our difference, has provided an experiential and embodied learning of Spivak's "double bind."[14] This necessary shuttling between different contested frames has perhaps been one of the most important strategies of survival for us and an important methodology for participating in mainstream spaces, necessary for sustainability yet requiring constant vigilance against neoliberal collection.

Though in today's context of expanded conversations about the multi-modality of this field we describe our work as "contemporary dance," we began by using the descriptor "contemporary Indian dance." This was our strategy to claim location in terms of choreographic and performance modes—the ways we reimagine meaning-making through dance and rehearse Black and brown femme empowerment, for instance—and acknowledge the aesthetic lineage of our movement style even as we rejected nationalized belongings. I have written elsewhere about how the descriptor "contemporary dance" masquerades as a universal signifier but is most often "white dance," connoting choreographies from the global North or located in Euro-North aesthetics.[15] Claiming contemporaneity in culturally specific ways then becomes an intervention into the hallowed zone of the avant-garde in concert dance, which seems to be reserved for Euro-North "hip" dance-making, relegating aesthetic difference to "tradition." It also pushes back against the gatekeeping of artistic practices and artists by the nation-state through grandstanding narratives of culture and tradition.

To claim that no movements in our technique come from established Western dance forms is not, however, an essentialist statement. Oppositional to rhetoric about purity and authenticity, our claim of Indianness was intended to emphasize our aesthetic alterity, assert the possibility of different sourcings for a contemporary expressivity, and uncouple South Asian performance from ideas of unmoving tradition. The particular ways in which our aesthetic is reimagined from core principles of distinct Indian movement forms, and some of our choreographic retelling of stories, have angered several traditionalists. Yet the articulation of this practice and the extension of our base training in the 1980s reconstruction of Odissi, by incorporating current research and the intersection of principles of vinyasa yoga and Mayurbhanj Chhau, is complex, requiring us to navigate carefully through entrapments in charged frames of first-world consumerism,

Western appropriation, nationalism, tradition, and local, intranational power plays.

We have also had to weave carefully through the tensions that inhere in arts contexts set up as a marketplace functioning within capitalism and the dichotomy of professional and community-engaged art. ADT was set up as a space where professionalism and an ethical and socially accountable artistic practice are mutually constitutive. Yet we have found that community-based art is often denigrated and equated with lack of depth or rigor. Often, though less frequently in current times, we have been invited to perform in community spaces, where the floor was cement and stone cold or carpeted, with no professional technical assistance available, and organizers presented it just like a talk or the entertainment. Often the audiences in such spaces are important for us to connect with, but the performance conditions are unsafe and difficult for dancers, and they obscure the layered, deliberately designed, and specifically marked staging of the choreography. Such spaces, generally underresourced, typically lack the capacity for fulfilling our "tech rider." It then becomes incumbent upon me, as artistic director, to adjust the choreography so we can share the work without risking injury and to negotiate some compensation for dancers' artistic labor and time. This tension is pressing for Black and brown women and femme artists working in alternative aesthetics: every time we participate in such spaces, we recognize that we are in a way remarginalizing ourselves, giving life to the fiction that perhaps this work could be done without adequate resources. Yet we also connect with individuals whose appreciation and stories provide vital affirmation for our dancing.

In working through such challenges and making complicated decisions, we have also grappled with the consequences of actively off-centering our work within the performance world. It is not like we ever desired centrality, but we work in a system where mandates for diversity and inclusion, putatively mobilized to make space for including "others," are manipulated to retain power at the center, and where resources and sustainability are ultimately connected to that structure of center and margin. This means we have to constantly balance our goals of engaging with underresourced communities, financially compensating our artists, and working within the nonprofit structure, which is its own industrial complex. Often these contesting demands feel overwhelming. The rigorous practice of hope in the choreographic process and the solidarities we have built in the many years of work in the field carry us through these difficult times.

NEW LANGUAGES

In 2012, ADT was one among fifteen organizations selected to be part of the ArtsLab, a peer-learning, capacity-building program of Arts MidWest. There were difficult lessons in this journey: for instance, building a culture of "giving" or creating sustainability for BIPOC-led organizations committed to social justice simply does not work in the same way as it does for mainstream and white-led arts organizations. Often we felt at odds with the lessons we were learning and struggled with the burden of having to dismantle the toolbox offered to us and to reimagine them for our context. We found ourselves in alliance with two similar organizations, one in visual arts, the other in theater, but ADT, with one of the smallest budgets in the room, had to work through yet another layer of self-definition and precariousness. Through this two-year period, we worked intensively to tell our story with clarity and effectiveness. What inevitably surfaced through the long hours of discussion was a shared recognition that our practice already contained the clues to a verbal articulation.

It is in this period that, looking at the work we have done and come to be known for in our communities, we arrived at the tagline descriptor of the company: "People-powered dances of transformation." This reflected our deepened understanding of our social justice mission and our commitment to a larger paradigm shift toward equity. We also parsed, named, and articulated the foundational principles of our work: (a) Yorchhā, the particular dance technique that I created by intersecting and extending the movement principles of Odissi (the traditional dance form from Odisha), Chhau (the martial art form from Odisha, with specific reference to the Mayurbhanj style), and the vinyasa style of yoga; (b) Shawngrām, the choreographic methodology of researching and juxtaposing the little-known lives and work of women and femmes from global BIPOC communities, the intentional crafting of dances in dynamic, overlapping spatial and temporal arcs, and the philosophy of resistance embodied in the thematic foci of our work; (c) Aanch, the practice of generating heat and desire for love, beauty, justice, and hope through physical and emotional investment in dancing, and the express intention of reaching out to audiences, knowing that we can catalyze shifts but need a broader movement for change to be effective; (d) Daak, the call to action that is part of all our work but manifests most clearly through the invitation to audiences to share space with dancers, negotiate their way through a group of strangers, or move with simple choreography or improvisation to embody intentional gestures. This last principle of the deliberate shifting of energy is inspired as much by Indigenous concepts of energy as by my fascination with grassroots movements such as Occupy Wall Street.

I had traveled to Spain for a performance/lecture engagement in the fall of 2011. In Madrid, I encountered the public protests that began as the Spanish Indignants Movement earlier that year and was fascinated by the way the group of young protesters surrounded the entrance to the city hall in the Puerto del Sol plaza. Returning to the United States, I began to study the Occupy Wall Street movement, which was gathering steam. While this movement reiterated some things we already knew about racial hierarchies, I was impressed with the organic growth of this movement without formal leadership, the principle of physical occupation of spaces, the commitment of showing up every day, and the innovative practice of the "people's mic" to amplify a speaker's voice. I was inspired especially by Angela Davis, who reminded us of the "complex unity" of the 99 percent when she spoke at Zuccotti Park in New York City, in October 2011, and about the urgency of recognizing different goals and conditions that had brought people together.[16] I had grown up in left-front-governed West Bengal, where the practices of *gherao*—physically surrounding centers and persons of authority to highlight a demand for justice—and protest processionals were quite common. And the practice of occupying public spaces over sustained periods of time resonated with my orientation to dance; it reminded me of histories of women and femmes from global Black and brown communities, of ADT dancers, showing up daily, filling spaces with breath and movement, changing their energetic frame.

ADT's directive to inhabit and fill dance emerges as much from the mission of social justice, which necessitates a broad platform of participation—the philosophy of Daak—as from our resistance to separating dance from daily life issues. After years of inviting audiences into our work through powerful dancing, reimagining conventional notions of beauty and staging stories of struggle and transformation, I wanted, by 2011, to engage audiences in ways different from the lobby exhibits, the conversations, and the workshops that we had been doing for years. I wanted to say to our audiences, who were by now primarily women and femmes, primarily Black and brown, and young: "For nearly a decade, we have been brokering hope through our dancing, we have embodied pain and devastation and have rehearsed the generating of light from darkness through many performances. For years, we have filled your imaginations and invited you to come along with us in this journey as we have spun dreams. We now invite you to join the stage as a space where change can be born, and accelerate its transformation into a space of possibility that can then inspire action in life processes." This strategy, which meant that I had to find ways for audiences to come into the experience of dancing with us, shifted my choreographic process. I began to choreograph "performance installations" in public spaces, which had as their premise audience participation or interaction with performers, and these became another stream of our work. Also, in concert performances I have been devising ways to invite audiences to join the dancers at particular moments: on the stage, from their seats, and in other ways.

Yet there was a substantial challenge for me in choreographing these experiences, sparked by Davis's call to heed the complex unity of people coming together to share a platform. Participatory art, for me, is not about making the audience experience more cool or even more engaged. Rather it is an intentional invitation to share the civic responsibility for our part in pushing back at a system riddled with multiple layers of injustices. I also have to ask: How can audiences have a material experience of the journey and of the hope being actively carved by women and femmes from global BIPOC communities? How can they experience this work as a re-cognition and thus dismantling of myths and stereotypes that we often internalize? What kind of participation will remain in muscle memory and resonate later, in ways that will provoke questions?

Troubling audience participation, filling it with thoughtfulness and intention, also meant analyzing histories of occupying, and separating that conceptual frame from its co-optation in histories of colonization. As BIPOC women and femmes doing social justice work in an alternative aesthetic, we knew marginalization well, although in very different ways. Yet our choice was to fill dance as it existed in the rarefied realm of the concert stage, to redefine it for ourselves, and to keep demanding resources and spaces that were supposedly for *all* artists but typically betrayed that broad reach. What did it mean to consciously inhabit such spaces and resources, to come to them with the intentional politics that characterized our work? Certainly, it meant that we were always vigilant, to veiled racisms, to moves to co-opt our presence as a validation of other agendas, to the ways in which representation was often used to mask inequities, and to other false equivalencies. It also meant an insistence on the collaborative leadership of Black and brown women and femmes, and a concomitant reckoning with the different histories and strategies they brought to the table, even as they stood together.

Part of this modality is reflected in the motif that became a critical part of my choreographic palette: artists repeatedly "dying" but returning to life to share their stories. For me, this was a reminder of the multiple assaults that constantly dog our lives. The cyclical returning of the women and femmes, not as spectral presences but as full-bodied dancers who bear histories of many murders, is for me a kind of hauntology, a commitment to life forces despite the threats of death and evisceration. When these artists reach their hands out to audience members to dance with them or hold audience members in their gaze, they prevent the eclipsing of the histories they carry, disallow a looking away, and refuse their disappearance in what Diana Taylor has described as "percepticide."[17]

Also through this period, ADT dancers came to claim a different descriptor for their work, perhaps in recognition of the broad spectrum of work they took on, and partly in recognition of the ways in which dance had come to be commodified, settled in public imagination as screenic activity and entertainment, framed in levity. I had coined the term "cultural activist" much earlier, but by 2010, dancers came to embrace it fully, emphasizing the twinning of the aesthetic and political decisions in the choreography and dancing.

UN-BALANCE / DIS-EASE / WE ARE NOT THE SAME

One of the discursive challenges that remain at the core of our work is the need to theorize energy. As dancers working with social justice, we experience in very real terms the movement of energy through our bodies and in the spaces we occupy. We experience it both in the heat of our dancing bodies and in the materiality of the sweat that drenches the floor as we dance, as well as the perceptible connections we experience with audiences. Because of the way new-ageists have appropriated the language of energy, it has been challenging for us to talk about its materiality and transmission. While thermodynamic theory is useful—energy is that which moves us—it does not yet fulfill the multidimensionality of this force, its spiritual, emotional, and political workings, or reveal how these multiple movings are interconnected. Similarly, while our practice of collective breathing has been integral to our work from the beginning, it has been challenging to speak about it as a radical practice, one that actually enables us to move the air around us, due to the commodification of yoga and pranayama methodologies.

It has also been difficult to communicate the complexities of belonging, even as exigencies of our work necessitate that we do so. As a company touring transnationally, we often find that we must describe ourselves as American artists, yet find ourselves, our work, and our bodies strangely misaligned with what audiences expect of American representation. This not-quite, not-there belonging that we repeatedly find ourselves articulating is always unsettling, yet deeply emancipatory. It has been urgent to deflect the neoliberal cosmopolitan impulse ("What a multicultural group you are!") and the limited toleration of otherness that cannot understand the entanglements-in-difference that Achille Mbembe talks about or the intentional solidarities inherent in Walter Mignolo's notion of the "horizon of pluriversality."[18] It has been urgent for me to practice speaking about citizenship in nuanced terms, understanding both the logistics of passports and travel policies to ensure the safety of ADT artists when traveling, for instance, to perform at the Harare International Festival of the Arts in Zimbabwe (in 2012), the Crossing Borders Festival in Addis Ababa, Ethiopia (in 2015), the Bethlehem International Performing Arts Festival in Bethlehem, Palestine (in 2018), and the Ocean Dance Festival in Cox's Bazar, Bangladesh (in 2020); and to simultaneously raise questions about identifying ourselves only in terms of ethnonational representative categories. Home, representation, belonging, and continuous refraction. Identity and concatenation.

Lastly, this decade of work has revealed the urgency of a politics of necessary inconvenience. We understand, for instance, that our necessary critique of Hindu fundamentalism and of the patriarchal and casteist toxicities enshrined in much of "classical" Indian dance, woven into my choreography, means that we are shut out from some festivals and resources. Indeed, our artistic and political choices have been rather inconvenient in terms of financial stability, growth, and sustainability. But we have learned to value critical analyses of systemic power and the ultimate global impact of daily, individual choices. We understand that choices made in alignment with a mission of social justice, certainly in the context of an arts and cultural field rigged to support the preeminence of what Slavoj Žižek has described as "the privileged *empty point of universality* from which one is able to appreciate (and depreciate) properly other cultures" cannot be easy.[19] It means that we have to take on particular kinds of labor, redefine the work of dancing as the deliberate creation of a community, and embrace thoughtfulness as daily practice. It guides us to balance our care of our bodies and our discipline of studio practice with attention to the sensory experiences of standing in the bitter cold at rallies held after the Michael Brown and

Trayvon Martin verdicts; understand the societal conditions that allow us to practice yogic breath, *pranayama*, at a time when Eric Garner's and George Floyd's repeated pleas for breath were unheeded; adjust our regular practice of footwork when we walk with activists along the Mississippi River, bracing ourselves as we slip on the snow; and spend much more time raising funds through community crowd-funding so we can construct our costumes in ethical ways.

We have learned that it is when we care about issues that might not affect us in direct ways, at least seemingly, and we act, create, dance, in alliance with a broader base of struggles for justice, that we are able to understand the deep structural connections in a politics of resistance to imperialism. This has led us to reimagine the scope of virtuosity, for instance, beyond fast footwork and dynamic jumps that produce excitement and charm audiences through the allure of extraordinary embodiment, to shared breath and mutually held gazes, deceptively simple but difficult to accomplish and involving much more than personal genius. This kind of caring is inconvenient because such work requires much more labor, detailed care, and energy, but often does not match audience expectation and desire. Yet it is a necessary cultural politics, one that recognizes how convenience often undergirds projects of colonialism and empire. Ultimately, this has pushed us to think differently about time, space, labor, and love. It has led me to rechoreograph the salutation with which we begin and end practice and performance, the *pranām* of Indian dance, in conversation with Dakota leader Janice BadMoccasin and Ojibwe leader Sharon Day, as a celebration of Mni Sota Makoce. And this different philosophy—our articulation of Shawngrām as a core value—shifts our dancing every day.

Today, as we dance in our Shawngrām Institute for Performance and Social Justice (established 2018), created from refurbishing an empty used car salesroom located in the historic Rondo neighborhood of Saint Paul, I am grateful to my comrades in ADT, whose courage and support are testament that when we match our inconvenient politics with ethical innovation and labor, we can combat the lack of resources. These artists remind me that we must affirm each other and value our work in our own terms. Witnessing their commitment to come together and dance every weekend morning for several hours in addition to other rehearsal days, virtually through the COVID pandemic of 2020, I am reminded that the space making we have engaged in has repeatedly challenged capitalist aggrandizing or monumentalizing. I remain in gratitude to the practice of radical love and our shared meditation on breath. And I invoke M. Jacqui Alexander, who dared to bring spiritual and feminine erotic forces into theorizing to disturb modernity's epistemes and ask for a pedagogy (just as applicable to artistry) that "summons subordinated knowledges that are produced in the context of the practices of marginalization in order that we might destabilize existing practices of knowing and thus cross the fictive boundaries of exclusion and marginalization."[20]

NOTES

1 Todd S. Purdum, "Mayor Dinkins; Dinkins Sworn In; Stresses Aid to Youth," "He Pledges to Be 'Mayor of All the People': Dinkins, Sworn as Mayor, Stresses Help for Children," *New York Times*, January 2, 1990, A1.

2 Allan Parachini, "NEA's Top Officials Assess the Impact of Funds Shift to States," *Los Angeles Times*, November 5, 1990, F10.

3 Parachini, "NEA's Top Officials Assess," F10.

4 Scholars, such as Hari Krishnan in *Celluloid Classicism: Early Tamil Cinema and the Making of Modern Bharatanatyam* (Middletown, CT: Wesleyan University Press, 2019), have troubled the naming of certain Indian dance forms as "classical," tying this nomenclature specifically to Brahminic privilege and caste dominance (6). Hence, even as I occasionally refer to the descriptor because it holds recognition in the widespread cultural imaginary, I immediately signal my dis-ease with it.

5 Sara Ahmed (*Strange Encounters: Embodied Others in Post-Coloniality* [New York: Routledge, 2000], 96) writes incisively about official policies of multiculturalism where "the welcoming of the strange culture's difference itself requires that culture *fit into this model of cultural diversity as a normative model of who 'we' already are*."

6 *Bol* is the syllabic accompaniment typical of Indian dance and music performance. Usually recited by the percussionist during dance, the sounds of the *bol* hold the time cycle for the movement.

7 Awam Amkpa, *Theatre and Postcolonial Desires* (London: Routledge, 2003), 13.

8 Joseph Roach, *Cities of the Dead: Circum-Atlantic Performance* (New York: Columbia University Press, 1996), 26.

9 Roach, *Cities of the Dead*, 26.

10 Pierre Nora, "Between Memory and History: *Les Lieux de Mémoire*," *Representations* 26 (Spring 1989): 11.

11 Nova, "Between Memory and History," 7.

12 Gayatri Chakravarty Spivak, "Subaltern Studies: Deconstructing Historiography," in *In Other Worlds: Essays in Cultural Politics* (New York: Methuen, 1987), 205.

13 Stanley Fish, "Boutique Multiculturalism, or Why Liberals Are Incapable of Thinking about Hate Speech," *Critical Inquiry* 23, no. 2 (Winter 1997): 378–95, 378.

14   Gayatri Chakravorty Spivak, *An Aesthetic Education in the Era of Globalization* (Cambridge, MA: Harvard University Press, 2012), 3.

15   Ananya Chatterjea, *Heat and Alterity in Contemporary Dance: South-South Choreographies*, (Cham: Palgrave McMillan, 2020), 72.

16   Transparent Film, "Angela Davis at Occupy Wall Street," YouTube, October 31, 2011, https://www.youtube.com/watch?v=D7gdNptUWlc.

17   Diana Taylor, *Disappearing Acts: Spectacles of Gender and Nationalism in Argentina's "Dirty War"* (Durham: Duke University Press, 1997), 27.

18   Achille Mbembe, *On the Postcolony* (Berkeley: University of California Press, 2001), 14–16; Walter Mignolo, *The Idea of Latin America* (Malden, MA: Blackwell, 2005), 156.

19   Slavoj Žižek, "Multiculturalism, or the Cultural Logic of Multinational Capitalism," *New Left Review* 1, no. 225 (September–October 1997): 44.

20   M. Jacqui Alexander, *Pedagogies of Crossing* (Durham: Duke University Press, 2005), 7.

2

"IT'S BEEN MY COMMUNITY"

Interview with Gina Lynn Kaur Kundan

ALESSANDRA LEBEA WILLIAMS

> Gina Kundan is a founding company member of Ananya Dance
> Theatre who performed with the company from 2005 to 2011. She
> is currently the president of the board of directors of the company.
> Alessandra Williams conducted this interview on November 1, 2012.

IT SOUNDED PERFECT. I WAS IN A BAD SPOT. I HAD THIS MANAGER
that made me out to be the "angry Black girl," because any time I spoke up,
the response would be, "Why are you so intense?" To be invited to join a
group that understood that was a godsend. My spouse, Jit, was out of town
the day the auditions were set, and I have two kids. I asked, "Can I set up
another time?" Ananya said, "Bring them. Children are welcome." I brought
them, and all three of us danced together. Ever since then, it's been my
community.

There are lots of organizations that say they do community outreach. We
say we are located in community, because community outreach has to do
with assimilating you and making you what I want. Whereas, in being a part
of community, we are reaching ourselves, but we don't see ourselves in an
ivory tower or any way separate from an organization. We want to learn with
and from community as much as we engage and teach, so that it's a mutually
beneficial involvement. Recently there has been more work with immigrant
communities and refugees, organizations that specifically work around
issues of violence against women and preserving culture and understanding
life in Minnesota. And we've worked with some Native communities in the

past. Some of the partnerships have not always gone so well. There was a group that came to watch a rehearsal and said, "You need to tone that down. That's too much. Our people are not going to be able to relate. It's too intense." That's kind of what we're all about. We're not going to do less facial expressions because you're frightened.

3

ANANYA DANCE THEATRE AS SOCIAL JUSTICE EXPERIMENT

Where We Were in 2005, Where We Are Now

SHANNON GIBNEY

WHATEVER YOU NEED AND CAN IMAGINE, YOU MUST CREATE.
This was the impetus, the urgency that undergirded our decision to form a women of color dance group in Minneapolis, Minnesota, more than fifteen years ago. I use "you" here in the collective sense of the term—as an invocation of community, especially marginalized ones. My use of the word "need" is equally specific: I am describing a condition of unrealized human potential, as opposed to material or even intellectual scarcity.

That is, there is something just outside your reach. Something that will change you and the landscape you stumble through daily, to such an extent that both context and character will be irrevocably altered. Place and person, although remaining the same, will mash up, evolve, complicate, disintegrate.

So, you reach.

We, Black, South Asian, East Asian, Native, Latina women, did not know each other individually, and we certainly did not know each other's collective cultural and social histories. This was why we kept on bumping up against each other roughly, our pointed defenses cutting and bleeding on each other. This was how the blinding Minnesota whiteness had divided though not yet conquered us. We were environmental justice activists, corporate scientists, nonprofit workers, university professors, writers and editors, social justice activists, private sector managers, dancers, stay-at-home moms, students, artists of all kinds, and even children of these artists, and we needed another canvas of expression. One that was big enough to hold all of our varied and complex experiences, but also small enough for us to see what we were doing while we were doing it.

This was not easy.

And although I am no longer formally part of the company, I understand that it is still not easy, this attempt to interrupt a dominant narrative via those who may be less centered, less palatable to the mainstream. Still, even then I understood the importance of what we were doing. Even then I saw myself, younger, less exhausted, less alienated, dancing in *chauk* with my Black woman thighs deeply sitting, each *mudra* articulating a story of escape and bondage in the South Asian language of Odissi. Not my language, but the language of this particular sisterhood, in this particular time, in this particular place.

———

Lying on our backs with our legs raised from the hips above, twenty women and I flex our heels and run through basic Odissi footwork during a warm-up at the University of Minnesota Barbara Barker Dance Building. It is a strange edifice, a piece of contemporary architecture with sharp edges jutting out at odd angles. The practice rooms are gorgeous, though, with state-of-the-art floors and huge windows and glass everywhere. It is what you would expect from a top-ranked Dance Department at a top university, but we obviously brown women, some of us young and some of us older, are not. Walking up the elegant staircase that morning, I saw several well-meaning twenty-something white girls look Kenna and me up and down, their eyes screaming, *What are* you *doing here?* And I can't say I blame them—it's a question I ask myself often enough. I am almost thirty years old at that time, not a young, lithe, skinny, hairless white girl gracefully leaping through the air. They are everywhere here, defining the landscape of the term "natural dancer," as well as the territory of dance itself. Every time I walk by them, "Minnesota nice" as can be, I feel that I am somehow polluting the pristine, clean space of young white womanhood, and the perversity of my personality makes me delight in it. The other women and I, stomping through footwork in the studio, stinking up the hall outside it with our greens and curries and seaweed, laughing too loudly, know *we are not supposed to be here*, so we have tacitly decided that *we will not be*

FIGURE 3.1. (From left) Chitra Vairavan, Lela Pierce, Renée Copeland, and Negest L. Woldeamanuale in *Tushaanal: Fires of Dry Grass* (2011). This image captures the dramatic interactions of Ananya Dance Theatre's work. Photo by Paul Virtucio. Courtesy of Ananya Dance Theatre.

supposed-to-be-here together. We are not intentionally reacting to whiteness. Once we are in the studio, working and sweating, whiteness is largely irrelevant. What we are doing is colliding our various kinds of brownness together, and seeing what it means and what it becomes (figure 3.1).

Through her academic appointment and sheer willpower, Ananya has somehow managed to get us this space and time. Everyone knows it is oppositional and a bit unorthodox, working with women from the community who are not trained dancers, but since everyone else in her Dance Department has their own dance companies, they cannot tell her how she should create her own. Ananya, whose name in Bengali means "Like Whom There Is No Other," is a known force of nature in these parts: part artistic genius, part visionary, part ass-kicker. If you're smart, you don't cross her unless you have to.

"Up! Up! Get those stomachs up off the ground!" Ananya shouts at us from the front of the room. She is leading us through the plank exercise, on our elbows and the balls of our feet, parallel to the floor.

"It buuuuurns us, Master," I say to Gina, in the voice of Gollum from *The Lord of the Rings*. She is huffing and puffing just like me in the pose.

She laughs, then rolls her eyes at me. "Nerd."

I stick my tongue out at her.

Hui giggles on my right side. She is five months pregnant with her second child, and her belly touches the floor when she does this exercise. Frankly, I have no idea how she trains with us at all in this condition. She is one of our lead dancers, and pregnancy seems to have only mildly slowed her down.

"Concentrate!" Ananya yells. "You will never have the stamina to complete the footwork if you don't train."

A drop of sweat drops from my forehead into my eye, and my stomach muscles are screaming.

"Fifteen more seconds!" she tells us.

Why is she built like a bird and can throw down like a wrestler? She looks like she could go on like this for fifteen more minutes, much less seconds. *The rest of us are mere mortals. Don't punish us for it.* Pain definitely brings out the meaner parts of me.

"Okay, that's it," Ananya says finally, the fifteen seconds finally up.

A chorus of groans floods the room, as all of us collectively collapse on the floor.

"And now, the side stretch," she says, balancing her weight on her right knee on the floor, stretching her left leg out long on the other side. As the rest of us are still getting our breath back from the last exercise, Ananya reaches her right arm out to the side, as long as she can, gradually pulls it up over her head and then all the way to the left, until she is all the way over her left leg, grasping her foot.

"For fuck sakes," I say.

Gina starts laughing outright, which makes me laugh, too.

Gina just shakes her head.

I am the problem child here. But it is okay, because I am not the Angry Black Girl Problem Child that I am instantly demoted to in most spaces. I am the Crazy Mxd Black Shannon Person Who You Adore Cause She Is, Always, Who She Is. I am "Shannu," Chitra and Pramila and Ananya and Ananya's nine year-old daughter Srija's affectionate Bengali name for me. This is whom I translate into among my South Asian sisters.

Ananya glares at me from the front of the room—part exasperation, part love—and then motions to me to get into position.

I raise my eyebrows and say, "I'll try," as I bend my right knee into position and extend my left leg. Trying is the best I can do, although it never feels like enough.

Later, we sit in check-in circle. It is something we do at some point in each rehearsal, to see where each of us is at emotionally, physically, and otherwise. I would hate all this touchy-feely stuff if I didn't love these women so much.

"Where is Amanthi?" Ruchika asks, looking around the circle.

Amanthi is a thirty-something Sri Lankan immigrant who is almost less of a natural dancer than I am (if such a thing is possible). She and I often find ourselves at the back of the room, trying desperately to follow an intricate set of footwork that everyone in front of us somehow seems to have already mastered. She has been in this country for a little over five years and has a husband and two small children. Like me, she does not have *a dancer's body*: she has hips, and thighs, and an ass, as well as some gray hairs.

"Her kids are sick," says Kayva absently. "She's at home with them."

Ananya frowns, registering her disapproval, I think. This irritates me.

"How dare she," I say sarcastically. "Putting the welfare of her children before rehearsal."

Some of the women laugh, and some of them just smile to themselves. Sometimes I think that Ananya and I might have been lovers in another life—we bring such intense energy to the space and often throw it at each other. Then everyone else is left to deal with the consequences. Of course no one has ever or will ever *say this*, but it is nonetheless absolutely and universally known, so that in these moments, mostly everyone has decided that the safest bet is to stay on the sidelines rather than risk the pain and futility of taking sides. They can feel that something is brewing, as can I.

"Yes, we hope they get better fast," Ananya says quietly. "We have six weeks till the show, which really means it's as good as tomorrow. We need all hands on deck—everyone here for every rehearsal. And when you're here, you can't be messing around anymore. Your head has to be here, too. As you well know, plenty of people will be looking for us to do sloppy footwork and inexact spacing. We cannot live up to their damaging expectations."

I sigh and look out the huge windows around us, full of the Minnesota winter light. I know that Ananya's dream, and many of ours for that matter as well, is to bust up the false community/professional binary in dance and art in general: The idea that "good" art can come only out of "professional" spaces (which are, of course, disproportionately white, middle class, and Eurocentric) and that art coming out of communities, particularly communities of color, is by default "bad." She has a point . . . but as two-hour rehearsals lengthen to three, and even four in the two weeks before the show, I start to feel in my body, to see in my brain why excellence is so often left to the purview of professionals. *Professionals are the only ones who have time for this shit*, I say to a bunch of us, exhausted and waiting in the wings for our entrance during tech week. Kenna and Chitra and Lela crack up, and I know they know exactly what I mean, being professional dancers themselves. In the end, the people who will stay in the company for the long haul will be the professional dancers. Those of us who are attracted to the social justice mission and philosophy of ADT and who want to learn how to express it through the medium of contemporary Indian dance will gradually leave the company over time, unable to commit the time and space to the ever-increasing demands of artistic excellence. When I finally see ADT perform *Neel: Blutopias of Radical Dreaming* at the Ordway Center in Saint Paul for their ten-year anniversary, I am astounded by many things: the sheer virtuosity of the dancers, the commanding footwork and articulate *mudras*, and the many pairings and groups of dancers the company is able to showcase in various scenes, because their talent and physical abilities are just that strong. The searing artistry of everyone involved. But I am also astounded by the relative youth of the dancers—pretty much everyone seems to be in their twenties. Maybe three women from the original company of which I was part remain, and they are all dancers first, social justice activists and teachers second. Something else has changed as well: maybe seven years into its tenure, Ananya and the company decided to work with white dancers. There aren't that many of them, maybe two total, but I would be lying if I didn't say that it means something different to see them on the stage amid so many different hues of brown. There is no denying their skill, talent, and sensitivity as dancers, even social justice thinkers. But there is something that happens when white bodies are contrasted with black and brown ones. We are socially conditioned in our culture (and most of the world) to notice and value the white bodies, *merely because of their whiteness*. Although we everyday African American, South Asian, East Asian women could not have ever executed the physical and artistic depth I consistently see the new ADT company present in its works, I would be lying if I didn't also sometimes wonder if something has been lost in this process of necessary evolution.

I like to think I could see all this complicated future, which would both exceed and diminish our expectations, back in 2005, sitting in circle with my fellow dancers and friends. I like to think of this fissure, this tension between a *community of dancers* and a *company of dancers* as a productive one. It is a space that in many ways cannot and should not be reconciled, or "fixed." It is a space of questioning. It is why I say, fifteen years ago, speaking with my sisters about Amanthi's absence, "What about the artistry of child-rearing? Of being in community that really supports this kind of creativity that demands time and space, and which women all over the world engage in every day, all the time? Where is the space for this—not just on the dance floor but for its own sake? Where is the recognition that this constitutes excellence, as well?"

───────

After months and months of practice, we are finally about to debut our first full-length work, at the Southern Theater, in May 2005. It is called *Bandh: A Meditation on Dream*, and it is a ninety-minute piece about women's resistance and community and movement building—especially women of color—and the dreams that fuel it. Sometimes I feel like a grand imposter here, and also more than a little ridiculous, in my tailored black pants that flare out widely at the bottom, shiny black tunic, and brilliant red-painted forehead. Who do I think I am, anyway? As a child I took years of ballet, and then turned my back on it to play soccer in sixth grade, and I have since taken various dance classes in other styles here and there. But never in my life have I devoted so much time and space to the process and product of dance. To be honest, I don't have the talent for it. When Pramila, Kenna, or Chitra tries to get me to articulate a particular *mudra* more exactly, or move my eyes counter to my torso in a group turn, I feel my feet flounder, my weight shift in the wrong places. They are patient women, my friends, and we joke, cajole, and sweat hard through rehearsals, but there is a reason why I am not one of the principal dancers, or even one of the second tier, who are featured in small group sections with Ananya. It is because my best skills lie elsewhere: in organizational infrastructure building, communication and writing, and social justice movement building and analysis. There is definitely a place for me here, but it is not first and foremost executing the Odissi footwork that is powerful enough to render most audiences silent when they encounter it. This is what I feel keenly while standing shoulder-to-shoulder behind the opening curtain with my fellow company members. I am hoping that my feet remember what my brain cannot. I am hoping that I don't inadvertently hit Hui in the face while enunciating Ananya's breathtaking arm movements. I am hoping against hope that I don't fuck the whole thing up.

Then, suddenly, abruptly, the curtain lifts, and blinding lights penetrate my sight. We are all standing in what Ananya calls turtle pose, our hands clasped with pinkie and index fingers pointed forward, elbows strong and up, legs squatting. Silence. Silence everywhere. Then we start to move. Front to back, a mass of twenty-five brown women's bodies, shifting forward by way of switching the soles of their feet back and forth on the floor, until we reach about the middle of the stage. Then Chitra begins to slowly pound out a rhythm with her right foot, at the front of the pack. *Ta-ka-dimi. Ta-ka-dimi.* Ball of foot on floor, whole foot on floor, back of foot on floor. Then the next row of women in the triangle join her, Mika, Ruchika, Kayva, Kenna, Pramila. The sound begins to swell on stage. Then Hui, Gina, Shalini, Tillana, Stefania, Anika join their soles to the struggle. And then finally, it is my turn to enunciate each syllable of resistance with my sisters. We have not yet started sweating in earnest tonight, but the memory of three-hour-plus rehearsals for the past month is marked in my muscles. They remember, even if my mind is amuck. *Laboring together, we build community,* I can almost hear Ananya say in my ear, as she has done in so many rehearsals. *There is nothing theoretical about it. We actually work to make something larger than ourselves, something new in the world, something that says something about our lives, the lives of women of color here and now in Minnesota.* I take a breath with all the women around me, and all at once we are moving across the floor en masse, a whirl of brown arms cutting through the humid, enclosed air of the theater, a freight train of legs and raised knees pounding our stories into the space. My brain forgets, for a moment, to think. Just for that moment I am just movement. Just free. Just nothing.

I breathe.

I stomp.

I wrestle with my story.

And then I arrive with the rest of the women at the end of this chapter, at the center of the stage, one breath caught in our throat. One red palm lifted above a binding grip.

4

THE GONE BIRD SONG

CHITRA VAIRAVAN

> Written during the choreographic process of her solo in *Moreechika* (2012), inspired by the images of birds stuck in the ocean after the Gulf oil spill, their wings heavy and weighted.

Years of dreaming die in one moment
Yearning flight
Calls with no sound
I collect for you and this is how you greet me.
The weight of it all
Collapses
Washed up with no water
Slick with history
Sounds of hope whisper nothing
I stand here
Still
Stuck
And beneath me

You, my sky
Feel the breeze
Pain
On your back burden
These eyes

5

DANCE OF THE SPIRALING GENERATIONS

On Love and Healing with Ananya Dance Theatre

HUI NIU WILCOX

FOR THE PAST FIFTEEN YEARS, I HAVE BEEN A MOTHER, A DANCER with Ananya Dance Theatre, and a sociology professor. My personal history is part of the often-untold collective history of women of color working from within the academy and other institutions, mobilizing creativity and community to "make it work" and mentoring our sisters and daughters along the way. In writing this history, I find myself doing the same thing that I have been doing throughout the last decade and a half: looking for ways to weave together all the things I love to do: dancing, mothering, teaching, working for social justice, and seeking pathways of healing and wholeness.

———

Upon seeing Ananya Dance Theatre's performances, my colleagues from the academy would ask, incredulously, "How do you do this?" I scramble to give logistic explanations, such as a strategy to integrate scholarship and dance work, a supportive partner and creative children who transform the dance studio and theater space into blissful playgrounds. Those are all true and essential parts of the equation. But deep down, what I really want to say is "How can I not do this?" My survival and growth within the academy as a transnational woman of color have depended on my embodied interaction and artistic exploration in the space of Ananya Dance Theatre. There has been ample research documenting women of color's traumatic experiences in predominantly white academic institutions.[1] My own experience has to be understood against the prevalent marginalization and isolation of faculty of color in these institutions. I am a survivor thanks to the sanctuary that is Ananya Dance Theatre—a safe space where I do the work of deep reflection, creative expression, and most importantly, decolonization of my own mind.

It was serendipity that Ananya sent out the first call for audition as I was about to embark on my post-PhD academic career. My daughter Claire was seven months old. Perhaps she was taking one of her daytime naps. Perhaps she was sitting in my lap as I checked my email at the kitchen table. "Calling all women of color who want to move. . . . Children are welcome in the space." My whole being was seized by excitement and anticipation. I knew that this was what I must do: to heed a call for action, by women of color, for women of color.

Saying yes to that call was the singular moment in my life that changed everything. I was to surrender to dance, I was to wrestle with the relationship between dance and justice, and I was to confront and reconcile with my restless spirit at the crossroads of dance, research, teaching, and the work of mothering and mentoring. I was to awaken my spirituality and my faith in human healing through the many injuries before and during this journey—both physical and psychological—and through exhilarating recoveries I have experienced while dancing alongside other women of color artists.

Having to endure injuries seems a negative part of dance. But I have learned along this journey that one gets stronger by pushing up against one's limits, taking risks, learning and relearning one's limits, and figuring out how to push up against new limits. This process of physical healing seems to work as a metaphor for spiritual development and healing from historical trauma. In 2009, we performed excerpts of *Kshoy!* at the National Women's Studies Association (NWSA) annual conference. The scene titled "Crow" has three of us (Ananya Chatterjea, Kenna Cottman, and me) downstage left in a triangle formation, facing the openness of the stage right, feet parallel, knees bent, back extended diagonally by hinging at the hip joints, hands gripping the front of our thighs. We pushed our tailbones back and thrust our heads back and forth, as if in motions of birth. *Kshoy!* was the first of ADT's quartet focusing on women's embodied experience of systemic violence. That particular scene evoked countless women's experience of having to birth in public.

After our performance, a Black woman in the audience spoke poignantly: "Your performance evoked so much pain for me. What should I do with the pain?" This is not an uncommon response from our audiences, who empathize with us kinesthetically and emotionally because of the intensity of our dance labor on stage. To the woman at NWSA I said, "We cannot heal without feeling and acknowledging the pain first." Perhaps one of the things ADT's work does well is to force our audience to confront their pain, both individual and collective, and to imagine pathways toward healing.

I have since been grappling with the possibility of healing and hope, even as we struggle with injuries, pain, and despair. Many of these injuries occur as a result of structural violence, institutionalized racism and sexism, both in the academy and in the arts world, manifested in grant rejections, exclusion from various spaces, and a multitude of microaggressions in our daily living. In my attempt to articulate personal pain and healing in the context of systemic violence, I find affirmation in M. Jacqui Alexander's "pedagogies of crossing" and Gloria Anzaldúa's "spiritual activism." Alexander links the idea of "wholeness" to the work of dismantling hierarchies, divisions, and colonization. She lays out the various dimensions of colonization: systemic exploitation, yes, but also, perhaps even more important, colonization of the mind. Our minds are imprisoned by "dualistic and hierarchical thinking." Consciously or otherwise, we abide by and reproduce many divisions, "among mind, body, spirit; between sacred and secular, male and female, heterosexual and homosexual"; between classes, nations, and so on. Alexander reminds us that our minds are also colonized by "the mistaken notion that only one kind of justice work could lead to freedom."[2]

Alexander's revelation that "the work of decolonization has to make room for wholeness" resonates with Anzaldúa's call for us to work on self-reflection and self-growth as foundations of dismantling injustice. Nearing the end of her journey on earth, Anzaldúa taught three important lessons regarding spiritual activism: (1) transformation of self must be part of a larger process of social transformation; (2) transformation is complicated, "filled with uncertainty and unanswered questions"; and (3) spiritual activists acknowledge the "violence, pain, and other forms of suffering in this world" and choose to live with contradictions.[3] The artists of Ananya Dance Theatre are spiritual activists, as we are invested in working on self-transformation as a stepping stone toward social transformation. Our technique of Yorchhā and its accompanying principles are demanding because they are out of the ordinary in the contemporary North American cultural landscape, where the majority of dancing bodies have been colonized by Western paradigms of ballet-based lines and biases masked in "arts for art's sake" neutrality and universal Reason. Most of the dancers who joined Ananya Dance Theatre recently have had years of training in mainstream institutions. I acknowledge the courage it must take for these young people to plunge into the space of Ananya Dance Theatre. They embrace the challenges, both technical and philosophical. They practice the lines, the footwork, and they peel off old skins of internalized oppression, as they grow new muscles of Yorchhā as well as those of critical, liberatory thinking. As they see the world through these lenses, they see themselves differently as well.

I am intrigued by and invested in these young dancers' transformation because I went through similar processes of disorientation and growth. My story began in China. The injustices I was keenly aware of pertained to class and gender. When I came to the United States as a graduate student in sociology, race, ethnicity, and even immigration were not on my mind. I identified as a working-class Chinese woman. As I spent eight years in graduate school, I came to see myself as an immigrant woman, a border crosser, a person in transience. But a woman of color? I was not sure how to relate to the term despite diligent study of race and ethnicity at the university. The readings and discussions strewn with jargon and statistics did not teach me what I should do with my experience of isolation and marginalization.

In our first year (2004), the women in Ananya Dance Theatre started the work of identity right away. I guess that's what happens when you gather a group of women with self-claimed descriptors such as biracial, Asian American, Chinese, Indian, African American, Latina, Native American, transracially adopted, and queer. We talked about our relationships to each other and our relationships to whiteness. We commiserated and disagreed. At times ADT gatherings felt like graduate seminars: we shared not only conversations but also book lists on race, class, gender, and sexuality. While all of this was going on, I was teaching classes in Critical Studies of Race/Ethnicity at Saint Catherine University. Things began to click, as I became a cultural worker with an antiracist agenda, sweating it out and talking it over with ADT's brown women. Somewhere on my journey with ADT and at St. Kate's, I became an immigrant woman of color, which is infinitely different from being an immigrant woman. The transformation happened amid many hours of warm-up sequences, footwork, and choreography drills. It happened when I tried to help students understand race, class, and gender, only to receive teaching evaluations that accused me of being overly passionate and biased when it comes to race.

Immersed in the daily practice of Ananya Dance Theatre, I knew that I was not alone in my struggle for identity. The words I found in academic writings started to make more sense—such as the following passage in *Feminist Genealogies*: "We were not born women of color but rather became women of color in the context of grappling with indigenous racisms within the United States and the insidious patterns of being differently positioned as Black and brown women."[4]

During 2006, my third year working with Ananya Dance Theatre, Ananya and I worked on a duet for *Pipaashaa*. The choreography of the piece was inspired by yoga and Taiji, reflecting both of our personal and cultural histories. That was a pivotal moment, when I realized that I had so much history in my body that I needed to process through dance. I felt possessed by my grandmothers' spirits, which made my body move in ways I never thought possible. I began to write also, reflecting on the process of getting to know Ananya, the process of peeling off layers of emotional armor that we have to wear in order to survive as women of color in white- and male-dominated institutions. It was significant that in November 2008, we restaged *Pipaashaa* as part of a residency at St. Kate's. In addition to the performance, we conducted a series of workshops designed to help my colleagues and students understand embodied ways of knowing. The most memorable moment of that residency involved the tearful embraces we shared as we watched, on the TV screen of the Green Room, Barack Obama being elected as president of the United States. We did not stop working. We were a group of women of color rehearsing a show to call attention to environmental racism. Women's work and dreams rarely have the glamour of a presidential election, but they are just as urgent and important.

Identity is a political matter. Identity work is an important part of teaching and justice work; as Parker Palmer says, "We teach who we are."[5] If colonization of our minds keeps us from freedom, then we have to prepare our minds and bodies for the work of liberation. Jacqui Alexander writes, "Both complicity [with colonization] and vigilance are learned in this complicated process of figuring out who we are and who we wish to become. The far more difficult question we must collectively engage has to do with the political positions . . . that we come to practice, not merely espouse."[6] So it is with Ananya Dance Theatre that I have begun the embodied political work of figuring out that, indeed, I wish to become a woman of color, and I wish to be at home with coalitions against racism, classism, sexism, heterosexism, and colonization at large.

––––––––

The collaborative nature of ADT's work also reminds me that decolonization does not stop with self-identification. There is no self without community. The dancer that is Hui Niu Wilcox does not exist without the ensemble of Ananya Dance Theatre. The ADT community is not confined by the walls of the studio or the circle we form as we workshop ideas and movements. The circle is always open, ready for new encounters. Our most powerful encounters have been with scholars, poets, and activists who insist on challenging dominant modes of knowing and insist on telling unheard stories not just with their words but also with their bodies and souls.

M. Jacqui Alexander is one of them. In 2005, Shannon Gibney, a fellow ADT dancer, introduced to me Alexander's groundbreaking new book *Pedagogies of Crossing: Meditations on Feminism, Sexual Politics, Memory, and the Sacred*. In 2010, I traveled with ADT to perform for the National Women's Studies Association's conference in Denver. Dr. Alexander was the most generous and enthusiastic spirit in the audience. She was also one of the few prominent scholars who mingled with graduate students and junior faculty—those of us low on the totem pole. At a supposedly casual gathering, Dr. Alexander started a conversation that went to such depth and length that we all pulled out chairs and sat down in a circle. She revealed to me a side of humanism that I had not thought about. Much of critical race theory and postmodern feminist theory that I'd studied offered a seething critique of the idea of universality presumed by modern humanism. The critique goes that humanism and universalism in the Western intellectual traditions tend to elide particular and historical social locations and as a result become Eurocentric by not seeing the particularity of the Western modernity project and its anchoring ideas of Reason and freedom.

I agree with this critique, but perhaps there is another side to the story of humanity besides our ability to rationalize empirical things and to strive for individual freedom. There was Jacqui Alexander, in her turquoise sweater and black-rimmed glasses, telling us that deep down, we share our humanness and all that comes with it. In her words, "Everybody has their own middle passage. Everyone has to find their own medicine, and then they can soar." She asked us, "What would happen if we start from a place of healing, instead of a place of injury?" Looking back, I can see that I was having a spiritual moment, sitting there with Jacqui and my ADT sisters. I came home and read *Pedagogies of Crossing* for the second time.

Along with *This Bridge Called My Back*, *Feminism without Borders*, and other feminist texts, *Pedagogies of Crossing* has influenced Ananya Dance Theatre's work in both politics and poetics. We share Alexander's concern with analyzing and critiquing interlocking systems of race, class, gender, and sexuality. We also share her critique of global capitalism, which she radically links to "the practice of imperialism." She reminds us that we are all complicit in the production and maintenance of hegemonic power. Alexander is as radical as a radical feminist can be.

When she speaks of pedagogy, however, Alexander takes an unexpected turn toward a politics of the sacred, desire, healing, and care. She writes, "The classroom is Sacred place. In any given semester a number of Souls are entrusted into our care and they come as openly and as transparently as they can."[7] As she sees it, all students come to us with a yearning, "faint or well-formed," to imagine communities and to be free of domination and colonization. At times, I have a hard time believing her, disheartened by encounters with the occasional students who refuse to engage or respond—what Palmer names "the Student from Hell."[8] But then I realize that Alexander's leap of faith, the faith that everyone yearns to be free and whole, is precisely what I need to keep teaching and dancing with conviction. It is this faith that empowers us to "listen to a voice before it is spoken."[9]

Alexander knows too well the struggle for those of us charged with the mission to teach and dance for justice, to demystify, or even to dismantle domination. She writes, "I have not always been successful in simply teaching in order to teach, to teach that which I most needed to learn. More often I intended my teaching to serve as a conduit to radicalization, which I now understand to mean a certain imprisonment that conflates the terms of domination with the essence of life. . . . The point is not to [replace] a radical curriculum. The question is whether we can simply teach in order to teach."[10]

These are easily the most profound pedagogical statements, perhaps controversial in some ways. How do we make sense of a critique of a radical women's studies curriculum coming from a radical feminist scholar? What does she mean by "simply teach in order to teach"? What does she mean by saying that the single-minded goal to radicalize our students could be understood as "imprisonment that conflates the terms of domination with the essence of life"?

I am still grappling. But I believe the second "teach" in that phrase encompasses a much bigger domain than the classroom. It is teaching in the deepest sense, teaching each other so that we can live together and care for each other in spite of difference. Domination is what we face, and yet change requires a vision where dismantling domination is not the ultimate goal but a step toward a future where we can *build* a new world and where we can all be fully human. It is what bell hooks calls teaching as a practice of freedom.[11] "What would happen if we start from a place of healing, instead of a place of injury?"

In a way, Ananya Dance Theatre started in a place of injury. Our work was and is still motivated by our rage at the "white supremacist capitalist patriarchy." Anger is important, but anger alone, a negative emotion toxic to our bodies and souls, does not sustain the work that needs to be done in the long run.[12] Love does. The women who have stayed connected with Ananya Dance Theatre over the years are sustained not so much by rage but by a deep love for each other, for community, for dance, and for the possibilities that dance always holds. During conversations that are part of the processes of all of our productions, the question of hope and healing always comes up. Having witnessed and sometimes walked together with communities that have experienced unspeakable historical traumas, we now understand that hope is not a luxury in life. Hope is the essence of life that is generated through women's daily work of sustaining selves and communities. This is why Ananya Dance Theatre explores the themes of women's work, dreaming, building, birthing, healing. Through dance, we have expanded and deepened our understanding of the interdependence of hope and work.

———

When I performed in ADT's premiere of *Bandh* in 2005, I was close to eight months pregnant with my second daughter, Lynn. I was getting so big that my fellow dancers and our director were talking about an emergency plan in case my water broke on stage. Perhaps that half worry, half joke remained in our creative subconscious, for the following year, in our production *Duurbaar: Journeys into Horizon*, we danced on a stage covered by actual water. In 2013, we came full circle to create *Mohona: Estuaries of Desire*, "inspired by stories of women and water and the violence that has resulted from the widespread corporatization of this community resource" (ADT program notes, 2013). Water, as metaphor and material reality, captures ADT's feminist aesthetics and politics, which reclaim and harness the paradoxical power of femininity, of a woman-centered space. Water is a paradox:

it is both gentle and forceful, both nourishing and menacing. The paradox of water is an antidote to the rigid, dichotomous ways of thinking that imprison our minds.

A friend who teaches at a private elementary school once shared with me the school's teaching philosophy, the gist of which is that the kids learn about Beauty first, and when they are older, they learn about Truth. This dichotomous thinking keeps us from seeing both beauty and truth in their ultimate interconnectedness. Truth is often revealed to us in the clearest way through beauty, even when it's an unsettling truth such as the devastation of our communities and ecosystems by unbridled capitalism. In fact, when the so-called ugly truth is evoked through the utmost beauty, the effect is often the most visceral and powerful. And who says there is no beauty in simply recognizing and confronting suffering? It is the tendency to cover up the dark crevices of our histories that keeps us from healing, both for individuals and nations. Truths and beauty cannot be separated because they both speak to the deepest yearnings of our souls.

Here I want to evoke the example of "Chemical Lawns," where the ADT ensemble uses precise, slicing movement of the arms, persistent footwork in patterns of seven and eight, and abrupt turns of the body to suggest a competitive, corporatized world in which we all must move fast and conform. At our audience empowerment workshop, we were asked, "How can you even bring yourselves to embody something that is so ugly?" Some of us did not enjoy learning that piece. I personally took it on as the ultimate physical and mental challenge. The piece required extraordinary physical stamina and mental focus. As we practiced more, the mental focus became even more challenging. But collectively we had a sense of mission: to convey our critique of capitalism; for our bodily critique to have an impact, we have to do this piece with full commitment. Beauty is paradoxical and multifaceted.

So is truth. The truth that we need the most is often the truth that makes us uncomfortable. Ananya Dance Theatre's artists invite activists and artists to make circles with us, year after year. As our circle grows bigger, we as a collective and as individuals grow older and wiser. I recall a moment of uncomfortable truth, of painful and yet necessary growth. In 2007 ADT dancers and guests participated in a workshop led by a Mexican woman artist, where we explored the devastating effects of the harsh US border policies. We walked in a circle and took turns spontaneously going to the center and enacting scenes of border crossing: interrogation, humiliation, and despair were recurring scenarios. We screamed, cried, pleaded, stripped, ran, leaped, fell down, crawled, dragged each other, and wobbled in each other's arms.

One of the Native participants chose to sit outside the circle. When we sat down and debriefed, she remained silent. Upon being invited to share her thoughts, she stated that sometimes borders *should* be safeguarded; Native Americans' displacement and genocide were a result of people not respecting preexisting borders. She said that some members in her community would ask "everyone to go home."

Silence. The tension was palpable in the air. A biracial Caribbean woman who's often identified as black spoke up: "I did not choose to come to America. My ancestors did not choose to come, either." A first-generation immigrant who had started a family here in Minnesota, I choked on my words: "Where is home? Where would home be for my children?"

In my life and work in the United States, I am confronted with these questions every day: for my academic work, I read and teach theories and histories of Asian Americans' alienation. But at that particular moment, to evoke the idea of home inflicted so much pain—I felt not just my own pain but also this Dakota woman's pain—when she spoke of the genocide and displacement of her people. But how do I sit with both my own pain and hers?

I gave her a tearful hug after the workshop was over and said, "I love you." I did love her for telling the truth as she saw it. The next day ADT women had a debriefing session. Many of us expressed feelings of discomfort at what she had said, and then placed what she had said under an analytical microscope: she did not distinguish colonizers and the colonized, and she did not place the immigrant's border-crossing experience in the global colonial context.

But we knew that we had more questions than answers. Our desire to dismantle the socially constructed national border must have seemed self-serving to this Dakota woman, whose politics was rightfully about sovereignty over the lost homeland. But what does it take for us to see that our histories are interconnected, not polarized? How do we connect both histories of genocide/displacement and histories of migration to colonization? Can alliances be built among a range of justice movements rooted in particular identities and communities? How do we work toward justice without erasing each other's pasts?

These questions would have eventually entered my mind somehow in my intellectual journey, but ADT has pushed me along on a fast track, and these face-to-face encounters with activists with many agendas have demanded that I make myself vulnerable, that I see my own complicity in the untelling of so many histories.

It was a moment of growing pain, the beginning of a long journey toward healing. Ananya Dance Theatre is a space of healing, precisely because the community has the courage and capacity to open up the space to reveal painful contradictions and to seek truth and beauty simultaneously. Six years later, we find our closest allies in doing water justice work in Ojibwe and Dakota women who also seek healing and hope for water and through water. We have learned that to collaborate means to spend time with each other and to walk with one another. We learned the lesson most powerfully from Sharon Day, who walks with water year after year and reminds us of the urgency of love in a confused world.

As we tried to reflect on our journey, we told the story of the 2007 workshop to our Dakota ally Janice BadMoccasin, who simply said, "I was there." We were astonished. But now I remembered how she apologized for not being able to sit on the floor. She sat in a folding chair, off to the side of the circle. The story has gone full circle in a sense, as we relived that painful moment and reflected on its significance. We now do all our work with the keen consciousness that we dance on Indigenous land and the institutions that we work within and with are built on the oppression of the Indigenous nations. Janice has offered her love to us, for which we are grateful and eager to reciprocate. But I am haunted still: How can we make sense of the fact that we did not see her in 2007? How do we reckon with the fact that her quiet, observant, and compassionate presence barely registered in our memory?

I have no easy answers to those questions, except that we have come a long way, and we have a long journey ahead of us. We'd like to think that we are on the right track with the clear goal of decolonization, accompanied by many loving spirits. I am inspired by *Black Atlantic*, a brilliant book that connects the global phenomenon of Black music with the painful histories of colonization and slavery. Paul Gilroy speaks of a "politics of transfiguration" that "refuses to accept that the political is a readily separable domain."[13] Artistic practices such as music and dance have the capacity to "conjure up and enact . . . new modes of friendship, happiness, and solidarity that are consequently the overcoming of . . . racial oppression."[14] Friendship, happiness, and solidarity: these are the things that sustained Ananya Dance Theatre's antiracist work. Our work is living proof that the true, the good, and the beautiful all reside in the estuaries of our desire—the desire to live, to be human, to dance, and to walk with each other.

———

I welcomed the year 2013 on Stone Arch Bridge in Minneapolis, huddled with Ananya and other ADT members, standing in vigil for a young Indian woman brutally raped and murdered in Delhi. Later, I talked about this experience with a family friend, who sneered at the fact that there were only nine of us there and that we didn't get any press for it. "But it's the spirit of solidarity that counts," I protested. This short conversation captured the conundrum of dancing for social justice. We do not make sweeping policy changes, and we do not make our way into the media spotlight. But in the end, it is the spirit that sustains our work and gives us hope, and it is the tremor of the souls touched by our dance that leads to action and change. Something magical happened on Stone Arch Bridge: I was a part of a very big thing, not just the eight people around me but also thousands of protesters in the streets of India and many more who desire collective healing from gender violence committed by both individuals and the state.

Life is a series of meetings. Ananya Dance Theatre is a crossroads where spectacular, transformative meetings take place. A few weeks after the vigil, Ananya invited me to watch a group of high school students perform a piece she had set on them during winter break. Her daughter, Srija, was among the students. Sitting in the dark watching Srija dance, I was surprised by my emotions, overwhelmed by the memories of nine-year-old Srija dancing with us on the same floor. She had stopped that work to be her rebellious teenage self. Now she was doing the work again. She had auditioned to be part of her mother's radical work. The dance was titled *Revolution*. Ananya and the students had made it in response to the Delhi rape and the government's sexist responses. I was moved by the young students' passion in conveying the idea of making a new world free of gender violence. A sense of hope surged in my body. Sitting in the audience with me were my own daughters, Claire and Lynn, nine and seven years old, who had started performing with ADT the year before. During rehearsal that day, Claire and Lynn helped improvise their own parts in our new project. We spent time talking about water justice. After rehearsal, when we walked into the dark, cold winter night, Claire asked, "So Ananya Dance Theatre is doing something that helps the world?" "Yes, Claire." I want to remember that moment—one of wholeness, however fleeting. It was a moment when dance, teaching, social justice, and motherhood came together.

———

At a postperformance reception, I spoke with a dance studies professor. Upon hearing that I was a sociology professor, she said, "Oh, so dancing is a hobby?" I paused for a moment and replied, "Sociology is work, but dance is life." To her, a dancer who is also a sociologist cannot also take up dancing as a profession. I have also encountered fellow sociologists who think I must not take my scholarship seriously enough to be so heavily involved in dance. I have grown used to being on the margin in both spheres. I would not have done things in any other way.

I can no longer abide by the binaries: of body and mind, of sociology and dance. I am aware of and grateful for all the subtle, embodied learnings that came to me through dance: my understanding of colonialism, cultural imperialism, racism, feminism, praxis, and so on. Only in dance do I get to put my whole being out there, both as a way of asserting my presence and as a way of figuring out how my body and my dance are viewed by the audience and are put in place by the institutions of the dance world and of the academy. I have come to see how ludicrous socially constructed borders are—the lines that divide artists and thinkers, Chineseness and Americanness, teaching and research, fun and serious work. To create means to play with ideas, objects, our bodies. In most of the academy, especially in the context of teaching, we have our hands, feet, and mind bound by traditions, habits, and even the unimaginatively designed and arranged furniture. To be creative in teaching does not come easy. It is unfortunate because teaching should be one of the most creative endeavors. I thank my experience of risk taking and playing in the space of ADT for my insatiable desire to be creative in teaching.

As I wrap up this essay, I think of my spiritual growth through opening my heart and mind to the influence of the women who inspire and are inspired by our dance. I think of Sharon Day's mesmerizing water song. I think of Jacqui Alexander's advice not to confuse "domination with the essence of life." The essence of life is all-encompassing; it evokes more questions than it gives answers. I straddle dance and academia because I cannot choose. Both worlds produce knowledges, sometimes converging, other times contradicting. I do not want to choose because I yearn for a glimpse of the essence of life that I imagine is not sliced into categories.

———

Ananya Dance Theatre has been dancing to decolonize for over fifteen years. Our dance stems from our dreams of deconstructing all ideas—

including that of dichotomy—and institutions that imprison our minds and bodies. When Ananya Dance Theatre was in her infancy, I danced and laughed along with my peers—women of color roughly my age or even twice as old as I was. As ADT grows as an organization, we have also grown older as people. Now most of the dancers are half my age. Sometimes I feel distanced from the conversations among the young dancers and nostalgic for the women-of-color sisterhood we built when we were younger. Then one day, twenty-year-old Lexi said, "When I grow up, I want to be just like Hui." I realized at that moment that dancing is not just a personal affair and that I am obligated to hold space for future generations with the awareness of our past that is stored in my body. So in this essay, my reflections on the past are not for nostalgia's sake but for the continued resistance and dance of the spiraling generations.

NOTES

1. Katherine Grace Hendrix, ed., *Neither White nor Male: Female Faculty of Color* (San Francisco: Jossey-Bass, 2007); Christine Stanley, *Faculty of Color: Teaching in Predominantly White Colleges and Universities* (Bolton, MA: Anker, 2006).
2. M. Jacqui Alexander, *Pedagogies of Crossing: Meditations on Feminism, Sexual Politics, Memory, and the Sacred* (Durham: Duke University Press, 2005), 505.
3. Ana Louise Keating, "I'm a Citizen of the 'Universe': Gloria Anzaldúa's Spiritual Activism as Catalyst for Social Change," *Feminist Studies* 34, nos. 1–2 (2008): 53–69.
4. M. Jacqui Alexander and Chandra Talpade Mohanty, *Feminist Genealogies, Colonial Legacies, Democratic Futures* (New York: Routledge, 1997), 9.
5. Parker J. Palmer, *The Courage to Teach: Exploring the Inner Landscape of a Teacher's Life* (San Francisco: Jossey-Bass, 1998).
6. Alexander, *Pedagogies of Crossing*, 272.
7. Alexander, *Pedagogies of Crossing*, 8.
8. Palmer, *The Courage to Teach*.
9. Alexander, *Pedagogies of Crossing*, 8.
10. Alexander, *Pedagogies of Crossing*, 8.
11. bell hooks, *Teaching to Transgress: Education as the Practice of Freedom* (New York: Routledge, 1994).
12. Audre Lorde, "The Uses of Anger: Women Responding to Racism," in *Sister Outsider: Essays and Speeches* (Berkeley, CA: Crossing Press, 2007).
13. Paul Gilroy, *The Black Atlantic: Modernity and Double Consciousness* (Cambridge, MA: Harvard University Press, 1993), 38.
14. Gilroy, *The Black Atlantic*, 38.

II

EMBODYING SOLIDARITIES AND INTERSECTIONS

Black and Brown Dancing

6

FEMININITY, BREAKING
THAT BOUNDARY

Interview with Orlando Zane Hunter Jr.

ALESSANDRA LEBEA WILLIAMS

> Orlando Hunter joined the company in 2011 and has performed
> with Ananya Dance Theatre intermittently since. Alessandra Lebea
> Williams conducted this interview on September 20, 2012, and she
> further corresponded with Hunter on December 9, 2020.

HERE WAS THE BASIS OF MY RESEARCH: TO DISMANTLE CONVEN-
tions that are placed on my body and that I even place on myself as a same-
gender-loving man. If femininity is perceived as a negative in a same-gender-
loving person, what choreography can you take on?

I work through softness. My body carries a lot of tension, a lot of bound
hardness because of how I grew up in North Minneapolis. You have people
calling you "fag"; you don't know where you're gonna have to fight for your
life. So being in this work helped me break up a lot of the things that I've
been thinking in my life. I've gained so much flexibility and more accessibil-
ity to different ways of becoming.

I was aware the second week I was rehearsing that I'm the only male in
the company. I'm the minority in the space. I'm in a room filled with women
of color, who in society are oppressed quadruple. I'm still male, and when
I walk out of here, I gain more access to some of the things that women in
the company would not gain. How do I function knowing that I am a male
with this male privilege and still work with women who are clearly working
against that? How do I build my alliance amid what society has already set

up for me? So, for one, I'm biologically privileged to move into this art form where there's just a shortage of men. So that's how I experience privilege in one way. But again, I'm a Black man.

I just don't want to be the stereotypical same-gender-loving Black male. The stereotypical same-gender-loving male is going to dance for Ailey, having a fierce or really snappy personality. There is this archetype of Black male dancer that people have in their mind, and I don't want to be that. That's why taking on this femininity is definitely breaking that boundary. And I wasn't performing hyperfemininity in "Plastic Desire" [of *Moreechika: Season of Mirage*]. I was not performing drag, the act of being a woman, putting on the air, fake boobs, having the appearance of a woman and not the becoming of the feminine energy, which I took on. In "Beauty," what Hui [Wilcox] was doing was hyperfemininity. I would go so far as to say that you could call that drag because Hui does not act like that every day. Performance heightens everyday life. That's when we take our personality higher.

I understand now that I am male-assigned at birth, I go by he, she, they, them pronouns. I showed up in this body to bring justice to it. The history of male bodies has caused tremendous violence in relation to women. I made the commitment to come into this plane of existence to fight the good fight alongside women and to help women heal. Ananya Dance Theatre was the place that allowed my authentic self to flourish with the principles of curvilinearity, flow, softness, earth, air, fire, and water. These elements combined transformed my body, mind, and spirit into a space that is more equipped to create harmony and work with more ease in interconnected relationships with the earth and its beings.

7

LOVING DEEPLY

Black and Brown Women and Femmes in the
Theatrical Jazz Aesthetic of Laurie Carlos and
the Yorchhā Practice of Ananya Dance Theatre

ALESSANDRA LEBEA WILLIAMS

> I don't agree with Ananya most days. It's very important that we
> have a difference in taste, in values, because I would never say about
> this company, "I work with women of color." I would never do that.
> That's really not my thing. But it is important that all of that be in
> the room at the same time. This is the only way, I believe, that real
> progress happens in art. I think this is the way that real love occurs
> in the room. You must be in the world fully knowing all of the ingre-
> dients. It's so important to live in that "yes" process. We don't have
> to agree. It's very important that we don't, very important that we
> don't. And it's important to love deeply. I love Ananya deeply. It's
> important to love deeply, because we don't agree. And that everything
> we do comes out of an action of love.
>
> —LAURIE CARLOS

ON NOVEMBER 20, 2012, IN SAINT PAUL, MINNESOTA, I INTER-
viewed the late Laurie Carlos about her work with Ananya Dance Theatre,
and her responses led me to prioritize "deep love" as the way artists collaborate across their particular differences. By this time, my reflections on
Ananya Dance Theatre had been building for many years. As an undergraduate student, I had viewed live performances of the earliest works,

Bandh: Meditation on Dream in 2005 and *Duurbaar: Journeys into Horizon* in 2006. Here artists of African descent such as Kenna and Beverly Cottman, Lela Pierce, Shannon Gibney, Stefania Strowder, Gina Kundan, and Omise'eke Natasha Tinsley performed alongside diverse Black and brown women and femmes in Indian dance forms to tell striking stories about dreaming. Later on, I joined as an artist for *Pipaashaa: Extreme Thirst* in 2007 and *Ashesh Barsha: Unending Monsoon* in 2009 to begin my training in Yorchhā, our technique practice in Odissi dance, the vinyasa style of yoga, and Chhau martial arts. In future years, when I was writing about the company during my PhD coursework in culture and performance at the University of California, Los Angeles, I spoke with Carlos as part of my research in the summer and early fall months of 2012.

Carlos had been collaborating with our artistic director and choreographer, Ananya Chatterjea, on *Moreechika: Season of Mirage*, a production that premiered at the Southern Theater in September of that year. As Carlos had worked with the company for two previous dances, *Tushaanal: Fires of Dry Grass* in 2011 and *Kshoy!/ Decay!* in 2010, she had thereby participated in the company's quartet of dances designed to examine women's different experiences of gender oppression as it concerned global resources. *Kshoy!* had explored land displacement, *Tushaanal* had focused on gold mining, *Moreechika* was interested in oil production, and the final piece in 2013, *Mohona: Estuaries of Desire*, would look at water pollution.

In our dialogue, Carlos was quite clear about how she differed from Ananya Dance Theatre's mission as a company that concentrated on Black and brown women and femmes. She held a complex position because she acknowledged that white supremacy existed institutionally, while she simultaneously understood how this overarching set of racial ideologies that privileged white bodies over others was indeed a mythology. I wondered, "How can Carlos and Chatterjea work together if they disagree about the company's roots in women of color stories and racial oppression?" Her responses have given me pause, especially in this unprecedented moment of racial justice and local antiracist Black Lives Matter protests in the Twin Cities and globally that have followed the murders of George Floyd, Breonna Taylor, Tony McDade, Ahmaud Arbery, and too many more. Enhancing my own disagreement with Carlos has been the reality of how social movements that challenge state-sanctioned violence have been consistently led by activists living at the intersection of multiple oppressions as Black, trans, and queer women and femmes.[1]

It became important to consider how Black women such as Carlos are not to be framed as a monolith; rather, their practices must be traced and analyzed closely. With Carlos in Ananya Dance Theatre, the tracking began with the theatrical jazz, an aesthetic described by scholar Omi Osun Joni L. Jones as a wide range of creative possibilities in nonlinear approaches to time, autobiographical writing, and physical vocabulary. And as Joni L. Jones accounted for how these layers of improvisation can lead aesthetic practitioners to resist dynamics of Black oppression, the space widened for me to examine the layers of racial and gender resonance in Carlos's artistic process.[2] And Carlos's own words about loving deeply continued to be integral as they further encouraged me to comprehend how Black and brown women and femmes express and forge multilayered intersections through Indian dance.

Through Ananya Dance Theatre's *Moreechika*, I came to appreciate how a duet between dancer Sherie Apungu and Chatterjea moved through Yorchhā's grounding in Odissi dance and vinyasa yoga to bring African and Asian women's bodies outside a singular notion of "woman." I found myself bearing witness to how artist Hui Niu Wilcox performed in relation to *Moreechika*'s set design, which had been influenced by East Asian puppetry, and how she connected this cultural practice to a particular Black feminist theory. I journeyed toward highlighting the role of dancer Orlando Zane Hunter Jr.'s Indian dance training and research on queer Black bodies as part of the company's critique of gender dynamics in the global production of vital resources such as oil. And I began to acknowledge what a theatrical jazz aesthetic, with its Africanist roots and insistence on improvisation with movement and emotion, brought to choreography. I learned it offered a practice that could be aligned with Indian dance principles, while remaining distinct in its work to deepen the audience's direct connection to a dance piece's take on grassroots social movements such as Occupy that have aimed to radically restructure access to resources in the hands of the 99 percent, rather than the further consolidation of wealth among the elite one percent. Overall, my admiration for the meeting of the Asian and African worlds of Yorchhā and the theatrical jazz aesthetic has been fully realized in the collaboration between Chatterjea and Carlos and in their different critical lenses on race, gender, and sexuality.

In what follows, I begin by outlining how these two artists came to meet across their multiple approaches to cultural practices. I continue with choreographic and performance analysis of Carlos, Chatterjea, Apungu,

Wilcox, and Hunter in *Moreechika* to reveal how Yorchhā and theatrical jazz shape perceptions of Black and brown women and femme persons in complex, layered, fluid, and specific ways. Throughout, my own Black femme body lives in this work as a witness, performer, researcher, and colleague who is immersed in our Indian dance aesthetic and submerged in the improvisatory process of theatrical jazz. This research method of being a part of the choreographic work leads me to argue that the deep love held by Black and brown women and femmes for their artistic practices, their collaborative work, and each other lays the foundation for a dance's capacity to comment on the crises that communities face in the world. Our disagreement and difference are the intimacies that build our intention to be actively engaged in the meaning of past and current social struggles.

LAURIE CARLOS AND THE THEATRICAL JAZZ AESTHETIC IN ANANYA DANCE THEATRE

The artistic lives of Ananya Chatterjea and Laurie Carlos have intersected as a result of an unwavering interest in cultural difference. In the 1980s, Chatterjea moved from Kolkata, West Bengal, India, where she had once trained with her teacher, Sanjukta Panigrahi, a student of Guru Kelucharan Mohapatra, who in 1957 had been central to stylizing "classical" Odissi dance out of what historically was a women's temple dancing practice.[3] Although she had specialized in the form with these world-renowned cultural proponents, Chatterjea eventually journeyed to New York to cultivate her "interest in difference."[4]

While completing her graduate studies in New York City in 1989, Chatterjea observed Carlos during a ceremony for a friend, artist Terri Cousar, and she thought to herself, "Laurie was collaborating, and I was like, 'That woman is fucking brilliant. I would so love to work with her.'" One year after moving to Minneapolis to begin her position as an assistant professor of dance at the University of Minnesota, Twin Cities, in 1998, she was reintroduced to Carlos at the Penumbra Theatre. She invited Carlos to create a "healing circle" as part of her performance *A Wife's Letter* in 2001.[5] Two years later, Carlos wrote the play *Marion's Terrible Time of Joy*, which included Chatterjea among its main themes. Chatterjea came to consider their work together as "jazz," which she defined as "the story of intersections between."

As Carlos and Chatterjea worked together, their shared path evolved to be one of holding on to their different ideas about race. According to Chatterjea, "Laurie refuses to have the race conversation. Whoever is right for the work are the people who are ready for it. My politics are different than Laurie's. I really want a company of women of color."[6] These artists disagreed over how the intersection of race and gender took precedence in a dance company. Now, just because Carlos might not have openly articulated certain thoughts about these social categories does not mean that her work has been postrace or color-blind, where she would absolutely refuse to be conscious of the sharp, everyday reality of these concerns.

An important example in this context was the 1976 staging of *For Colored Girls Who Have Considered Suicide / When the Rainbow Is Enuf.* The role of the Lady in Blue was first brought to fruition by Carlos:

> we deal wit emotion too much
> so why dont we go on ahead and be white then/
> & make everything dry & abstract wit no rhythm & no
> reelin for sheer sensual pleasure/yes let's go on & be
> white/we're right in the middle of it/no use holdin
> out/holdin onto ourselves/[7]

In this excerpt, a sense of irony suggests that women who claim a subjectivity as Black and as a woman might as well exist as white persons if they let go of the experiences that shaped them. Again, Carlos's position on these issues has been complex; as she once said, "I have always worked as a feminist person."[8] As her creative efforts have offered ample space for dealing with multiple oppressions of race and gender, I find that her artistry has an undeniable root in Black feminism. Critical race and gender studies scholar bell hooks has examined how Black women can speak from the margins to move through the struggle of existing on the periphery so that we develop a critical consciousness about suffering.[9] Carlos's feminist framework has highlighted women's self- and collective empowerment in order to resist any presumption that racial subjugation had been a controlling force in her daily life.

Eventually immersing herself in the livelihoods of women of African descent, as expressed in *For Colored Girls*, Chatterjea served as the choreographer for the staging of this play at Penumbra Theatre in 2018.[10] As part of her process of movement instruction, she brought the artists who were performing in the roles of the Lady in Brown, Lady in Yellow, Lady in Red, Lady in Green, Lady in Purple, Lady in Blue, and Lady in Orange to the working base of Ananya Dance Theatre, the Shawngrām Institute for Performance and Social Justice in Saint Paul. This way, they could be more

fully immersed in the details of how our training in Yorchhā was foundational to our preparation for upcoming productions. When executing
their own learning of Yorchhā in the final staging of *For Colored Girls*, the
artists embodied our gestural work in their articulations of hand gestures
such as *hamsasya* by pressing together the thumb and index finger and
leaving the remaining fingers open, or as they accentuated the spinal
curvature of postures such as *tribhangi* pose. Through her work in *For
Colored Girls*, Chatterjea found yet another means by which to intersect
her Indian dance techniques with the kind of theatrical processes that
Carlos had dedicated her artistry to.

In further examples, Carlos's creative work has continued to underscore issues of oppression. Regarding her play *White Chocolate for My
Father* (1990), Joni L. Jones has described how it included a "female ancestor" to explain how she negotiated "repeated rapes by placing a bag over her
head."[11] As the play highlighted issues of minstrelsy and its history of performers dressing up in blackface with the application of burnt cork to their
faces, Carlos encouraged "contemporary contemplation on racism." These
thoughts offer important insight into the racial politics in her practice. And
to return to Chatterjea's point, Carlos has chosen to prioritize the artists
best prepared for the performative process, rather than those with a racial,
cultural biology as woman of color. Yet the very context of her creativity
has consistently indicated that artists had better be ready to engage in the
intersections of gender and race that surely might arise in the work.

In fact, Carlos has been integral to supporting the company as it shifted
toward a new politics on the participation of white women and queer Black
and brown male bodies. The first year that Carlos began collaborating with
ADT in 2009 also coincided with the period that the company worked with
two white female artists, Renée Copeland and Sarah Beck-Esmay. The time
of Carlos's third collaboration with ADT in late 2011 included the company's first queer male-bodied Black artist, Orlando Hunter Jr. Acknowledging the role that Carlos played in the company's shift toward a different
framing around Black and brown women and femme identities, Chatterjea
once posited, "Carlos has given me the courage to move forward in this
journey."[12] Carlos's perspective on race and gender in dance has offered
Chatterjea a lens through which to be empowered as the company's politics
on the ethnic and gender makeup of its artists has changed.

Perhaps even more than this, their performing together on stage has
best captured the nature of their capacity to collaborate across these differences. While they coconceived three of the company's pieces in the Quartet

(2010–13)—*Kshoy! Decay!* (2010), *Tushaanal: Fires of Dry Grass* (2011), and *Moreechika: Season of Mirage* (2012)—the distinct layers of their partnership also extended into the performance sequences. In *Kshoy!*, Carlos and Chatterjea had a duet that exemplified how they had grounded themselves in their individual artistry.[13] At the start of this piece, Chatterjea's fingers were lengthened and placed close together while Carlos reached her arm forward with a rounded palm and softened fingers. Carlos released her body fully to the ground with the tops of the feet resting on the floor, as Chatterjea's knees planted down with the toes tucked under behind her. Chatterjea lifted up to stand in a fixed lunge pose with straightened arms lengthening toward Carlos, who remained on the floor, whispering as the inside of one hand caressed the ground. Meanwhile, sound artist and vocalist Mankwe Ndosi sat downstage, accenting Carlos's voice with her own humming. Chatterjea folded over Carlos, her body also reflecting a sudden fall, but she kept her knee sharply lifted. They both rose from the floor, and while Chatterjea went downstage, Carlos turned away, moving in a set of steady circles with her arms folding in and out from the chest. Ndosi's voice quickened in pace, her vocals offering a beating pulse to the energetic shift. Chatterjea ran swiftly into Carlos, who was ready to embrace her even as she kept one arm up, reaching toward the area that Chatterjea had just deserted. They both released, folding their bodies down. As they rose slowly, Carlos rubbed her fingers together rhythmically as Chatterjea rolled up through her spine to standing. Their arms lifted up, and they both gazed toward the front corner of the stage. They bent down to touch the floor with their fingers. Carlos continued to murmur with her breath and to hold a vowel sound intermittently as they both walked forward, twiddling their fingertips to their palms. As Carlos stepped easily, freely forward, Chatterjea paced herself with clear bent knees and parallel legs. Ndosi picked up the tempo by hitting her unique form of percussion, an instrument made of two crutches. Carlos and Chatterjea's movements also increased in pace, with Chatterjea going down to the floor to turn on her knees while twirling her arms overhead and Carlos remaining upright, holding her weight unevenly on one side for a moment, as she moved one palm away from her body and back in, pushed her chest away from her arm and lifted her head up, and vibrated her own voice from high to low.

Carlos's movements and sound work revealed her rootedness in a theatrical jazz aesthetic that is deeply Africanist, because of her practice of embracing conflict. Her flow through a cool, calm presence was matched with the juxtaposition of the continuous shifting of her arms, head, and upper body.[14] Carlos held Chatterjea up once again, this time at the front of her body, on her back, and on her side. Chatterjea fell to the floor, and Carlos kept on singing, walking, and bringing her hand to her chest as she walked off. Their bodies fell down, but Carlos continued to hold her song strong and carry on with the steady fluidity of her movements, while Chatterjea bore her own strength in the specificity of her posture. Chatterjea sought out Carlos's assistance, while Carlos was prepared to shoulder this weight and carry her own. Their individualized, shared dancing in the technique specificity of Yorchhā and an improvisational, Africanist foundation of a theatrical jazz aesthetic underscored the Quartet's thematic focus on how differently women and femme bodies experience and cope with oppression on the basis of gender. As they held their distinct artistic practices, they illuminated how bodies gendered as "woman" have continued to exist in their diverse stories rather than a general monolith.

Carlos's work in the duet also revealed her participation in the recorded sound composition and live performance. Through music compositions designed by Greg Schutte, Carlos's voice has been compiled alongside the musicality of Pooja Goswami Pavan, who is a composer, instructor, and scholar of Hindustani, North Indian classical music.[15] While Carlos's vocal work has functioned within the diverse compilations and selections of audible breath, "bits of blues, jazz, rock and roll, children's rhymes, and Western classical,"[16] Pavan's semiclassical practice has relied on devotional Sufi music and poetry from India. Pavan has described her exposure to different styles in the Twin Cities through the metaphor of curry: "When you are exposed to different styles, something new comes up but you can see the old flavors."[17] Through their respective processes of theatrical jazz and semiclassical music, Pavan and Carlos have revealed how aesthetics can be multidisciplinary and culturally diverse. Such practices operate in direct opposition to dominant framings of multiculturalism that bring communities together only to reduce "different ways of life to superficial tokens that they can harness as style."[18] Carlos's placement in the sound composition of ADT has been central to the artistic production's sole purpose: to bolster the Quartet's focus on racial and gender impacts of the global consumption of essential resources. Here, Carlos has been part of the company's efforts to move its multicultural endeavor away from any artificial premise and to insist on a larger politics of resisting systemic violence.

Still, Carlos's contributions have not been limited to sound and live performance, as they have also included her codirection of multiple theatrical elements to help fulfill the set design and to nourish the physical and emotional skills necessary for performance. For the third piece of the Quartet, *Moreechika*, designer Annie Katsura Rollins made five handheld figures that were placed on a projector and then displayed on the back wall of the theater for audiences to view. Carved with small limbs, large heads, and protruding bellies and known as "hungry ghosts," these figures were based on Tibetan and Chinese mythologies about the need to make urgent changes in the present day to solve the negative effects of past tragedies. Based on the overall vision for these figures to gradually move behind and above dancers in the production, Carlos made it possible for Chatterjea—as dancer and the other coconceiver of the work—to both make decisions about the puppetry while simultaneously dancing in the ensemble. In this case, the formation of the partnership between them has been based on reciprocity: Carlos has been called to lean in with her perspectives about how dancers might move alongside puppets and has been required to know when to step back and let Chatterjea's leadership on the subject come forward.[19]

The kind of direction that Carlos has provided on how artists might solidify their theatrical work has been a process credited to her previous periods of mentorship in breath and movement. "Being able to make these works under the auspices of Dianne McIntyre," she said, "—that taught me a lot about how, as an actor, I go and I find the emotion that I need because the breath ignites the body."[20] This instruction helped her to live with asthma, as well as a condition called myasthenia gravis, where "there were days when muscularly everything was closed out, so I was basically paralyzed." Fortunately, because she learned from Dianne McIntyre, she hasn't taken medication since 1994. McIntytre's own words have recalled how artists of Carlos's generation, such as Ntozake Shange, came to her Sounds in Motion studio to take classes. Her company was focused on "race consciousness, arts, music," and many Black women artists emerged from her studio, such as Marlies Yearby and Jawole Willa Jo Zollar.[21] And with music as a major center of McIntyre's work, how to appropriately categorize her practice became an issue as critics wondered whether to send a dance or music reviewer to her performances.[22]

In ADT, Carlos's own multilayered artistic work has deepened dancers' emotional capacity in a way that has offered yet another difference from specific Indian principles. In one rehearsal in 2012, she asked dancers to create a circle in the center of the theater.[23] She told artists to lift their forearms parallel to the floor with their palms facing upward. In silence, dancers gazed at one another and breathed as their bodies turned from stillness to finding a fluid movement of the legs and careful shifting of the torso. She suggested that dancers be in touch with all aspects of their experience: "Your emotional life is not to be disregarded in your work. Bring it in with you and use it." The exercise, along with the verbal context Carlos provided, reflected the theatrical jazz aesthetic's process of weaving one's own mythology so that others can build connections between their own stories.[24] Carlos's teachings aided artists in leveraging their lived experience for the performative work, while maintaining awareness of the breath of others. All of this was the substance that could lead to deepening audiences' potential to tap into their own stories as they witness a performance that moves across African American and Indian aesthetics.

As Carlos formulated an aesthetic practice rooted in emotion, she offered a lens that could be distinguished from elements of Chatterjea's training. Because Chatterjea once studied Odissi dance with Sanjukta Panigrahi, *rasa*, or the use of mood and emotion as stylized devices in performances, was critical to her earliest dance practice. Scholars of performance studies have framed a relationship between *rasa* and the notion of aesthetics by coining the term "rasaesthetics" to highlight how the emotion crafted by the performer must be separated from an artist's actual feelings so that the piece's communicative work is well understood.[25] Carlos's aesthetic certainly cultivated artists' work to mobilize their emotions, yet pieces such as *Kshoy!* seemed to resonate strongly with Africanist principles. For instance, Brenda Dixon-Gottschild has outlined how this transformation of aesthetic emotion in *rasa* relates to an improvisatory worldview in Black performance genres but with "more a matter of bringing real life within the domain of the art form than making a separation between life and art."[26] When Carlos guided dancers to take hold of their lives, it was a call to intentionally galvanize these specific histories to perform inside of one's own power. In *Kshoy!*, that memory of reclaiming her breath in McIntyre's studio might be an example of how Carlos grounded herself in strength and vigilance when being consistently ready to hold up Chatterjea's body in the duet, while remaining rooted in in the calm, flowing energy of her steps. Carlos has brought to ADT this different layer of emotion through the Africanist presences of theatrical jazz.

LAURIE CARLOS, ANANYA CHATTERJEA, AND SHERIE APUNGU IN *MOREECHIKA: SEASON OF MIRAGE*

Laurie Carlos is a poetic narrator in the opening to the third piece of ADT's Quartet on gender-based violence, *Moreechika: Season of Mirage*. This production explores how oil spills and other chemical crises have led to concerns for the environment and critical resources in Black and brown communities. As audience members sit in their chairs in the Southern Theater in Minneapolis, Carlos emerges among them, walking down the stairs with questions such as "Where is Bhopal?" and spoken words announcing, "The refinery blew up in the night."[27] By the time she reaches the stage, the dance ensemble has created a horrific scene: their bodies are encased in crumpled black plastic. Dancers thrust their limbs and stretch their tongues out of the fabrics that have enclosed them. Urging an energetic shift, Carlos cries out, "Dance your anger and your joy, dance the guns to silence!"

This moment of the piece intersects two different histories of chemical tragedies in India and Nigeria. On December 2, 1984, at the US-owned Union Carbide Plant in Bhopal, Madhya Pradesh, the poisonous gas methyl isocyanate killed approximately 15,000 largely poor residents in the surrounding region and injured many more overnight as they slept.[28] At the same time, it lifts up the poetry of the late Ken Saro-Wiwa, whose writing called out, "Dance oppression and injustice to death. Dance the end of Shell's ecological war of thirty years. Dance my people for we have seen tomorrow."[29] Saro-Wiwa was an activist-author of Nigeria's Ogoni people who mobilized communities against Shell Oil Company's lack of accountability for its oil spills. Tragically, under Sani Abacha's military governance, he was sentenced to death and executed in 1995. In *Moreechika*, Carlos's poetry, as she circulates through the audience and makes her way to the dancers, offers a link between environmental crises caused by multinational corporations with a capitalist presence in West African and South Asian communities. Carlos brings a form of theatrical jazz into ADT's Indian dance practice that bridges Black and brown experiences to create an integrated world and dismantle historical problems.[30]

Even as Carlos's work is highlighted and foregrounded in *Moreechika*, her aesthetic is consistently placed alongside Yorchhā technique. As these distinct forms share the stage, they further express a relationship across national and racial boundaries and explore the diverse position of particular Black and brown women—in this case, Ananya Chatterjea and Sherie Apungu. During the same harrowing scene of Carlos's poetic entry, one artist, Sherie Apungu, comes to the stage sharply, her legs and arms outstretched, trembling at her navel region until the plastic no longer covers her body. All around her, dancers grip with tension and turn slowly within the layers of their plastic. She lies there exposed, convulsing her abdominals until Chatterjea struggles out of her own plastic to come near her. Reflecting

FIGURE 7.1. (From left) Ananya Chatterjea and Sherie C. M. Apungu dancing a vision in interaction with puppets manipulated by Alessandra Lebea Williams in *Moreechika: Season of Mirage* (2012). Photo by Paul Virtucio. Courtesy of Ananya Dance Theatre.

on this kind of dancing, Apungu has considered her own ancestry as an African artist originally from Kenya and what it can mean to intersect with Asian women in dance: "Ananya and I did not meet by chance. I do believe our paths were destined to interact."[31] She goes on to say, "Ananya's passion and her intention to do right in the communities from which she is from and those communities that are oppressed" has inspired her own effort to "dig deep into the stuff that is me, to consolidate foreign stories into my own story and then transform the movement space to convince audiences to take the emotional journey in the piece with me." To perform in a narrative about the global oppressive condition of chemical spills is to strike a balance between larger issues and memories surrounding one's own bodily experience. Her words certainly reflect the framing of theatrical jazz that Carlos has offered in ADT's rehearsals to enhance dancers' grounding in emotion for performance purposes.

When Apungu begins that journey with Chatterjea in the performance, the ensemble of dancers has left the stage, leaving these two artists to begin their duet with a focus on the yoga practice that underlies Yorchhā (figure 7.1). Chatterjea presses both palms to the floor, straightens her arms, and lengthens both legs behind her to form yoga's low plank posture.

Reversing the pose, she opens the front of the body upward to the ceiling and relaxes her head back. Apungu then lifts from the floor with her hips open and rises over Chatterjea's body. Apungu presses a single hand into the floor, lifts the other hand to the ceiling, and stretches her legs long to bring her body to face the audience. Balancing on the edges of her feet, she shifts fully into yoga's side plank pose. Meanwhile, Chatterjea lies on her back in yoga's supine hero pose, with her spine on the floor, her bent knees coming to touch, and her shins embracing the floor. She presses both palms down, straightens her arms, and lengthens both legs behind her. Opening up the pose, she lifts the front of her body toward the ceiling and relaxes her head back, as Apungu also comes up from the floor to rise over Chatterjea's body. These artists' labor in Yorchhā is part of the company's effort to work in vinyasa, the form of yoga that makes particular alignments between the joints and enlivens the energy all along the body through breath.[32] And as they weave, encircle, twist, open, and separate, they reveal how Chatterjea's choreography resists displaying bodies in the generalized category of "woman," which essentially lacks cultural and historical specificity.[33] This reversal of universal ideas about women in the world lives in how dancers articulate a complex uniformity that highlights their varied spinal structures, torso curvatures, and flexibility.

When they come to stand, these artists establish their immersion in multiple Indian forms, as they build on the yoga poses with Odissi-based techniques. They sit in Odissi's square position of *chauk* with feet wide apart, knees bent, hips sitting low to the floor, and torso upright. As if being struck again by the horrendous visual of dancers' bodies easing and pressing in and out of plastic, Apungu leans her chest forward. Pulling her away from this gazing outward, Chatterjea lifts her leg onto Apungu's thigh. Their upper torsos oscillate to the front and back until Apungu launches Chatterjea ahead, her face meeting the center of her palm with fingers stretched out widely to form the hand gesture of *alapadma*. This surge, lunging ahead and downward, mirrors the program brochure's description of the partnering as "a vision terrifying, horrifying, epic" of "past-present-future" through "the shadows of death."And their grounding and flow in Yorchhā elevates the role of practice in establishing a Black and brown relation that gives spectators time to witness their individual diversity as women. Their bodies remain separate in distinct yoga postures and become uniform at particular moments in Odissi poses, with their crossing and layering of upper body parts and different foundations of the pelvis. The company describes this Odissi dance vocabulary as the "use of spirals in the upper part of the body, sculptural balances, extensions of the hip, subtle movements of the torso, active limbic extremities, and curvilinear extensions of the spine."[34] While Carlos's opening text forges together fragments of Asian and African contexts, the dancers' own layered technique expresses the complex turnings, curves, angles by which these stories differentiate and align. If a "counter-discourse to western modernity" emerges "precisely when it eschews the temptations of culturalism and raciology,"[35] according to Afro-Asian theorist Bill V. Mullen, then the duet's physical work brings together African and Asian realms by way of resisting a one-dimensional framing of Black and brown women.

Dancers further resist singularity and initiate dialogue across cultural differences through enduring bodily efforts. Prior to *Moreechika*, Apungu had danced in the first installment of the company's quartet, *Kshoy!/ Decay!* in 2010, which featured her in a solo.[36] The lighting hold and opening of her face as it turned toward the audience and the unwavering, unrelenting presence of her body as it lowered to the ground bolstered *Kshoy!*'s focus on the displacement of women and femmes from land. Rather than a mere perception of African women in a perpetual state of ethnic clashes, her dancing might expand our attention to coping, resisting, mourning, and surviving historical tensions and charges toward peace in a community. With Apungu's dancing in both *Kshoy!* and *Moreechika*, her capacity to dance her difference alongside Chatterjea has been built through an investment in multiple pieces of the Quartet.

Analysis of the moment that follows the duet between Apungu and Chatterjea shows how dancers wrestle with integrating the technique they have long shared and established. After the duet, Chatterjea has a solo that reconfigures movements from her former dancing. With Apungu, her hands had formed the lengthened fingers and rounded palm of the *mudra*, or hand gesture, known as *alapadma*. In this solo, the *alapadma* returns in a different vitality as her arms shake, knees bend, and legs open parallel to each other. Adding to the hand gestures, she forms *tripataka* by lengthening her fingers, bringing them to touch, and lowering only the third finger halfway to the palm of the hand. While holding *tripataka*, she presses one hand away from the body and brings the other hand toward her face. As she had done alongside Apungu, she then frames her eyes with her hands. She circles her arms in the shape of a figure eight, which had been the formation of Apungu's torso during her own exit. Yet here she balances on one leg and grabs her foot to form yoga's hand-to-big-toe pose. Then she shifts to landing in double *chauk* pose. This physical connection resonates with the purpose of yoga, as *yuj*, a Sanskrit term meaning to bind one's concentration on unity and communion.[37] She effectively rearticulates and transforms movement from the duet to the solo, revealing how African and Asian unity is about finding your gendered position and continuing to process and adjust these moments of intersection. Our solidarities as Black and brown persons are never static, but always change through meditation on each other's bodies and a willingness to return to the shape of our cross-cultural intersections again and again. That capacity to look back at the work, rework it, and build on it is a source of "loving deeply" in this Black and brown context.

LAURIE CARLOS, HUI NIU WILCOX, AND THE HUNGRY GHOST PUPPETS

The use of puppetry in *Moreechika* illustrates how dancers work to deal with historically rooted tensions. Ananya Dance Theatre artists such as Hui Niu Wilcox position themselves in relation to the figures on display. For the performance at the Southern Theater, I serve as the puppeteer who places these transparent objects on the projector, and I am guided by Laurie Carlos's ideas on improvisation and the artists' own thoughts about hungry ghosts.

As the puppeteer, I am driven toward conducting research on what they symbolize and how they get defined philosophically, and then matching these frameworks with Carlos's own directions. My main text to comprehend this idea of a hungry ghost is Padmasambhava in *The Tibetan Book of the Dead*.[38] Hungry ghosts can be understood as anguished spirits "under the sway of attachment" to unsolved cravings in history; they teach us to learn about how our habits generate the path of our future existence. To prevent negative past events from repeating themselves, adequate changes have to be made in the present to radically shift this natural law. In other words, the only pathway to liberation from a devastating history is the "skillful transformation" of the ordinary states of human reality.[39] In the context of *Moreechika*, then, the hungry ghosts serve the purpose of recalling the lives lost to industrial disasters and reflecting on how specific historical tendencies toward capitalist gain have harmed particular communities.

Alongside this focus on cyclical conditions, Carlos adds an emphasis on play in my initial practice with the puppets. Our designer, Annie Katsura Rollins, had made the five figures with small handles so I can more easily place them on the projector. Immediately, I begin trying to find an identifiable, memorable structure by which I can grab one of the puppets and put them on the lit screen in a way that I can recall efficiently for the performance.

Carlos cautions me against this claim I was making to rigidity so early on, instead advising me to refuse simply landing on a singular practice and rather focus on experimentation and improvisation.[40] In this way, Carlos exemplifies an understanding of her theatrical aesthetic as Oya, the Yoruba cosmic formation of wind and the intense energy of storms, to account for the dynamic flow of her creativity.[41] While guiding me toward a process of continuous reinvention, she also directs me to remember my previous history of dancing with the company in *Pipaashaa: Extreme Thirst* (2007) and *Ashesh Barsha: Unending Monsoon* (2009) so that every move I make with the puppets backstage will allow these figures to be in direct participation with the movement happening on stage.[42] This latter concern, though, seems to be a call to not only focus on overhauling my method of working with the puppets to better appreciate jazz but also to fully acknowledge the precise craft of the artists in the ensemble.

Hui Wilcox is critical to watch in *Moreechika* when it comes to making clearer connections between the puppets and the dancing. When the artists emerge on stage incrementally at the beginning of the dance, each covered in an individual parcel of black plastic, Wilcox stretches her own plastic, moving one step at a time with one arm reaching high and the other arm parallel to the floor to create a triangular shape with her upper limbs. Turning her body clockwise in this position, she tightens the plastic more closely around her legs. Continuing to turn, she crouches down to the floor to begin crawling off, her arms and head slowly revealed as she scrapes her way off stage. The sense of experimentation exists on stage, as each artist embodies an individual process of crafting imagery with the plastic. Through Wilcox's movements, it becomes evident how many times artists have repeatedly rehearsed with plastic to accomplish the different visuals that allow them to perform with the precision necessary to hold the body in distinct postures and reshape and dissolve these sculptures while maintaining a gripping sensation.

As part of her craft and emotional work, Wilcox reflects on a particular women's history. She recalls her grandmother's experience enduring multiple famines in China and how she stored bags of grain, rice, and flour to be prepared for future disasters. Hungry ghosts are a sign of the physical results of starvation or suffering from ingesting unhealthy food: "I said this narrative to myself. I am a hungry ghost. Reincarnated in different forms. In 'Almost Gone,' I'm wrapped in plastic. My tongue—capitalism—clogged in a machine. We are a hungry ghost. So I try to connect those pieces."[43] One of the famines has been discussed by journalist Yang Jisheng as resulting in thirty-six million deaths between 1958 and 1962 because of the Great Leap Forward created by Chairman Mao. The "mandated rapid industrialization" led to "exaggerated production reports from below" that could not be delivered.[44] The state provided no assistance when food became scarce, and by the end of 1960, China's population was ten million less than the previous year. Wilcox brings these larger experiences of her family into the performance as she holds the plastic taut against her body and underscores the notion of cause and effect that is tied to the hungry ghosts. She demonstrates how ADT dancers articulate global experiences through their lives, lest they risk merely voicing "Other" people's concerns from afar and not putting their own selves on the line.

The more attention I pay to the dancing, the more I can seek to also understand my position as a person of African descent who is manipulating puppets that are framed by East Asian philosophies. My maternal grandparents were African American sharecroppers in northeastern Louisiana who were furnished by a landowner to plant cotton, and at harvest, were required to pay back the advance and about half of the crop yield. This agricultural framework held Black farmers in deep poverty and economic disenfranchisement for generations. Burdened by obligatory debts and stripped of the possibility to sell their crops, sharecroppers "lived under the twin yoke of race oppression and economic peonage" even as cotton prices increased during World War I, explains historian Theodore Rosengarten.[45] Now, I did not have to endure my grandparents' tremendous labor of cultivating a seed only to reap barely any benefit from this system or, more tragically, to enter into debt. Similarly, Wilcox did not herself endure the era of famines survived by her family members. So reflecting on these histories as dancers in a performance about petroleum and chemical spills brings us back to Carlos's statement about how your "emotional life is not to be disregarded in your work." The hungry ghosts become a call to engage with the traumatic circumstances of our histories. And being fully present in this memory better sustains the kind of tension required in the body to accomplish Wilcox's performance with the plastic. Our labor as artists expressing the many theatrical dynamics and global concerns of *Moreechika* is to do the research necessary to hold bodies firmly in relation to the larger visual of the performance, which includes the decrepit look of the puppets above the dancers, beckoning us to respond actively to past tragedies and disadvantages (see the hungry ghosts on the back wall of dancers in figure 7.1).

And since the objective of our work with the hungry ghosts is to initiate "skillful transformation," it can also be our process to consider the existence of healing in the present moment. Wilcox has found a feminist framework useful in imagining this change in the continuum: M. Jacqui Alexander's theory of "the Crossing" describes the important ways in which formerly enslaved persons might still be yearning to tell their stories and how we can best bring these narratives to fruition through recreating and reinventing our practices. We learn here to coexist with one another through solidarity, interdependence, and relationality, and we can apply these ways of knowing to plots against violent, oppressive norms.[46] In Wilcox's words, when building a coalition and an "understanding of self, we are telling our stories, we are talking about ideologies."[47] Knowing our own catastrophic histories is the underlying layer of what allows us to be in solidarity with the large-scale issues facing Black and brown communities.

As we participate in enacting *Moreechika*'s inquiry into the human impact of oil through dance, sound, and puppetry, it is essential that we not lose sight of the value in intersecting our own present and past. For instance, as I engaged in the improvisatory play expected of me, Wilcox's two young daughters consistently tried their own hand at different positions, sitting with me, observing, and demonstrating their own ideas about various maneuvers with the figures. In response to this memory, Wilcox posits, "The hungry ghosts probably resonate somehow."[48] She has always hoped for her children to "have a community, a real community, of real women," because "my kids are my future—that's also part of healing." Our work in ADT is a kind of Black and brown world in its mapping across multiple oppressions to create connections in our communities. This movement between diverse social and political histories of peoples of African and Asian descent is described by Nico Slate as a history that "framed commonalities of struggle between 'colored' peoples fighting for their rights throughout the world."[49] In our context, the unity across Black and brown peoples is a dance production out of which particular forms of strife, survival, and a search for healing are forged. And this practice is tied to the care we share for one another as an act of loving concentration on shaping intentional communities.

LAURIE CARLOS AND ORLANDO ZANE HUNTER JR. IN "PLASTIC DESIRE"

How do women and femmes contribute to the exploitation of vital resources through their complicity within functions of power? Ananya Chatterjea and dancer Orlando Zane Hunter Jr. carry out this questioning in their research for a section of *Moreechika* called "Plastic Desire." This area of work takes issue with any assumption that Ananya Dance Theatre, as a primarily Black and brown company, refuses to acknowledge the role such bodies play in these issues. As the program outlines, "Plastic Desire" delves into the place of "power and femininity" in a "world run by the grab for resources." The performance's featuring of Hunter, the first person in the company to be normatively perceived by others as a "male" body, suggests that the category of "woman," with its restrictive norms on the feminine and its binary opposition to masculine notions, raises conflicts to be wrestled with in Yorchhā technique.

At the heart of their research is the leadership of Maria das Graças Foster, her control of Brazil's state-led petroleum company, and what a dancing body can unveil about gender. As Hunter pinpoints, the significance is the intersection between Foster's "emotions as a woman who is the head of this huge oil company that is predominately male-driven in that industry and the fact that the oil company is harming women and children and water resources."[50] For instance, an oil spill unleashed three thousand barrels in 2012 at Chevron's Frade Field development project, where Brazil's Petrobas petroleum company was a partner.[51] And as *Moreechika* moves away from gender norms, it holds its own matrix of critiques: the normative position of queer and male-presenting bodies in performance; the role of women in deepening the chemical spill crises; and the consumerist desire for products such as cosmetics, which contain toxic substances. Here is how Hunter describes the rigid dynamics that can exist in dance: "A lot of the time, [same-gender-loving male bodies] are placed in that heteronormative role. It's counter to their everyday life, to being able to express themselves and have more whole ideas onstage." It is useful to call this a kind of "queer of color critique," American studies scholar Roderick Ferguson's term for how nonheteronormative persons of color resist and perpetuate norms to "contradict the idea of the liberal nation-state and capital as sites of resolution, perfection, progress, and confirmation."[52] Through a Black queer embodiment, "Plastic Desire" explores a relationship among authority, gender, and capitalist structures.

It is one of Yorchhā's major forms, Odissi dance, that best articulates these body politics. Hunter (they, them, their pronouns) shapes a sari, a traditional Indian garment worn by women and femmes where fabric is held at the waist and taken over one shoulder to leave the sides of the body open. In this piece, though, the sari is made out of a large plastic garb. Hunter emerges upstage to begin a long, calculated walk at a diagonal across stage. The walk takes place in parallel, with their bodily weight coming onto one limb while the other leg moves forward with knees bent and feet flexed. The shape of one foot lifting and returning to the floor is done with such clarity that it creates a necessary mode of our training: a half-moon foot. Reaching closer downstage, Hunter grabs the long stream of plastic that has formed behind, whips it firmly up and around to the front, and continues walking toward the audience until they reach the corner of the stage. In the time it has taken to reach this point, Hunter has given us a moment to reflect on the image of a body appearing to be "male" moving through this concentrated effort of the hips slowly accentuating fully sideward, while the torso reacts to form its own upward pendulum swing. In this case, the so-called feminine traits of soft, seductive sensuality are not limited to a cisgender, female person. While dancers Renée Copeland and Brittany Radke come farther upstage, Hunter starts to form a sari out of the plastic by turning away from the audience and placing the plastic around their hips. Facing forward to lean down and grab the plastic, pleats are then formed by stretching the plastic and folding it around their hand. All the while, Hunter bends their knees, shifting between hips in Odissi's *tribhangi* pose, where the body accomplishes three bends: the weight comes to one hip, the leg of the other hip reaches forward and out at a diagonal, both knees remain lowered, and the upper torso circles away from that initial standing hip, followed by a tilt of the chin. Completing the sari, the plastic is lifted over the shoulder to stretch the fabric across the chest and behind the body. For the final touches, Hunter lengthens the sari down over their legs, tightens it around their waist, pleats again near their right hip, and then steps into one of the exercises of our Odissi training in *tribhangi* pose. The heel of the front foot meets the ground, and balancing there, the back foot lifts momentarily while keeping the hip extended. The back foot returns to the floor, and the front heel gets reshaped into a flat foot to create sound when planting back down.

And from the start of Hunter's walk, Laurie Carlos sings in the recorded composition:

Always one-hundred percent petroleum jelly
Royal Crown
Dixie Peach
Tar Road
Flames in the kitchen
Flames

Nooo!
Nooo!
Nooo!
Nooo!
Nooo!
Nooo!

During these vocals, Carlos's voice builds toward a punchy, irritated sound as if her face is clenching tightly. In the short pauses between terms, listeners have an opportunity to reflect on the use of petroleum jelly as a beauty product, a way of moisturizing and treating dry skin. This dance is not only about higher profile leadership, but also our own daily actions for beauty and whether these healing practices reveal a need to critique our own complicity.

The layers of gender, sexuality, and race in this moment are numerous. Hunter's movements are exacting, with the placement of specific parts of the feet on the floor and the flexion of the extremities necessary to balance on the heel while lengthening the hip. An everyday use of the sari in dressing an Indian female body is being used on a same-gender-loving Black person who performs in the context of how women leaders can better hold themselves accountable for the toxic harm faced by communities. Our artistic director's intimacy with Odissi dance evolves into a space of critique through the qualities of the practice itself. It is not enough to present a deep love for the beauty of Odissi dance on the concert stage, as Chatterjea has expressed her own desire to "deconstruct the sari on my body" so that the "classical" script for Odissi dance as having a seamless history gets replaced with a claim to a radical space. She takes an interest in choreographers making a direct address to internal hierarchies of gender and class so that relationships across difference can be discovered.[53] On the topic of Indian dance and the sari, dance scholar Priya Srinivasan clarifies how it can position bodies of South Asian descent as an inverse to white identity norms and simultaneously preserve the idea of a citizen that is heteronormative, patriarchal, and stereotypically Orientalist in their features.[54] In "Plastic Desire," the sari helps make sense of current global issues, because Chatterjea, as the choreographer, places ADT's dancing bodies at the intersection of African American experience and nonheteronormative existence. And in this case, Black and brown femme practice exists in the expressive quality that is embodied by queer Black artists training in the work, as well as the artistic contributions of Carlos in vocals and poetic narrative.

CONCLUSION: LAURIE CARLOS IN "OCCUPY"

At the end, Laurie Carlos's improvisation brings audiences onto a stage molded by a global Black and brown lens. "Occupy" is the title of this section, which is described in the program as being inspired by scholar-activist Angela Y. Davis's "statement at the Occupy rally in Philadelphia: 'the unity of the 99% must be a complex unity!'" On September 17, 2011, in New York, the Occupy movement began when "protestors set up camp for the night in Zuccotti Park in Lower Manhattan," claiming to represent the 99 percent of the US population and to be in "opposition to the 1 percent elite."[55] This piece continues *Moreechika*'s inquiry into corporate grabs for vital resources as artists invite the audience to occupy a stage filled with rice, but to enter with clarity about the dance's exploration of oil disasters and chemical spills that communities have endured.

In this moment, artists' hips lower toward the floor and their knees open in double *chauk* pose in placing the body downward with the feet wide apart. As they move with the fallen particles, dancers perform variations of a sequence. They drop down, swirl the rice around their bodies, pour it in front of their faces, or shake a fist full of it and let it fly out into space. In Yorchhā form, Chatterjea creates the clenched fingers of *mushti* by bringing together all the digits of the right hand. She releases the rice particles in front of her face and opens her mouth wide. With her knees touching the floor, she lifts her torso up and releases her head back. In this yoga camel pose, she throws rice directly at her navel. While on her knees, Chatterjea places her hand in the rice and swirls her arm out to begin creating images with it. In this way, she demonstrates how spectators can move intentionally with the rice, after Carlos has invited them on stage.

As dancers move, Carlos's voice and bodily actions are directed toward the audience as a way of helping spectators prepare to enter the performance space. Carlos walks as she says the words "Dance your guns to silence," the same poetic phrase that is based on Ken Saro-Wiwa's work. Her vocals are reminiscent of jazz artists whose singing protested the horrific violence Black bodies have historically endured in "translat[ing] an antiracist literary text into a dynamic musical work whose enduring meaning stemmed from the way she chose to render it as song."[56] Carlos's poetic words and bodily positioning are rooted in a social movement of the 99 percent, and her practice foreshadows her imminent return to audience seating to request that viewers cultivate their story. In the style of theatrical jazz, she calls on others to move into the space created by artists and to physically connect themselves to the work.

Carlos acts with great calculation by (1) connecting with the audience through gaze and movement in space, (2) entering into the audience with intention, (3) inviting a spectator to come with her onstage, (4) showing the spectator how to handle rice, and (5) returning to the audience to bring more spectators to the performance space. Preparing, Carlos gazes out toward the observers. She moves closer to the audience seating, walking downstage to stand directly in front of the spectators. Pausing, she looks at the visual of the artists moving in the rice. She turns her head toward and then away from spectators, saying, "Your anger and your joy." Moving farther from the audience, she walks to the back wall, stops momentarily, and re-adjusts the placement of her costume over her shoulder. Forthrightly, she walks down the stage into the audience, goes up the stairs, and pauses in front of a spectator. The recorded sound composition presents Carlos saying, "Raw to the sky, to you. This is the long, held note."

While holding Carlos's hand, the spectator (they/them pronouns) rises from the seat and walks down the steps and onto stage. Carlos bends over to grab some rice on the ground. The spectator waits there, turned away from the audience. Carlos puts rice into the spectator's hands, momentarily holding their palm close to her own. Carlos gazes at the spectator and they look directly into her eyes. While backing away, Carlos continues to look at the person before turning away to return to the audience and collect another person.

As Carlos ensures that spectators are aware of what is required to handle the rice, these actions resonate with the intention needed in social movements. She guides the audience toward a concentrated focus, because these witnesses are entering a space in which artists have danced side by side to negotiate their different physical bodies with care, have performed with full-bodied expression in relation to puppetry, and have held multiple articulations of gender and sexuality in their Yorchhā training. As Angela Davis posits, "There are major responsibilities attached to this decision to forge such an expansive community of resistance."[57] And this training in complete awareness, prior to stepping into this space that has been filled with dancers' labor, is quite valuable in grassroots efforts so that activists do not lose sight of the often unrecognized labor of Black, queer, and trans women and femmes who have long pioneered resistance movements.[58] Carlos's focused attention on them, her careful guidance on how to pick up rice and how to create with it, encourages audience members not to make careless gestures but rather to take seriously the task of crafting a story with the fallen rice. Each spectator's intent is critical, because they are being invited into a site of love that holds space for multiple perspectives and experiences of race, gender, culture, and sexuality and that has emerged in relation to dancers' commitment to researching toxic spills and oil pollution in particular communities.

"Occupy" is the culmination of ADT's *Moreechika*, in which disagreement and difference are alive in the creative realm, enhancing how we build up to the performance, how we carry out our research engagement, and how we envision and critique the intimacy embedded in our connections across each other's Black and brown histories. This deep love has been traced across multiple diversities in which the dancers' expression of Yorchhā technique reveals the complexity of connections established between women, as well as the role of femme bodies in shaking up the assumptions made around gender binaries. When brown and Black artists such as Ananya Chatterjea and Laurie Carlos insist on working through love to bridge their ideological and creative differences, the possibilities for aesthetic experimentation and technical rigor in performance grow immensely.

NOTES

Epigraph: Laurie Carlos, interview with the author, November 20, 2012.

1 I am referring here, for instance, to the leadership of Black Visions Collective in the movement to divest from police and reinvest in communities in the Twin Cities and also the cofounders Patrisse Cullors, Alicia Garza, and Opal Tometi of Black Lives Matter.

2 Omi Osun Joni L. Jones, *Theatrical Jazz: Performance, Àṣẹ, and the Power of the Present Moment* (Columbus: Ohio State University Press, 2015), 36.

3 Ananya Chatterjea, "Contestations: Constructing a Historical Narrative for Odissi," in *Rethinking Dance History*, ed. Alexandra Carter (New York: Routledge, 2004).

4 Ananya Chatterjea, interview with the author, November 3, 2012. In a further communication on January 3, 2021, Chatterjea conveyed that it is more accurate to say that she came here with the "hopes of working with artists from different parts of the global South, not so much 'multiculturalism' because I didn't quite understand that conceptual frame and its implications, and also India was deeply multicultural. It was the specificity of meeting artists from different global South locations that was exciting to me."

5 In this case, the practice of a healing circle—when an artist creates a space to be immersed in the full embodiment and expression of one's experience—is attached to experiments with physical and vocal expression.

6 Ananya Chatterjea, interview with the author, November 3, 2012. Note: currently, Chatterjea defines the company as consisting of Black and brown women and femmes.

7 Ntozake Shange, *For Colored Girls Who Have Considered Suicide When the Rainbow Is Enuf: A Choreopoem* (New York: Bantam Books, 1975), 47.

8 Laurie Carlos, interview with the author, November 20, 2012.

9 bell hooks, *Yearning: Race, Gender, and Cultural Politics* (Boston: South End, 1990), 152–53.

10 Ntozake Shange's *For Colored Girls Who Have Considered Suicide / When the Rainbow Is Enuf*, directed by Sarah Bellamy and Lou Bellamy, choreography by Ananya Chatterjea, performed by Cristina Florencia Castro, Khanisha Foster, Sun Mee Chomet, Audrey Park, Ashe Jaafaru, Rajané Katurah Brown, and Am'Ber Montgomery, and choreography assisted by Kealoha Ferreira (Penumbra Theatre, September 18–October 14, 2018).

11 Omi Osun Joni L. Jones, *Theatrical Jazz*, 40.

12 Ananya Chatterjea, postperformance dialogue, *Moreechika: Season of Mirage*, Southern Theater, Minneapolis, September 8, 2012.

13 *Kshoy!/ Decay!*, Southern Theater, Minneapolis, September 9, 2010.

14 Brenda Dixon Gottschild, *Digging the Africanist Aesthetic in American Performance: Dance and Other Contexts* (Westport: Greenwood Press, 1996), 13–17.

15 "Dr. Pooja Goswami Pavan," accessed May 28, 2020, http://www.ananyadance theatre.org/bios/dr-pooja-goswami-pavan/.

16 Omi Osun Joni L. Jones, *Theatrical Jazz*, 38.

17 "MN Original: Pooja Goswami Pavan," February 14, 2016, https://www.pbs.org /video/Pooja-Goswami-Pavan-655954H-1/.

18 Vijay Prashad, *Everybody Was Kung Fu Fighting: Afro-Asian Connections and the Myth of Cultural Purity* (Boston: Beacon Press, 2001), 39.

19 Her words resonated with Brent Hayes Edwards's theory of the term "diaspora," or those lives of persons such as African Americans whose residences in the United States place them outside an authentic place of origin on the African continent. Edwards considers the practice of 1920s literary authors of African descent as a search for reciprocity across their very different ways of resisting global racism and colonialism. Brent Hayes Edwards, *The Practice of Diaspora: Literature, Translation, and the Rise of Black Internationalism* (Cambridge, MA: Harvard University Press, 2003).

20 Laurie Carlos, interview with the author, November 20, 2012.

21 Dianne McIntyre, "A Dance Life: Race, Gender, Politics Art, Diane McIntyre," paper presented at the Collegium for African Diaspora Dance Conference, Duke University, Durham, North Carolina, February 23, 2020.

22 Dance historian Veta Goler captures this layering in stating that McIntyre was sensitive to dance and music, especially "classic and avant-garde jazz, rhythm-and-blues tunes, hymns, and historical Black music." Veta Goler, "Moves on Top of Blues," in *Dancing Many Drums: Excavations in African American Dance*, ed. Thomas F. DeFrantz (Madison: University of Wisconsin Press, 2002), 209.

23 Laurie Carlos, Ananya Dance Theatre rehearsal, University of Minnesota, Twin Cities, Minneapolis, July 8, 2012.

24 Omi Osun Joni L. Jones, *Theatrical Jazz*, 39.

25 Richard Schechner, "Rasaesthetics," *TDR* 45, no. 3 (Autumn 2001): 32.

26 Brenda Dixon Gottschild, *The Black Dancing Body: A Geography From Coon to Cool* (New York: Palgrave Macmillan, 2003), 257.

27 *Moreechika: Season of Mirage*, Southern Theater, Minneapolis, September 2012.

28 Alan Taylor, "Bhopal: The World's Worst Industrial Disaster 30 Years Later," *The Atlantic*, December 2, 2014, https://www.theatlantic.com/photo/2014/12/bhopal-the-worlds-worst-industrial-disaster-30-years-later/100864/.

29 "Remembering Ken Saro-Wiwa—the Ogoni People and the Greed for Oil," *African Perspectives*, July 22, 2011, http://afriperspectives.com/2011/07/22/remembering-ken-saro-wiwa/.

30 I am referring to the late choreographer Ranjabati Sircar, "Contemporary Indian Dance," in *Rasa: The Indian Performing Arts in the Last Twenty-Five Years* I (Music and Dance), ed. Bimal Mukherjee and Sunil Kothari (Calcutta: Anamika Kala Sangam, 1995), 259–60.

31 Sherie Apungu, interview with the author, January 27, 2013.

32 "Yorchha (Technique)," Vimeo (from Ananya Dance Theatre), January 6, 2016, https://vimeo.com/106247485.

33 Chandra Talpade Mohanty, *Feminism without Borders: Decolonizing Theory, Practicing Solidarity* (Durham: Duke University Press, 2003), 31.

34 "Yorchha," accessed February 10, 2019, https://www.ananyadancetheatre.org/philosophy/yorchha/.

35 Bill V. Mullen, *Afro-Orientalism* (Minneapolis: University of Minnesota Press, 2004), xx.

36 *K'Shoy! Decay!*, Minneapolis, 2010.

37 B. K. S. Iyengar, *Light on Yoga* (New York: Schocken Books, 1966), 19.

38 "Introductory Commentary by His Holiness the XIVth Dalai Lama," in Padmasambhava, *The Tibetan Book of the Dead* (The Great Liberation by Hearing in the Intermediate States), trans. Gyurme Durje (New York: Penguin, 2006), xv.

39 Padmasambhava, *The Tibetan Book of the Dead*, xv.

40 Laurie Carlos, Ananya Dance Theatre Rehearsal (University of Minnesota, Twin Cities, Minneapolis, July 9, 2102).

41 Omi Osun Joni L. Jones, *Theatrical Jazz*, 46.

42 Laurie Carlos, rehearsal, July 9, 2102.

43 Hui Wilcox, interview by the author, October 7, 2012.

44 Yang Jisheng, "China's Great Shame," *New York Times*, November 13, 2012, http://www.nytimes.com/2012/11/14/opinion/chinas-great-shame.html?_r=0.

45 Theodore Rosengarten, *All God's Dangers: The Life of Nate Shaw* (New York: Alfred A. Knopf, 1974), xvii.

46 M. Jacqui Alexander, *Pedagogies of Crossing: Meditations on Feminism, Sexual Politics, Memory, and the Sacred* (Durham: Duke University Press, 2005), 8.

47 Hui Wilcox, roundtable, New Waves! Dance and Performance Institute, Port-of-Spain, Trinidad, July 28, 2012.

48 Hui Wilcox, interview by the author, October 7, 2012.

49 Nico Slate, *Colored Cosmopolitanism: The Shared Struggle for Freedom in the United States and India* (Cambridge, MA: Harvard University Press, 2012), 66.

50 Orlando Zane Hunter Jr., interview with the author, 2012.

51 Rodrigo Orihuela and Peter Millard, "Petrobras First Female CEO Is Rousseff's Response to Delayed Oil," *Bloomberg.com*, May 31, 2012, http://www.bloom berg.com/news/articles/2012-06-01/petrobras-first-female-ceo-is-rousseff-s -response-to-delayed-oil.

52 Roderick Ferguson, *Aberrations in Black: Toward a Queer of Color Critique* (Minneapolis: University of Minnesota Press, 2004), 3.

53 Ananya Chatterjea, "Dancing Fugitive Futures," roundtable, University of Minnesota Twin Cities, September 11, 2012, Minneapolis.

54 Priya Srinivasan, *Sweating Saris: Indian Dance as Transnational Labor* (Philadelphia: Temple University Press, 2012), 119.

55 Eithne Quinn, "Occupy Wall Street, Racial Neoliberalism, and New York's Hip-Hop Moguls," *American Quarterly* 68, no. 1 (2016).

56 Angela Y. Davis, *Blues Legacies and Black Feminism: Gertrude "Ma" Rainey, Bessie Smith, and Billie Holiday* (New York: First Vintage Books, 1998), 185.

57 Angela Davis, "The 99%: A Community of Resistance," *The Guardian*, November 15, 2011, http://www.theguardian.com/commentisfree/cifamerica/2011/nov /15/99-percent-community-resistance.

58 I am reflecting here on the leadership of Ida B. Wells-Barnett in the antilynching movement; Fannie Lou Hamer in voting rights access and democracy in Mississippi; Ella Baker in her essential support of youth-led movements, specifically the Student Nonviolent Coordinating Committee; and Black feminist leadership and scholarship, such as Angela Davis and Ruth Wilson Gilmore, for the prison abolition movement.

8

EMERALD CITY

RENÉE COPELAND

This poem/song was written during the process of making
Moreechika (2012), while reflecting on the ruthless oil drilling
and fracking ventures in the small towns of rural Minnesota.

Nothin' ever happened on a Friday night
People tend to keep to their close-knit ways
The wind seeped in like a rattlesnake bite
Some of them stoop to the poison daze
and on and off and under and over and around
until the town broke down

The men on the wind said, listen my kin
underneath the ground there's a gold to take
It looks of boiled black salamander skin,
but we've got all the tools to help it take its shape
and on and off an under and over and around
until the town broke down

Good folks don't let your spirit go
to those bright lights
they don't mean right

The citizens of burrowin got used to the drill
they could fly and drive, yet mainly sat in lanes
tapping their toes to tunes halfway round the world
the highways led to wars and many died in the maze

and on and off and under and over and around
until the world broke down

Good folks don't let your spirit go
to those bright lights
they don't mean right

9

DANCING BLACK MILITANCIES

Written Meditation on Performance,
Black(female)ness, and Dance as Ecological
Resistance in Ananya Dance Theatre

ZENZELE ISOKE, WITH NAIMAH PETIGNY

FIERCE. ELECTRIFYING. FAMILIAR. THESE ARE JUST A FEW WORDS
that can be used to describe Ananya Dance Theatre's performance of
Kshoy!/Decay! (2010) and *Tushaanal: Fires of Dry Grass* (2011). Through
movement, rhythm, and sound, these Black and brown dancing bodies tell
stories that challenge, entice, and inspire us to theorize Blackness and Black
gender performativity in ways that crisscross cultural and geographic land-
scapes. Fundamentally, Ananya Dance Theatre is about the political
embodiment of global gender struggle through movement and embodied
storytelling. Within the space of the company, there are overtures toward
Black histories and creative forces that allow audiences and artists alike to
confront the terror of multigenerational, transnational greed, capitalist
exploitation, and racialized gender violence. It is through a multiplicity of
moving female bodies on stage that Blackness comes into being in the company. Blackness here is not overdetermined by skin color or a particular
historical legacy, nor is it encased within the prism of a singular identity.
Instead, Blackness enters the performative realm through multifaceted
sets of culturally embodied movements—ancestral, archetypal, and late
modern—which are mobilized in and through the physicality of the femme

body-in-resistance. Through choreography that combines aural and sonic forms, ADT challenges us to expand our understanding of Blackness to include a willingness to rethink the predictable yet contrived boundaries of time, place, skin color, and culture in order to imagine new assemblages of Black relationality and, ultimately, urban political resistance.

Through a sustained and intense meditation on what Hortense Spillers once described as "the irreducible materiality of femaleness," this chapter sits with ADT's entangled assemblages of Blackened female empowerment by directly refuting monolithic understandings of Blackness. As such, our analysis of ADT urges a critical reconsideration of contemporary performative iterations of Black femaleness. We place ADT within a localized ecology of urbanity in the Twin Cities, a geopolitical landscape that forces diverse communities of color to practice a transversal politics of artistic crossing that hinges upon migration, remembrance, movement, and the practice of freedom in the face of robust manifestations protesting police killings of Black male civilians, including Jamar Clark, Philando Castile, and most recently George Floyd and Daunte Wright. We also position ADT within a microclimate of Black resistance politics that strategically engages across converging diasporas—Black/African/Asian/FirstNations/Palestinian/Dalit/(anti-)white supremacy—and challenge anti-Black racism in the Twin Cities. We draw from firsthand accounts of ADT's artistic and choreographic practices and theorize Blackness simultaneously through the lens of performance and social ecology.

In the Twin Cities, Black performance appears through both intentional and spontaneous acts of protest and spiritual militancy. It is through forging intense political relationships with the Blackened *other* that new ecologies of Black resiliency are made manifest. In this paper, social ecology refers to the broad network of mutually assistive relationships among artists, activists, and scholars that generate and incite radical critiques of power in urban spaces. Social ecologies enable community members to confront the trauma of sudden death produced by state and extrajudicial violence, cultural isolation, as well as the hard fact of our own complicity in the severe patterns of economic and social hardship that are pervasive here in the Twin Cities. Black ecological resilience doesn't just emphasize physical survival or the cultural reclamation and preservation of African Americanness. Rather, it refers more widely to the cultivation of complex networks of friendship, learning, healing, and art-making that hold affirmative cultural space—which in the Twin Cities is more often than not actually multiracial—to support Black creatives. In the Twin Cities, storytelling, dance, and poetry are the raw materials through which Black resiliency is transformed into Black militancy. In our thinking, ADT cannot reasonably be severed from the rich legacy of Black arts in the Twin Cities because it is intrinsically part and parcel of an explosive geography of cultural resistance that moves both within and across Black artistic communities that, due to economic and social minoritization, are forced to negotiate racial, cultural, and ethnic difference at every turn in order for Blackness itself to survive.

In this essay, when we speak of Black militancy, we speak of an unleashing and reinhabiting of liberatory traditions wherein people historically *Blackened* by violence and history move with their ancestors as spiritual-political resources for their contemporary, embodied radical practices. Rather than solely performative—meaning organized around the act of calling out names of well-known "leaders"—these remembrance practices represent forms of spiritual militancy *as* Black feminist praxis, and thus unfold through choreographed explorations of archetypal glyphs that surface buried histories of our femaleness, which, we argue, bring us closer to certain underexamined truths of Blackness. Within the paradigmatic lens of US Black feminism, militancy is predicated upon seeking out and nurturing social affinities that counter pervasive experiences of Black (female) isolation, cultural intolerance, and outright hatred. ADT provides a collaborative movement-making space for remembrances and performances of living histories that center movement, breath, and Black corporeal utterance—*body speak*. From our vantage point, ADT engages points of Black feminist praxis through untethering the body and its movement practices from the biopolitics of heteromasculinist articulations of Black expressive culture, which insist that Blackness only resides in phenotypically Black visual apparency and necessarily segregated African-descended bodies. Alternatively, we envision Blackness as something that moves in, through, and across bodies and cultures, dancing its way through time/space and history in unpredictable yet unmistakably decipherable and familiar ways (figure 9.1).

ADT moves in concert with Black social ecologies activated by the realization of social justice projects that bring diverse social actors into moving formation to protest xenophobic bigotry, racial/ethnic territoriality, and anti-Black state violence. By providing a stage for people of color (most often femme, gender nonbinary, and/or female-identified persons) to practice social justice activism through dance, ADT works against institutional and social norms that erode trust among Blackened people by opening up time/

FIGURE 9.1. (From left) Toan Thanh Doan, Magnolia Yang Sao Yia, Hui Niu Wilcox, Orlando Zane Hunter Jr., Julia Gay, Lizzette Chapa, Kealoha Ferreira, Ananya Chatterjea, Renée Copeland, Laichee Yang, and Alexandra Eady in a dance that talks back to structures of power from *Sutrajāl: Revelations of Gossamer* (2019). Photo by Paul Virtucio. Courtesy of Ananya Dance Theatre.

space/memory and physical and psychic energy for collective, multiracial acts of cultural insurgency. Transnational feminist storytelling through dance is the hallmark method through which ADT ignites the cultural practice of movement-making within and between bodies and communities that must exist through the continual onslaught of racialized generational trauma.

The dance methodologies and practices of ADT form a unique thread in the dynamic tapestry of protest-performance in the Twin Cities. The company is unquestionably assistive in a variety of struggles that work to disrupt the logics of anti-Blackness and capitalist heteropatriarchy operating in the world of dance and the uneven urban geographies in which ADT dance is locally produced. Although for many years, ADT dancers have warmed up, stretched, developed, and cocreated choreography in Barber Barker Dance Center, located just blocks away from the Cedar-Riverside Somali community on the West Bank of the Mississippi in Minneapolis, we see ADT dance artists everywhere—but most often protesting against racialized gender violence in the streets of the Twin Cities. Whether performing a phrase of an upcoming dance at a dusk-to-dawn annual arts festival in downtown

Saint Paul; dying-in at the Hennepin County Government Center Black Lives Matter protest in defense of Black life,[1] or dancing at a student-faculty rally demanding accountability, as well as genuine and observable ethnic and racial justice, from the University of Minnesota, ADT is present and making movement in the Twin Cities. Ananya and her dancers stoke the fires of protest by inciting us, *all of us*, to dance our rage, dance our grief, dance our sadness, and dance our dreams of freedom. In this way, ADT brings us home to Blackness.

Ananya Dance Theatre exists within a constellation of movers who illuminate underexamined practices and articulations of Blackness that both depart from and bring us back to familiar geographies of Black life that are linked to crossings associated with the Middle Passage. In the Twin Cities, revisiting the truth of this history is essential for our survival. African Americans historically migrated north to Minnesota by following the Mississippi River (i.e., New Orleans, Jackson, Memphis, Saint Louis, Chicago, Des Moines, Minneapolis, and finally, Duluth). In the Twin Cities, the descendants of enslaved Africans who were kidnapped from Africa and exploited for slave labor on American plantations since the 1600s are the true ethnic minority in a sea of other Black peoples who have more recently migrated (under similarly deadly circumstances) from Liberia, Somalia, Ethiopia, and Eritrea to the Midwest. With this said, in the Twin Cities and globally, Blackness of skin still *fails* to be a reliable marker of solidarity or cultural affinity, although it certainly marks us for state-endorsed surveillance, harassment, containment, and physical violence. Instead, militant performance exists as a locale where we—Blackened people—are allowed to re-remember our shared histories of hauling water, tilling the soil, burying our children, and more importantly, critiquing the necropolitical logic of race that makes Black femme materiality so devastatingly *real*.

In ADT Blackness lives in those muddied spaces between memory: it is through the poetry of ancient transcontinental movements that Blackness itself irrupts cartographies of dispossession, economic and cultural marginality, and racial containment that constitute the urban in Minnesota. Black performance art—whether through choreographed movement, experimental vocalism, spoken word, or other forms of stage work—is the most important modality of sustained political resistance and dissent that flourishes within Black social life in the Upper Midwest. Ananya Dance Theatre is an important yet poorly understood part of this local ecology of Blackness. And ADT forges space for Blackness to reground itself within its female roots.

ADT, as a militant dance troupe, insists upon an ethics of rootedness and intimacy with unacknowledged yet intermingled pasts of people of color that kindle our desire to resist and transform violence in the present. Through dance, ADT visualizes the emancipatory possibilities of becoming fluent in each other's stories. Flesh against flesh, the metaphysics of global Blackness is brought to life as dancers work through choreographic inquiries into the relationship between the earth, multiracial communities of struggle, and gender violence that shapes the everyday existence of women and femaled others on this planet.

When we place the Black femme, the expressiveness of Black female materiality, at the locus of Black gender performance theory and transnational feminist praxis, we open ourselves to thinking Blackness in new ways. So we ask: What is at stake in reading ADT as a part of Black social ecology in the Twin Cities? What do we gain and what do we lose? How does ADT allow us to see and make legible unrecognized formations of Blackness that sustain Black life-making practices (like dance) within a racialized geopolitical landscape in which Black lives are constantly threatened with annihilation? What new remembrances are made possible when we detach Blackness from the familiar tropes of African American suffering, and instead theorize it through grammar of global anti-Blackfemaleness? What happens when anti-Blackness is displaced as the only referent for thinking Blackness in our contemporary moment? Here the performance of Blackness is no performance at all—rather it is an embodied meditation, an actualized, materialized audiovisual discourse on the Blackfemaled soul. Could there be such a thing? We're not so quick to deny it. In the following prose segments we explore these difficult questions through fieldnotes, conversation, and critical reflections.

KSHOY! /DECAY!

Under Ananya's seemingly demanding instruction the soles of the dancer's bare feet smash against the floor of the stage. Every finger, every toe, every tendon of the dancers' extended limbs are stretched to the brink of exhaustion. Women—mothers with broad shoulders and thick waistlines, wide hips and plump breasts, move in tandem. Slender, muscular, old, and young move together Black, beaten, and laboring under the power of a polyrhythm that can only be felt, not observed. I could close my eyes and see the story. Dancers leap between vocabularies of culture that speak a similar truth of birthing, caring, rejection, dejection, death, and letting go. Every breath feels choreographed, every sigh syncopated, and every quivering muscle of the dancers suspended in an impossibly complex rhythm that moves between the unseen worlds of the spirit. Ananya and her dancers unleash untold histories seared into female flesh—sweating, bleeding, hurting, moving, abandonment, loss, struggle. It's all there. But how does she do it? Ananya traffics dancing bodies across the stage, sucking the audience into a nightmare that is both beautiful and familiar, leaving us all breathless, depleted, and strangely exploited. Like the earth. Like women. Golden. We bought tickets for this, and Ananya sold them to us. She is not fucking around.

BLACKNESS IN THE BREAK: READING ADT THROUGH MOTEN'S THEORY OF BLACK PERFORMATIVITY

ADT paints Blackness on other women's bodies, but you have to be Black to see it. Blackness can't be seen with the eyes; it is seen with the body. It is a particular kind of energetic resonance that reverberates through the body and ignites the soul. It slips, glides opaquely. It's the feeling of knowing-ness . . . the groove . . . a moving back and forth between the beat, between pain and pleasure, an amplification of in-betweenness. Like Fred Moten says, "It is in the break." More specifically, ADT delineates "an ontological field wherein Black radicalism is set to work."[2] Our reading of Blackness rejects easy multiculturalist perspectives that privilege cosmetic solidarity and shallow practices of coalition-building for the purposes of inclusion. Rather our work attends to horizontal and necessarily multiracial/multi-ethnic psychic imaginaries that nurture multiple and differential ways of being Black. In ADT, Blackness is more than just skin color, more than the affective attachment to Middle Passage epistemologies (however profound and meaningful they are to us survivors), and more than just the concentra-tion of dark *bodies* through violent practices of racialization and urban containment. Rather Blackness refers to life-giving practices that express the "irreducible materiality of the female." This exists in the fire bearing down to push a human infant skull through our vaginal canals and into the world, and in the fire of the leather whip that tears open Black flesh. This femaleness is the Black beingness of life in the face of uncertain death. Femaleness lies in that moment of not knowing the difference between life and death; it is the ferocious ecstasy of deep embodiment, even when we are not able to care if we live. It is that moment when the bullet explodes from a pig's nine-millimeter semiautomatic handgun pressed up to our temples as we lie handcuffed on the cold concrete, after our terrified lover has called "for help."

(We remember you, Jamar Clark.)

This is the Blackfemaleness of George Floyd's belly deep groaning call for his Black mama as Derek Chauvin asphyxiated him to death. These are the sublime tragedies of Blackness that are exorcised through Black, brown, femaled bodies in ADT.

(Come home, baby, come on home.)

An ecological engagement that Blackness pushes us to think through involves the assistive intimacies that allow Blackness to simply be—because and in spite of anti-Blackness. It is not an appeal to an ideology or a world-view; rather it is an assertion of ease with *Black female presence*. In other words, an ecological perspective pushes us to explore the different kinds of communities and social networks that invite refusals to relate to Blackness in an inherently exploitative and violent way. Black people may never be the true majority, but Black presences can be found in their circuits. It is not the Blackness of the token or the Blackness of the hopeless, beaten down, despairing, and thingified. Instead it is the Blackness of yearning—looking into another's eyes and seeing scenes of your ancestor pains in the faces of another whose sufferances were birthed on another continent. It is a Blackness that consists of a *knowing* that both of our great-great-grandmothers slapped old garments soaked with river water against a washboard twelve times, up and down, down and up before rinsing. They did it, even though it hurt, and found joy in the *doing*. Freedom was found in the repetition of care. Caring hurts. Like Blackness hurts.

In ADT we come closer to the reality that so many of our mothers, fore-mothers, and other mothers were left alone to raise us and our siblings. Female mothers felt their bodies change from slender and tight to fleshy and sagging after years of carrying babies on their backs until they learned to walk while also hauling a ten-pound bag of dried beans from the market back home. That beautiful young mother, worn down from years of caring, heard someone say that the water was dirty with something called "run-off" from a poultry processing factory thirty miles north of the town that she lived in her whole life. She still simmered fabaceae in ᏏᎩᏦ, origan, yàn, *perejil fresco*, চিলি মরিচ, from her small garden in boiling river water for six hours before serving them to her children and their father(s) (when they bothered to stop by). The language is different but the meaning is the same. The mother cooked beans to feed her family. One day, the young mother aged and fell ill with unforgiving tumors in her uterus. Her lymph nodes swelled with poison, until her body surrendered into the final comfort of death. The mother's children and grandchildren remembered that they loved her for cooking beans in contaminated river water, but only one adult child let the fading Black mother in on this tender truth before she passed over into the world of ghosts. She lived her life as a Blackened woman even though the color of her was the color of warmed butter. These are the stories of Blackness that Ananya Dance Theatre tells using the vernacular of yogic transnational praxis.

Blackness here is not dependent upon articulating its presence or calling it Black. Rather, it's ushered in through the physical conjuring of a space that permits Blackness to express itself in all its diverse multiplicity. Blackness as enough, without conditions—not politicized or politically correct—not inherently radical or dissident, but *as it be,* in its *femaleness.* We find that this has been a central component of ADT's artistic brilliance. Somehow ADT facilitates ubiquitous space for Blackfemaleness (even on Black-maled bodies) rather than confining it to a prescribed geographical or even phenotypical historical imaginary. But both ironically and inevitably, though, of course it is the chestnut-skinned dancer undeniably, and most convincingly, that conjures this Black imaginary. Those Black bodies are essential to the telling of genuine female struggle. Ananya knows this.

TUSHAANAL: FIRES OF DRY GRASS

To experience her work is to experience a truth that goes untold and unseen by the coloniality of dominant culture. Not just the pain and suffering but the woman who is a life-giving force on this planet. You see how the beauty and sacredness that we hold in our body are used as a tool for commodification and capitalist exploitation. To see the struggle as we experience it as women creates a space of recognition. Ananya creates a place of fellowship, love, and affirmation. Mirroring aspects of ourselves that are not allowed to be seen in dominant culture.

If there is a tiny hole of light in our suffering she stretches it open and holds the truth wide open for us to see.

In her choreographic work, Ananya has deconstructed specific movement forms—Odissi, yoga, Chhau—in order to (re)build them among a community of brown women who bring in their own narratives and aesthetics of struggle, resilience, and embodiment, thus generating choreography that resituates itself as it settles in different bodies and is specifically deconstructed and hybridized to tell a complex, diasporic story. In Ananya's production the female does not simply reproduce the relations of production. She produces value itself. Human value is Blackness. The Blackness of ADT is not expressed solely through what Thomas DeFrantz describes as corporeal oratures, or what we prefer to call "body speak," which reference specifically US Black historical events or the unique contemporary circumstance of African familial affiliations. Rather the Blackness of ADT rests in its ability to tap into the global denigration and exploitation of femaleness, which is realized in its totality through the treatment, or *Blackening*, of femaled others in the global South—when our land and waters are stolen for exploitation of oil, coal, gold, and other rare earth minerals. When entire species are eradicated to increase the quarterly earnings of a corporation. For most of us Blackened femmes, as the externalities of the anthropocenic world order, our outrage and horror are not expressed through our mouths. They are involuntarily expressed through our bodies. Body speak is the sound of our flesh as we press forcefully against each other, incoherent words caught between a belabored breath as we try our best not to say what it is we want to say but can't quite bring to mind the right words to say. The sayability of the truth locked within the clenched muscles of our stomachs by centuries of unresolved heartbreak. Body speak is the grunts emitted as we lift heavy objects that strain our weary backs and legs—which ache deeply, moving back and forth between our feet and hips as we walk ten blocks home from the bus stop at the end of a long day. Body speak is the scream stuck deep in our chest as we study the contorted face of our lifeless child on the coroner's table again, and yet again.

We remember you, Philando Castile.
(And you, too, Black mother survivor, Auntie Val!)

Body speak is the sigh of acceptance of the inevitability of life and death, as we realize for at least a brief time that we are not really alone in this one moment. Body speak is the ecstasy of riding with that impossible note that finds the bliss in hardness of our lives. ADT taps into these aspects of Black-femaleness without relying on *a* singular expressive vernacular or a single story.

ADT confronts the audience with underexamined physical codes that are inherent to our Blackness but can only be expressed through unfaltering engagement with what Spillers describes as the zero-degree materiality of femaleness. Not the curving and swerving and recoiling of the hips associated with heteronormative female (re)productivity, but femaled bodies that are forced into violent conversation with the earth: how we were beaten into mutilating it, digging in it, snatching up and poisoning weeds, ruthlessly thinning crowded seedlings that might otherwise strangle the realization and reproduction of profits for white supremacist capitalists of all hues thirsty with greed (or, just maybe, our contemporary socialized inclination to keep up with the Joneses).

In ADT, the dancers work the interstitial space between objectification and humanness. Between breath and breathlessness, love and a relentless avalanche of despair, the dancers create a rhythmic energetic field that is familiar yet seems so far away from the crashing tides of urbanity that define so much of contemporary Blackness in Minnesota. In *Kshoy!/Decay* and *Tushsaanal* Ananya's treatment of femaleness wrestles Blackfemaleness away from the countrified grammar of mammyism, Jezebel, Sapphire, and the Hottentot Venus; instead she is placing us (Black females) within a too-long-*un*referenced relationship with land, water, earth, air, fire—the basic elements that constitute the fact of our physicality instead of the fiction of their representations. Sandra Bland comes home.

> (Whisper)
> Blackness begins and ends with the mother.
> Belaboring utterance and response.
> The m/other.
> *She hurts*,
> Finding belonging in knowing that we hurt together.
> Black m/other
> Dancing her dreams
> Hurts.
> Black m/other.
> Singing her pain.
> Black m/other.
> Living her life.
> Beauty so deep and dark.
> Black m/other.

BLACK FEMINIST MILITANCY: A CONVERSATION
BETWEEN ZENZELE AND NAIMAH

ZENZELE: As a Black performance theorist, what do you find to
be especially significant about Ananya Dance Theatre?

NAIMAH: One of the first things is the creative research process
and the use of techniques that really synthesize field research,
community empowerment, and rigorous technical training.
ADT uses movement and spoken word in tandem. Thus when
we are moving together, we are also carrying narratives with
us, *in our bodies*. ADT also places value on the input of all of
the movement artists in the company—and not just with the
choreography but with the core emotional and theoretical themes
of the movement work. ADT attempts to center the *artists'
visions* of what they want the performance to enliven and the
effects they want the audience to struggle through. Because the
dancers travel and are artist-activist-scholars from all over the
world, they also bring acute understandings of globalized suffering and resistance with them and infuse it into the work. In
ADT artists learn from activists [and vice versa]. This allows
ADT to create performances that [genuinely] fuse art, social
justice, and societal transformation. Another crucial element of
ADT is the way the performances reflect overlapping and divergent historical legacies, traumas, and violences in an attempt to
illuminate the interconnected legacies of [community] defense
and resilience. If we look at Yorchhā, the ADT-specific dance
form and choreographic style, we see that it demands that
dancers take up space on the stage and be fully inside the form.
In other words, in dancing Yorchhā there is no room nor desire
for westernized, or balletic, forms of movement. [As a result]
the dancer's bodies reverberate on the stage, unapologetically
and with sharp intentionality. [You can hear this in their breath-
work, the soles of their feet pounding against the floor.]

ZI: Yes, it is magnificent to see that different kinds of bodies from
women from different cultural locales are able to be present on
the stage together.

NP: Yes, indeed! I don't believe the goal is to blend in or to transcend
experience, as is the case with so many other forms of dance (like

ballet), which for me are inherently disembodied, especially for women of color. In ADT, the goal is for each of us to be fully present in their own stories as well as in the collective narrative that we tell through movement and emotion. The goal is to practice an almost (militant) mode of embodiment. [We can see this] in the percussive footwork, [the Odissi] that [anchors] [the vocabulary] and the stories that are told with the bodies of women of color.

ZI: This is reminiscent of a resonant theme in people of color feminism—learning how to be fluent in each other's stories. How does ADT relate to other forms and modalities of Black movement that you are familiar with?

NP: The Odissi footwork that ADT works with is quite reminiscent of the percussiveness of West African and Afro-Caribbean dance, and stepping, or step dancing, in African American dance traditions, especially when Black women perform the technique. The footwork is polyrhythmic and requires a certain level of precision, balance, and presence [with the body] to be performed, as well an awareness of holding multiple scales of time and timing at once. [Let us take, for example,] Bomba, an Afro–Puerto Rican improvisational style of dance founded in the seventeenth century which is an important modality of dia-sporic Blackness created by escaped free Blacks on the island, in the areas of Loiza, Santurce, Mayagüez, and Ponce. These spaces are also known as some of the Blackest parts of the island. Different styles of Bomba have varying basic steps, or *paso basicos*, but all rely heavily on improvisation and the innate sensing of both the dancers' and drummers' bodies. Bomba is also a dance that pays homage to the orishas and to the spiritual energies that guide Afro-Caribbean dance. It is a very hip-, chest-, and shoulders-centric form that has an urgency subsumed in its movements that marks it as very simi-lar to Yorchhā. Through the movement, dance and sound lead each other; toning [of the drums] and the stomping of the dancers' feet are in sync. Bomba footwork uses precisely exe-cuted patterns that feel so freeing for the spirit. The movements we use are repetitive and demonstrate the forced urgency of working the land under harsh conditions. Dancers are often left exhausted yet renewed by the form, and there is a seriousness and an urgency to the drilling of phrases and particular steps. I see this kind and quality of movement in ADT, especially in the exacting physicality of particular phrases that can be repeated over and over again. Another aspect is the wrist work in Bomba—[it is] at the same time sharp and precise as well as fluid and soft. The dancer also illuminates the beauty of the sheer materiality of the movements: repetitive, intuitive, militant, yet fluid and in unison. There is labor to be performed through these movements, and it is something that dancers don't shy away from. It is something that they dive into with an intensity and fearlessness that is fierce, and that's the beautiful part.

ZI: One of the things that is truly remarkable about ADT is just how much of Black women's collective history the ADT imagery allows us to remember. When we think about Black enslavement and often-forgotten histories of fugitivity and maroonage, we often forget just how much our histories are intertwined with the wildlife of the jungle. When our ancestors dared to escape slavery and live as fugitives, we also had to sleep in the bush in the presence of big cats, snakes, alligators, and other animals that could have very well have killed us if we got too close. Even prior to that initial crossing of the Atlantic Ocean, we Black people of the diaspora also learned to live side by side with these awesome beasts. This is a part of our history, a part of our survival that is preserved in our blood, our DNA. ADT, while also working through choreography that is telling the story of village women in India who have to live side by side with magnificent but potentially deadly creatures, helps us remember our own relationship with the nonhuman—an aspect of our own Blackness that we often are not provided with space to acknowledge, unless it is in the context of the most vicious anti-Black, anti-African stereotypes. I think ADT helps us remember past lives that we have forgotten. I like to think about these as forgotten archetypes that are part of the Black collective unconscious experience. It is a history that links us with other women of color on the Indian subcontinent, in Southeast Asia, and in different parts of Africa and the Americas to this very day. I believe that Ananya provides us, African diasporic women, with an opportunity to remember these histories through other contemporary women's stories of struggle for survival.

zɪ: Along with the Yorchhā footwork, ADT draws upon contemporary vinyasa yoga as the foundation for developing strength, flexibility, spine strength, and a general philosophy of how to cultivate presence with the body. This brings me back to modern understandings and embodiments of Blackness: today, many African American folks, especially middle-class Black folks like myself, are both attracted to and practice yoga in our cities, provided that we can afford it or it is offered free or at reduced cost. We learn to come consciously to our breath through yogic breathing practices and movement. As for myself, I learned to relate to my body, its physical potentiality, differently. As a former dancer—way back in high school—I learned to appreciate my body because of how it looked or what it could visually achieve through movement. After having my first child, it was through yoga, and specifically kundalini yoga, that I began to appreciate the movement of my body because of how it makes me feel. I learned to take pleasure in my body for its own sake, not for how it appears through the eyes of others. My own spiritual development as a contemporary Black mother is very much connected to yogic practice.

NP: Yes! I love that more and more there are burgeoning networks of Black women and girls practicing and studying yoga across the United States! Have you heard about Black Girl Om? They are building a whole embodied movement committed to Black visions of wellness, pleasure, and liberation! Yoga is a unique part of ADT because only rarely do we see yoga philosophies and practices outside of yoga studios. Yogic-centered movement and intentionality is a part of the philosophy of the dance company and is used both in the warm-up and technical training as well as in the choreography.

NP: Yes, Yorchhā really pulls from yogic breath and movement practices alike! Having yoga exist in this different framework is really important. In ADT yogic movements are incorporated within movements that serrate—loud stomping, sharp twists of the body with audible exhales. This blends with Odissi footwork, another movement practice that is associated with brown bodies. Here yogic movements are retooled for community resilience to explicitly address the daily trauma and violence that Black women and other women of color face—they take on a radically different meaning. I think meditation also holds this potential, a potentiality of presence, embodiment, and healing. Yogic meditation offers us a medium for clearing. Yogic meditation can then become a tool for community self-defense and a method of healing.

ZI: For me, ADT reappropriates yoga from the deadening abstractions of white middle-class womanhood. Yoga is no longer an expression of ableist normativity. Instead, the fire of yogic unification of body, breath, and interplanetary and interspecies consciousness is fed through movement. The elements of the fire of insurgency are stirred up deep down in our bones—the deep dark red Blackness that sits at the seat of spine or deep down in the womb.

ZI: Naimah, as a scholar of Black female embodiment and protest, what might young women, especially those of African descent, gain from experimenting with the specific dance forms that emerge from South Asia and especially the Bengali tradition of percussive footwork?

NP: It is so important for young women of color to be comfortable with taking up a lot of space! Women of color are taught to make themselves smaller—not to talk too loudly, to be quiet, to settle down and shrink themselves. But ADT encourages us to be expansive and make our presences known. Seeing other women of color be expansive is important. The histories and contemporary issues that the company focuses on, such as land rights, water, and state violence, all mirror contemporary struggles in this country. Homelessness, unjust detention—which is all detention—gender violence and anti-immigrant racial violence. Elements of all these issues can be explored, transnationally, within performance rooted in social change, and this is so important for young folks to witness. It should be our goal to think about these violences as locally and globally anchored. When you have work that does this, the joint articulations of politics and artistic essence can be easily read.

ZI: In academia, appeals to ancestral energies and healing modalities are either ignored completely or submerged within dense texts that are often inaccessible to those without access to advanced courses in higher education. How do dance and performance, and especially thinking about dance and social justice together, go against the winds of secularism in higher education?

NP: I love this question. I think it illuminates disembodiment as a structural foundation of contemporary education. Not only do you learn in disembodied ways, but you are also required to be disembodied to learn, in a traditional sense. *Leave your body at the door of the classroom.* These structures of learning become more violent when Blackness, and its expressions in and through the body, are abstracted. It [embodied performance] requires a centering of the raw materials that academia is out of touch with. I think this happens because we delink our labor and knowledge production from the materiality of the body. Even in the embrace of healing modalities we still see it as not as important as our reading, writing, or scholarship. Studying dance and performance undoes the abstraction of our training and discipline. It requires us to be present with what is moving and shifting in front of us, and I think that once we are attentive to that . . . or in a process of connecting knowledge and the body, the connection between movement and social justice happens quickly. The more we move, the more our research practices and tools of analysis become malleable technologies for learning. The more we practice studying or being in the space of performance, of protest, the more accessible our work can become.

ZI: When we think about Black women and feminist knowledge production, there are a few things that our minds forget but our bodies remember: Our bodies were never intended to survive on this continent; neither were our ideas. To insist on the value of Black (female) embodiment and Black thought is a militant stance against the logics of whiteness that are often articulated under the guise of multiculturalism. In ADT different bodies do the same dance moves, but still, we can see the specificity of how certain stories live in, on, and through particular bodies. In some moments in her [Ananya's] pieces, specifically in *Kshoy!*, it was incredible to see how articulations of Blackness were emboldened to exist both in tension and in solidarity with expressions of female alterity from different parts of the world, or to be more specific, through *different diasporas*. Black, Asian, Indian, Palestinian. . . . Diasporas are forged through memories that live in bodies that move—across the stage, across the state, across the ocean. . . . ADT opens up space and opportunities to move closer to body memory.

zi: Back to your question, though. Black intellectual militancy is a refusal of the exploitative idea of the unity of Blackness. It allows Blackness to move freely within and through multiple frames, methods, writings, aesthetics, and imaginaries. Our intellectual choices, or more precisely, the ethics that govern the aesthetic of knowledge production, are always in conversation with communities of struggle. In the writing of feminists like M. Jacqui Alexander, and following her specifically in Ruth Nicole Brown's book *Hear Our Truths: The Creative Potential of Black Girlhood*, Omi Osun Jones's *Theatrical Jazz: Performance, Àṣẹ, and the Power of the Present Moment*, and more recently, Alexis Pauline Gumb's *Spill: Scenes of Black Feminist Fugitivity*, we see that there is a way in which genuine intellectual and artistic freedom is central to both the content and structure of their writing.[3] Blackness and Blackfemaleness is both a commitment and a practice. I find that ADT really provides a political and cultural space for women of color that permits the liberatory imagination to flourish. In other words, ADT provides a way for us to be present in each other's art-making structures without falling into state-endorsed practices of multicultural liberalism. It is also important to note that other Twin Cities artists, specifically Shá Cage and Signe Harriday of Mama Mosaic Theater, also engage in practices of staging Blackness in its multiplicity—for example, their ensemble performance, *Blacker the Berry*, includes artists of different ethnic, cultural, and racial backgrounds—however, the articulation of Blackness in the production of their work is, in my opinion, unmistakably, *Black* and female for that matter.

FINAL THOUGHTS: ADT AND BLACK SOCIAL ECOLOGIES IN THE TWIN CITIES

In environmental studies, social ecologies have largely referred to human beings' relationship to the land, the natural environment, and its resources.

In the social ecology literature, all human beings are equally attributed responsibility for the destruction and depletion of natural, land-based resources. Humans are appropriately conceived of as encroachers and plunderers of the land and natural environment, much to the detriment of other species, especially large nonhuman species, and the planetary atmosphere itself. Human beings have appropriately been associated with creating toxic atmospheric conditions that produce cancers. We have (although certainly not equally) participated in the emission of carbon dioxide into the air, the release of dioxins in our air and water supplies, and multiple forms of toxic runoff that make our natural habitat more or less unsustainable.

Such being said, this is a very whitewashed understanding of ecology that is based solely upon the dominant classes' historic relationship to the land, air, and natural resources. Such a perspective omits critical thinking about how enslavement, Black gender, class, land and water theft, migration, and racial difference have structured particular communities' relationships to the exploitation and damage of the earth and Indigenous communities that preceded Western colonization. Dominant notions of social ecology dismiss the social, emotional, and psychic pollution created by extenuated histories of colonization, forced migration, marginalization, and violence enacted upon human beings *and* their environments as an effort to control resources, reap profits, and eradicate peoples, cultures, and histories that the dominant classes have deemed inferior.

Global white supremacy through coloniality has not just attempted to destroy the planet; it has also sought to enslave peoples to racial capitalism and its structural antagonisms, as well as eradicate entire groups of people and their remembrances from the face of the planet. Luckily, coloniality has not succeeded. BIPOC people—Black, African, Indigenous, Asian, Indian, Arab, Muslim, mixed-raced people, and others—still constitute the majority of human beings on this planet. Even though we suffer, and suffer greatly, we are still here. We still make art, make community, and find ways to sustain our bodies, communities, and cultures in spite of the coloniality of power. We are still here! We dance. Being here, being oppressed and struggling anyway, with other people who have been made into strangers is a form of Blackness that is more powerful than melanin in our skin.

From this perspective, we have argued here that Ananya Dance Theatre, a so-called Contemporary Indian American Dance Company, should be considered a unique and important element of the unique social ecology of Blackness in the Twin Cities. By social ecology, we mean the intellectual and creative vitality of Black and also majority African-descendent spaces of cultural diversity in Minneapolis and Saint Paul. I believe that ADT offers a robust and compelling articulation and critique of practices of Blackness that should be studied, celebrated, critiqued, and enjoyed. ADT, as an institution, and Ananya Chatterjea, as a Bengali-American dancer, choreographer, and director, are part of local and localizing spaces of arts-based cultural production that work to constitute the power and potential of Black liveness in the Twin Cities.

In these cities, social ecologies are produced by the spaces that enable Black people to make sense of our world and our places in it. Cultural institutions like Capri Theater, Pillsbury Theater, Penumbra Theatre, Mama Mosaic Theater, Intermedia Arts, Juxtaposition Arts, Mixed Blood Theater, TU Dance, and from our perspectives ADT (among many, many others) are places that allow Black artistry to unfold on its own terms without the burdensome weight of ideological nationalist and heteromasculinist political dogmas. In these institutions, which are really nonprofit and community-sustained buildings, Black performance artists like Tish Jones, Shá Cage, Signe Harriday, Hawona Sullivan, Beverly, Bill, and Kenna Cottman, Mankwe Ndosi, Andrea Jenkins, Gabrielle Civil, our ancestor Laurie Carlos, and so many others are able to cultivate ethics that are resistant, dissident, liberatory, and *Black*. They help us, Twin Cities residents who may be reluctant to claim the identity of artist, imagine decolonizing and ultimately abolitionist cultural systems and community practices. In particular, they help us, Black and African-descendant females specifically, to make meaningful and invigorating connections among the diversity of people and places in which we study, eat, play, rest our heads, and live out our social and political lives. They are part of an ecology that promotes life-giving practices that give us the space, encouragement, and emotional incentives to breathe.

Often, we, Black and queer people of color, who live side by side with each other in cities, often emit toxic emotions, toxic words, and toxic energies into our social environment. Make no mistake: many BIPOC people in Minnesota are anti-Black and don't even know it. I believe that, along with the poisoning of the earth, poor nutrition, and lack of exercise, we are dying of cancer, mental illness, diabetes, stress, and other autoimmune diseases. Speaking poorly about other community members, failing to see, identify, and seek out opportunities for collaboration with people who are wounded and flawed, produces toxic relationships with each other. Often, we do not make a conscious effort to treat each other with care, genuine attentiveness, and respect. These maladaptive behaviors are, of course, the byproducts of whiteness and white supremacy that we too often unwittingly consume— and that activists in ADT help us to see, understand, and ultimately move toward eradicating.

NOTES

This essay is based on Isoke's twelve years as a Black feminist Twin Cities educator and scholar who attended countless performances and community gatherings sponsored by Ananya Dance Theatre. Isoke also had the opportunity of interviewing four ADT Black female collaborators who have deep roots in the Black artist movements in the Twin Cities, including Mankwe Ndosi, Kenna Cottman, and Tish Jones. Naimah Petigny, who briefly rehearsed with ADT, also contributed to this essay in the form of an extensive free-form interview featured in the section on Black feminist militancy.

1   These protests centered the lives and legacies of several young Black men, including Jamar Clark, Philando Castile, and Thurman Blevins Jr., who were brutally murdered at the hands of Minnesota police officers.

2   Fred Moten, *In the Break: The Aesthetics of the Black Radical Tradition* (Minneapolis: University of Minnesota Press, 2003).

3   Ruth Nicole Brown, *Hear Our Truths: The Creative Potential of Black Girlhood* (Urbana: University of Illinois Press, 2013); Omi Osun Joni L. Jones, *Theatrical Jazz: Performance, Àṣẹ, and the Power of the Present Moment* (Columbus: Ohio State University Press, 2015); Alexis Pauline Gumbs, *Spill: Scenes of Black Feminist Fugitivity*, ed. Inc Ebrary (Durham: Duke University Press, 2016).

III

TRANSGRESSING SPACE AND BORDERS

Local Politics, Transnational Epistemes

10

MINDFUL SPACE-MAKING

Crossing Boundaries with Ananya Dance Theatre

SURAFEL WONDIMU ABEBE

PROLOGUE

STAGING AN INTERNATIONAL FESTIVAL IN ETHIOPIA BY INVITING companies like Ananya Dance Theatre signifies precarious but meaningful crossings since it took place amid the state-sanctioned primordial identity politics that obliterated trans-sectional (beyond any ethnocentric model of identity) epistemologies of social justice. My reflective fragmentary stories engage with the tensions in these multiple crossings. The Crossing Boundaries (CB) festival-conference took place on September 23–27, 2015, in Addis Ababa, Ethiopia. Initiated by three Ethiopian performing artists, Azeb Worku, Meaza Worku, and myself, CB was organized by the Ethiopian Theatre Professionals' Association. It was one of the events that were staged in sixteen countries in collaboration with Performance Studies International, which decided in 2013 to decenter its global North–centered festivals and conferences under the rubric Fluid States: Performance of Unknowing.

Yet, as much as it was the first Performance Studies International event in Africa, CB was also a result of previous conversations that happened between Northeast African performing artists who wanted to build on and depart from foreign initiatives that collapsed whenever interest in the global North changed. As an Ethiopian participant, I witnessed, for example, when the Swedish International Development Cooperation and Sundance Institute staged and diverted their focus/politics. Then they withdrew funding from their programs, East African Theatre Institute, Performing Arts Cooperation between Sweden and EATI, and Sundance Theatre Program in East Africa. CB encountered ADT when it was attempting to understand and change such conditions so that African initiatives could thrive.

Coming to Ethiopia as a group for the first time, ADT gave the keynote performance at the Ethiopian National Theatre at the CB festival before 1,200 spectators. ADT received a standing ovation. The warm reception was for the wonderful performance, which exposed the edge of capital that cuts bodies, particularly bodies of women of color who labored for the survival of nature/humanity in the global capitalist onslaught. Mainly it is because of this attention to and critical engagement with issues of global humanities that CB invited ADT to its festival-conference. ADT's keynote performance at the Ethiopian National Theatre, *Roktim: Nurture Incarnadine*, invoked musings.

Attending to the audience members' engagement with *Roktim*, an Ethiopian female art critic, Tibebesilassie Tigabu, posed this question: "How would the world turn out if it is controlled by Monsanto-like overlords?"[1] This is a very important question in that on August 14, 2015 (almost two months before the CB festival-conference), Ethiopia amended a law on biosafety enacted in 2009.[2] Monsanto was urging Ethiopia to change its previous biosafety law.[3] Otherwise known for global leadership in protecting biodiversity, Ethiopia started to ease the regulatory framework so that the state could import genetically modified seeds like Bt cotton for its ambitious industrial park projects.[4]

Whereas authoritative neoliberal recommendations and seductions have been permeating through various spaces, the Ethiopian National Theatre, as the federal government's major cultural apparatus, is invested in dancing identity politics. The state's metanarrative of ethnicity became hegemonic after the Ethiopian People's Revolutionary Democratic Front (EPRDF) came to power in 1991.[5] As a matter of fact, ethnicity has been politicized for almost six decades in reaction to historical injustices. Yet the current identity politics works from the site of historicism, or what Walter Benjamin calls homogenization of time and space.[6] When I say identity politics, I am referring to uncritical pan-Ethiopian and ethnonationalist discourses. Both flatten out interlaced and fragmentary issues such as class/capital, ethnicity/race, gender, sexuality, disability, and religion. To make the freedom question more complex, TPLF-EPRDF acted as a "developmental state" discursively centering the poor. Nonetheless, the elites of TPLF (Tigray People's Liberation Front) and its allies captured the state and the government in order to create their own business empire. In so doing, the coalition, particularly TPLF, thought and acted as a heteropatriarchal neoliberal force despite its claim that it worked for the benefit of the historically marginalized people.

When the National Theatre makes a major commitment to "preserve" and "advance" the cultures and arts of "nations, nationalities, and peoples," it principally participates in the abstraction of reality. Given that the coalition negotiates with the West (particularly with the International Monetary Fund and World Bank) and China in view of controlling Ethiopia's market, these complex webs of relations woven between local and global (paradoxical) alliances cut (across) various heterogeneous categories and bodies. CB invited ADT to dance on the National Theatre's stage to speak to and expose such kinds of political economy using performance as one aesthetic-ethical intervention to envision multiple futures.

However, in a world where certain bodies are punctuated by complex markers of imperial fantasy that incessantly work to name, locate, and fix those bodies, the postcolonial desire for movement and acts of crossing always happen with all their precariousness.[7] While imperial webs are woven to entrap and direct movements in avenues based on neoliberal choreographies, itineraries that pass through interstitial spaces, twisting and making constant detours, become necessary. It is the dialectical tension between dis/placements imposed by strategies of power and multiple tactics of insurgencies that make ADT and CB's encounter imperative. In fact, this was not just an encounter but a moving and crossing together.

It needs to be noted that togetherness is also mediated by power. This kind of co-crossing wants us to go beyond the notion of self-reflexivity and consider the consequences of differences in global relations, including the conflicts and inequalities re/produced in the global South.[8] When they met in September 2015 in Addis Ababa, CB and ADT crossed together epistemic, disciplinary, identity-based, gendered, classed, raced, faithed, and other literal and figurative boundaries. That demanded a critical understanding of difference, respective local historicities, and global conditions of humanity. Both CB organizers and ADT were reflexive about the labor embedded in their encounter as well as crossings. Going beyond reflexivity, we engaged in critical conversations spelling out how our respective historicity would inform the ways in which we think through questions of inequality and re/productions of relations. We never tried to forge sameness, nor did we attempt to resolve issues. Neither of us allowed con-versing (dishonest/uncritical poetics) to happen between us. We rather wanted to have critical open-ended co-performing or co-re-creation. That is what both the CB festival-conference and ADT understood as a mindful act of space making. CB's "postcolonial desire" pushes against the fixture of bodies in places and calls for a Fanonian notion of freedom, which is not a restful condition but a "lasting tension," which reminds us to engage with "endless" "[re]creation" of self.[9]

What is at stake is the re-creation of spaces of critical conversation, and thus the reinvention of space for life, healing, hope, and beauty. It is about coperforming to unsettle heteropatriarchal neoliberal power, which organizes spaces based on local identity politics, national interest, and transnational pacts of capital and security. Northeast Africa, which CB takes in this edition as a point of departure and critical intervention, is an interesting space to probe into these issues. CB basically takes the claims made by East Africans regarding the multiple sources of the Nile and the attendant question of in/equitable use of the river as an occasion to envision multiple entry and exit points.

EAST AFRICANS IN THE UNITED STATES

Organizers at CB had been aware that ADT critically engaged with and creatively engendered social justice in and beyond the Twin Cities in Minnesota. I had a chance to be part of artistic activities in Minnesota, particularly with East African communities, who have a huge presence in the Twin Cities. Despite its performance of nicety, Minnesota inflicts much pain on bodies of color that have been historically wounded and continue to bleed due to structural violence. For instance, East African immigrant bodies, who are marked by politics of race, capital, and the post-9/11 raced religious discourses, live under constant state surveillance. Such surveillance is evidenced by the so-called safety center, a police garrison set up in the Cedar-Riverside neighborhood, where many East Africans, mainly Somali immigrants, reside. The state posits the safety center as a neutral objective space where police and the community in this neighborhood would mitigate issues of safety that refer to and are instigated by security problems related to loitering, killing, drug sales, and terrorism with links to Al-Shabab and ISIS. The owners of the Cedar-Riverside Plaza gave the space, which had been used by one of the youth organizations of the neighborhood, to the safety center. Without engaging the community but taking this space away from them, the top-down safety approach was hailed as a national model to be replicated by other states. This model frames the issue in terms of safety/security and pathologizes the community to place constant surveillance in the building.[10]

For the United States, the issue of security is mainly defined by its "national interest," whose apparatuses are stretched from the immigrants' residence in the Twin Cities to East African land, air, and sea, where drones land and fly and warships sail. Being a strategic US security ally, Ethiopia enacts American foreign policy in Somalia in joining the fight against Al-Shabab. One of the most important issues CB posited was the idea of security, with all its political, economic, and environmental implications.

Interrogating the notion of security that is defined by global-local powers in terms of trans/national interests, the festival-conference creates a space to converse on the political rationales of security. It creates a space that allows participants to ask and understand what it means to be human, who decides who should live and die, and what the meaning of home is. This probing has a great deal of importance for peoples who inhabit the Northeast African region, which has been ravaged by political violence, drought, and famine (which is a function of authoritarianism). It also resonates to the world at large, where lives are being governed by the logic of profit and loss and the post-9/11 technologies of antiterrorism, which are vernacularized by local powers to stifle freedom of speech, performances of dissent, and the transformation of lives. CB questioned "the positive and normative discussion of 'security'" and invited participants "to see the historical and material conditions that make the invention of state in/security and the disposal of bodies as logics of governance possible."[11]

As a dance theater group that works hard to remain engaged with communities of color in the Twin Cities, ADT is well aware of the realities in which East African communities live in the Twin Cities. Given that they also reside in sites of marginality as women of color, ADT dancers know that East African immigrants inhabit a similar time-space riddled with gendered and sexed white supremacy. In its encounter with East African immigrants, neoliberalism reinvents itself through logics of securitization and racialization. The stress gets intensified when those laboring bodies are female immigrants and Muslims. In the middle of such pain, ADT's and East African members' radical healing arrives as wound-care nursing: an act of singing, dancing, poetry or spoken word performance, conversations that critique the fundamental logics of raced neoliberalism, and the mindful act of coming together to alter the hierarchical space. In the face of the intricate oppressive system, they dream together.[12]

Hence, inviting ADT to East Africa, to Ethiopia, was important. This invitation provided ADT with the opportunity to extend its radical engagement from the microcosm of the East African communities in the Twin Cities to the larger geopolitical space called the Horn. Crossing the Atlantic to Africa as women of color with this politics of healing signifies these women artists' readiness to surrender to another. This act of surrendering allowed feminists at ADT to take solidarity not as given but as a work of love.[13] That opened up avenues where they would translate each other through critical reflexive dialoguing and coperforming.

TRANSNATIONAL POLITICAL PERFORMATIVES

Since its inception, ADT has been doing transnational feminist activism by going beyond the boundaries of the nation-state. Its transnational move is a critical way of questioning global/izing capitalism. In spite of its particular manifestations in local spaces, naming the global acts of capital opens an avenue for activists of the global South to engender subversive desires resisting a continued coloniality that cuts particular bodies, such as women of color.[14]

CB created a platform where artists of color come together and work through intersectional questions. Moreover, because discourses of identities currently circulating in Ethiopia often lose sight of the workings of heteropatriarchy and the neoliberal order, CB foregrounded issues of gender with all of their intricacies. Women of color presented both the keynote performance and the keynote story/speech. Three senior female scholars (two of whom are performers) were panelists in the roundtable discussion, which was moderated by a veteran female African activist-scholar. CB also gave a lifetime achievement award to the ninety-four-year-old Ethiopian actress Askale Amenshewa, whose body carried and survived the weight of colonial, imperial, and vulgar Marxist historicist histories. Her story is not just about surviving post/colonial oppressions (she lived in Madamismo, a colonial concubinage in East Africa, during the late 1930s) but also about engendering postcolonial desires, as was evident in her participation in the 1974 revolution, which changed her position as a marginalized female performer.

African artists and intellectuals, particularly those who reside in the Nile basin, met with members of ADT in Addis Ababa to think about global humanities and forge collaborations while they addressed their region-specific questions. CB's invitation of other African artists and ADT made possible a critique of neoliberal projects and the wounds they inflict upon women's bodies.[15] Articulating such critiques on the stage of the National Theatre is near impossible for local artists, though some have carved space for dancing notions of identity. However, the folkloric performance arts (*twfitawi tiwn tibebat*) are concerned with building Ethiopian image through "ethnic cultures." The plays and music performances in the special and regular repertoire are expected either to be "ethnic-developmental" or politically benign toward the state. These performance arts are not fully successful in probing the political economy, which sustains and incubates multilayered oppressions, including even ethnic domination. The elite forces of the ethnic-federal Ethiopian state profited from local-global neoliberal alliances. CB staged ADT's dance theater piece *Roktim* (which means "blood-red"), walking around the curves of power so as to also critique similar global-local capitalist projects that obtain benefits at the expense of the environment, the ecosystem, and the bodies of the poor, the working class, and women's communities.

MAGNIFICENT PETALS OF FLOWERS: HIDING THE RED BLOOD

The state-owned media in East Africa portrays the flower farm businesses as beneficial to the nation, particularly to women. However, the peril of floriculture in East Africa is horrendous. Kenya has the largest floriculture industry in Africa, while Ethiopia stands second, despite being a latecomer to the scene. White, yellow, pink, oatmeal, soft brown, red, and other kinds of roses that Europeans enjoy seem to be signs of love and sympathy. The freshness of the flowers adds to the intensity of the affect. Yet the petals enact a double abstraction. While they symbolize life, they also carry signs of agony and death, particularly the agony of women. Sixty percent of workers in Kenya's flower industry are women, as well as 75 percent of workers in Ethiopia's floriculture business. These figures would be a sign of hope if the industry did not involve serious threats against women who work their fingers to the bone. The adverse effect of floriculture in East Africa has already been documented, although more studies and analytic engagements are yet to come.[16]

It seems that the freshness of a flower cannot be attained without using lots of pesticides. Further, floriculture, unlike other aspects of horticulture, uses dangerous fertilizers, insecticides, nematicides, and fungicides. In particular, the farm labourers who work in the greenhouses suffer from various kinds of health issues, including respiratory and dermal problems.

The inorganic chemicals pollute the air, water bodies, and animals. Due to the logic of agglomeration that the floriculture industry uses for productivity, flower farms intensify global warming: the pesticides used in a greenhouse spread across 1,500 miles. Fish are perishing. Lakes are drying. Bees are vanishing. In his theorization of orature, in relation to the connectivity of humans with nature, Ngũgĩ Wa Thiong'o says, "Eliminate all bees and butterflies, and famine will threaten human life."[17] It is in the middle of such developments in the East African region that ADT staged its pertinent dance theater, *Roktim*.

ADT AT THE ETHIOPIAN NATIONAL THEATRE:
ROKTIM: NURTURE INCARNADINE

Through its keynote performance, *Roktim: Nurture Incarnadine*, ADT used dance theater, songs, poetry, and visuals that allowed audiences to actively engage with the performers. ADT took women's daily lives seriously and worked through questions of the human, relating the social issues with planetary ones. That connection between the realms of humanity and nature did not lose sight of history, but imagined historical narrativization as contingent. *Roktim* is a story about women's toil in the farms. It is about the survival of their lives and of the seeds. ADT's performers labored, gasped, sweated, staggered, fell, stood up, walked, and ran on the stage—the agricultural field. They showed us how transnational corporates and their neoliberal projects pricked the bodies of women of color as they rushed to control seeds. Yet *Roktim* was not a performance of defeat. It was rather a story of struggle, resilience, and re-creation.

The audience at the Ethiopian National Theatre, who came from more than fifteen countries, including many Ethiopians, identified with the lives of those women in the agricultural field. Many international participants were from the Northeast African region, where big industrialization projects have been dispossessing people in many ways. They were aware, for instance, that the floriculture industry was wreaking havoc in the Horn of Africa. Women who were fighting against transnational corporations were harassed and even killed. Farmers—women, men, and children—were protesting against these industries that profit over people's lives in the name of job creation. Huge agribusiness companies were making predatory moves to control African seeds, and thereby lives.

Hence, the audiences at the National Theatre saw the sweat, blood, and bones of the fighting women on the stage as a confirmation of their experiences. Yet the reaction was also a conscious move: naming the enemy. According to a local newspaper, "The audience at the National Theater was fully engaged with this social justice–themed dance performance and was cheering after each section of the production."[18] It was like, "Hey ADT, we hear you, we see you, we see our red blood through *Roktim*, and we need to do something about it." ADT and the audience were already doing something together.

THE TALE OF TWO PERFORMANCES: "DROPLETS OF DUST, PARTICLES OF WATER" AND *ROKTIM*

Along with the nineteen performances staged by artists of eleven countries in eleven venues throughout Addis Ababa, including at Africa's biggest open air market, Mercato, a conference was held in three places: Alle School of Fine Arts and Design (College of Visual and Performing Arts), Mekonnen Hall (Institute of Ethiopian Studies), and the Goethe Cultural Institute.

A keynote story/speech, "Droplets of Dust, Particles of Water: Portraits of Survival from Lake Turkana Desert," presented by Mshai Mwangola, a performance studies scholar who works at the African Leadership Center in Kenya, conversed with ADT's *Roktim: Nurture Incarnadine*. Mwangola's keynote raised critical questions on the tensions around the arid wilderness of Lake Turkana, which she posited as a "liminal space of borderlands where Kenya meets its northern neighbors, Uganda, Ethiopia, and South Sudan."[19] A storyteller-thinker, she worked through women's stories to engage with ideas of security, humanity, boundaries, home, and industrialization.

Mwangola says that her performance project "reflects the landscape of possibilities challenging imposed political boundaries as fluid as the rhythms of those whose cartographies are determined less by state-imposed legalities, and more by the changing realities of the environments of their existence."[20] Her work engages with the daily lives of four women who share a fleeting temporality and spatiality in and with the people(s) named Turkana, like the lake, the land, and the language inhabiting the liminal space between Turkana and the Nile.

Mwangola performed her keynote speech through the narration of stories as ADT staged stories of humanity through dance theater. Humans, for both, were neither abstract concepts nor neoliberal individuals who wandered alone, but historical subjects who were socially related. They were particularly interested in the daily lives of marginalized women. They showed how big industrial projects threatened women's lives, pointing to the global-local nexus of power. Environment was an issue for both. They articulated women's struggles against the raced neoliberal conditions in their attempts to alter their position in society. Mwangola's stories complicated the problem by probing the global circulation of capital, whose encounter and alliance with the nation-state renders women's bodies in certain localities expendable. Yet her stories, like those staged by ADT, were reenacted not to proclaim the obvious domination and insurgency but to throw the seemingly rigid border construction into relief and to show how marginalized female bodies of Turkana navigate those fluid spaces.

ADT's artistic director, Ananya Chatterjea, joined the roundtable discussion, "Movement, Ideas, and Bodies," with Mshai Mwangola and Elizabeth Wolde Giorgis, director of Gebre Kirstos Desta Center–Modern Art Museum at Addis Ababa University. Zenebework Taddesse, the veteran African feminist scholar and activist, facilitated the discussion. The CB conference invited scholars to the roundtable discussion to work through questions of the movement of thoughts and bodies in the postcolonial present. The conference was particularly interested in rethinking coloniality, knowledge formation, and acts of space making by marginalized people, particularly by women of color.

ACTIVISTS ENCOUNTER: YELLOW GOES TO MINNESOTA

The Yellow Movement (YM) was founded by a female professor of law, Blen Sahilu, and a group of female students from the same department at Addis Ababa University. Choosing yellow as a sign of hope to generate courage in the face of patriarchy, YM has been mainly working toward challenging gender inequality and assisting poor female students at Addis Ababa University.

The movement sessions allowed ADT and YM to dance together and unravel the position of distant observer and get closer to one another, to intersperse. In this regard, Aklile Solomon, a member of YM, has the following to say: "It was really liberating for the YM to see advocacy through art and performance."[21] As YM received energy from ADT as they conversed and danced together, it sent stories of passion and hope to Minnesota through ADT. "We have [now] Yellow in Minnesota," said members of YM after they met ADT.[22]

On September 28, YM took members of ADT to a safe house called Association for Women's Sanctuary and Development (AWSAD). AWSAD serves as a sanctuary for women and girls who have survived violence. AWSAD gives twenty-four-hour medical care, counseling, legal aid, and training in life skills and employment.[23] With all the critical sensibilities of "surrendering" to the Other or understanding their own historicity and differences, women of color from ADT joined Ethiopian women at YM to celebrate Meskel with the wounded women at AWSAD.[24]

The Christian women at AWSAD were not able to—rather, the violence of patriarchy did not allow them to—join the 700,000 or so people who gathered at Meskel Square to be part of the spectacular religious ceremony, which was staged around a huge bonfire. In fact, it needs to be noted that ADT members were invited to be spectators in the Meskel celebration the day before with the 700,000 people. While ADT's position in the global North privileges its members in getting access to local spaces in the global South, the wounded women at AWSAD were not able to participate in one of their public religious and social rituals. This shows how the dialectical tension within a space and between different fields of power is constant.

In addition to their attempt to learn Ethiopian languages from East African communities found in Minnesota, dancers of ADT created space and time to learn the others' dances. Despite the fact that the others' languages have their own hierarchies, the gesture toward surrendering allowed ADT and YM (which of course has established relations with the women at AWSAD) to craft a mindful space of solidarity. The children at the safe house danced with and taught members of ADT how to perform some Ethiopian dances. These performances blurred the patient/visitor divide and threw the possibility of boundary crossing into relief. Yet the act of surrendering is not a one-time visit but a constant act of critical revisiting, re-creation of global critical black solidarity. This calls for a labor of love for constant struggle against global oppressions through incessant and inventive solidarities.

PRECARIOUS MOVES

I want to reiterate that mobility is mediated by power. Marked by various factors and being re/presented, artists of color have encountered various challenges whenever they want to cross boundaries and meet fellow artists. Particularly for artists who come from the South, a space that is also full of tensions and contradictions, raising funds and asking for and getting a visa are a wearying experience. Though humanities and arts are universally underprivileged due to the Cartesian epistemic regime, the political economy of cultural mobility animates the experiences of people of color differently. Seeming to be close to one another, it is strangely more probable for Kenyan and Ethiopian artists to meet in New York, Berlin, or Stockholm, on platforms sponsored and choreographed by the North, rather than in Addis and Nairobi.

I said in a speech given at the opening night at CB festival, "Though we do not miss the fact that our attempts are precarious and part of varying negotiations, it is also a reality that we are capable of inventing a space where we can come together, perform, converse and confront our artistic, social, economic and political positions in a reflexive manner."[25] That reflexivity has allowed CB to tap into the resources embedded in social wealth and to negotiate with the neoliberal world of sponsorship.

It was from this site of negotiations that CB invited ADT to widen and complicate its modest experiment of space making. ADT and CB worked closely to bring *Roktim* to Ethiopia as a keynote performance, applying to various funding organizations. Coupled with its precarity as a women of color dance group, the fact that ADT wanted to come to Africa impacted its mobility, since its performance was not for white consumption but for the re-creation of critical alliances in/with the South. It turned out that ADT's travel to Ethiopia required funding secured from the US State Department. The funding made possible the boundary crossing and Black solidarity for ADT and CB, but in a precarious way. If striking a balance is untenable, what would mindful movement and negotiation look like? Working from within and against becomes the political in boundary crossings.

In the process of keeping the tension, another vital question needs to be raised: What does it mean to negotiate with power (be it empire or a state in the global South) without falling into its traps? Or how would one walk between subversion and slippage? While we were in dire need of funding for the organization of our festival, a female colleague from the College of Visual and Performing Arts advised us to approach a lawyer-artist who also does fundraising. In a couple of months, this fundraiser brought in $500,000. Even though we had discussed with him what kind of politics our festival-conference wanted to do, this fundraiser brought money from the very regime that we needed to critique. Led by TPLF's guru, the so-called Ethiopian International Institute for Peace and Development from which the fundraiser artist got the money is one of the regime's machines used to sustain the status quo.[26] The fundraiser also told the organizers that CB should also be staged in Mekelle, where he wanted CB to join the anniversary celebration for TPLF. Along with their allies, the elites of this party are responsible for imprisoning, torturing, and killing people to amass capital.

CB's organizing committee unanimously decided that we had to decline the funding, knowing that would defeat our struggle for social justice. Because we live under authoritarian rule, declining the offer would be equally hazardous. The situation reveals the political economy of refusal. Hence, we had to cautiously tell the fundraiser that Performance Studies International had to postpone our event as it reshuffled its series of global events.

It is through such detours that ADT and African artist-thinkers could traverse borders to meet and grapple with global currents of power while they attend to their own nuances.

EPILOGUE

A few months after ADT's keynote performance at the Ethiopian National Theatre, people who were displaced from their lands and suffered from the global-local alliance of capital destroyed a number of flower farms in various parts of Ethiopia. Following the unrest that spread in many parts of the country, particularly among the diverse Oromo- and Amharic-speaking peoples, the Ethiopian state repeatedly imposed states of emergency. Neither frightened by state-sanctioned imprisonment and torture nor intimidated by the militarized state security, the Ethiopian peoples forced the TPLF-EPRDF regime to undergo serious changes. Fundamental systemic transformation is yet to come, however.

It was on the eve of a larger social movement that ADT met African artists from Egypt, Sudan, South Sudan, Ethiopia, Kenya, Uganda, Rwanda, Burundi, and Tanzania, as well as Ethio-Israeli performers. Mindful space-making brought these performer-thinkers together. Coupled with its encounter with graduate students at the School of Theatre Arts at Addis Ababa University and Destino Dance Group, where it was able to exchange ideas and compare movements of social justice, ADT met with YM, talked with Ethiopian women at the AWSAD safe house, and danced with other Northeast African performers looking for ways in which future performances of healing and other kinds of collaboration would be possible. Surviving multifaceted challenges, ADT has continued to imagine and re-create performances of and for social justice: *Horidraa: Golden Healing*

(2016), *Shyamali: Sprouting Words* (2017), *Shaatranga: Women Weaving Worlds* (2018), and *Sutrajāl: Revelations of Gossamer* (2019).

To create CB as an annual event, its organizers have been working to stage the second edition under the rubric Crossing Boundaries II: Performance, Climate, and the Human Condition. Such aesthetic intervention is urgent for multiple reasons. As Ethiopia is passing through transitional time-space, which is shadowed by and riddled with global neoliberal prescriptions and a local tendency to succumb to that strain, the threat of flower farms is intensified by new aggressive agribusiness projects such as that of Monsanto/Bayer. It is already being reported that Bt cotton farms are affecting bees. When greed eliminates bees, Ngũgĩ Wa Thiong'o would say, famine will follow. The paradox is that agribusiness companies encroach on lives in the name of eliminating famine but not bees.[27]

That is why we need to have a continuous act of exposing the logics of capital so as to envision other utopias. In a world where a state of emergency has always already been declared, crossing boundaries becomes a way of life to fight anti-Blackness that is embedded not just in police departments but also in the raced-gendered-sexed global capitalist logics and institutions. ADT and CB's paths need to cross again, then.

NOTES

1 Tibebeselassie Tigabu, "Crossing Boundaries," *The Reporter*, October 3, 2015, 38.
2 Ethiopian Federal Democratic Republic, "Proclamation No. 896/2015: A Proclamation To Amend the Biosafety Proclamation," *Federal Negarit Gazette* 21, no. 66 (August 2015): 8308–17.
3 Adane Abraham, "Toward a Workable Biosafety System for Regulating Genetically Modified Organisms in Ethiopia: Balancing Conservation and Competitiveness," *GM Crops and Food* 4, no. 1 (January 2013): 28–35.
4 Abu Tefera. "Agricultural Biotechnology Annual," United States Department of Agriculture, Foreign Agricultural Service, February 2020.
5 In Ethiopian politics various groups and individuals grappled with issues of ethnic domination, arguing that the "Christian-Amhara-Tigrean" (religious and ethnic) empire marginalized the eighty-plus "nations and nationalities" of Ethiopia. See, for instance, Walelign Mekonnen, "On the Question of Nationalities in Ethiopia," *Struggle* 2, no. 2 (November 1969). However, the Tigray People's Liberation Front (TPLF) invented the ethnicity question as an object absolving Tigrean elites from the empire's late nineteenth- and twentieth-century hegemony. Using the suffering that Tigrigna-speaking people had to endure, TPLF invented the predominantly Amharic-speaking heterogeneous peoples as one "chauvinist" group called Amhara. See, for example, Adhane Haile Adhane, "Mutation of Statehood and Contemporary Politics," in

Ethiopia in Change: Peasantry, Nationalism and Democracy, ed. Abebe Zegeye and Siegfried Pausewang (New York: British Academic Press, 1994), 12–29. TPLF, whose founders were part of the 1974 Marxist Student Movement, toppled socialist military dictatorial rule, winning a seventeen-year civil war in 1991. Ideologically leading the Ethiopian Peoples' Revolutionary Democratic Front (EPRDF) for about twenty-seven years, TPLF collaborated with groups such as the Oromo Liberation Front (OLF) to remap Ethiopia along ethnic federalism. This radical restructuring constructed the Amharic-speaking opposition (and by extension certain classified people) as "chauvinist" while it designated OLF (including "disloyal" Oromo-speaking political groups and societies) as "narrow" ethnonationalists. In so doing, the regime created a binary between good (TPLF and its allies) and bad ("chauvinist and narrow") nationalists. It always invokes a hypothetical condition of Armageddon/genocide in the absence of TPLF. And it installed itself as an imminent arbiter until the continued struggle troubled the regime to the core, particularly in 2016–18. TPLF then retreated to Tigray, and other elements from within EPRDF underwent self-baptism as the Prosperity Party, continuing to rule the country with new promises. The multifaceted and protracted tensions between TPLF and the federal government or Prosperity Party culminated in armed conflict in November 2020. The war has imposed inestimable costs. Thousands of people have died. Internal displacement, migrations to neighboring countries, and famine have wreaked havoc in different parts of the country. Hundreds of women suffered from rape and other kinds of sexual assaults perpetrated by multiple forces involved in the conflicts, including the Eritrean army. It needs to be noted that this essay was written in December 2016, aside from minor additions about current developments.

6 Walter Benjamin, "On the Concept of History," in *Walter Benjamin: Selected Writings*, vol. 4, *1938–1940*, ed. Howard Eiland and Michael W. Jennings (Cambridge: Harvard University Press, 2003).

7 Here I am thinking with Awam Amkpa, who posits "postcolonial desire" as "an act of refusal to assume the passive, static, essentialist identity of [the] 'Other.'" Awam Amkpa, *Theatre and Postcolonial Desires* (New York: Routledge, 2004), 10–11.

8 I am thinking with Gayatri Spivak's notion of "reproductive heteronormativity," in which she invites us to see how one would reproduce regimes of oppression unless she/he/they build the epistemic and physical infrastructures in view of subverting global-local inequalities. See Gayatri Chakravorty Spivak, *An Aesthetic Education in the Era of Globalization* (Cambridge, MA: Harvard University Press, 2012), 429–42.

9 In respect to this idea of re-creation, see Frantz Fanon, *Black Skin White Masks* (London: Pluto Press, 1952), 179–81.

10 See "Cedar Riverside Safety Committee to Sign Area Safety Plan Agreement," e-democracy, June 23, 2011, http://forums.e-democracy.org/groups/mplscr/messages/topic/6rLsbH7dNmfAyooJ1qD8Fl; Julia Nikessa, "Confrontation in Cedar Riverside over Planned Safety Center," July 9, 2011, https://www.tcdailyplanet

.net/confrontation-cedar-riverside-over-planned-safety-center/; David Chanen, "Minneapolis Police Outreach to Somali Community Offers a National Model: Somali-Focused Effort Could Be a Model for Police Serving Immigrant Populations," *Star Tribune*, July 27, 2014, http://www.startribune.com/mpls-police-outreach-to-somalis-offers-national-model/268749491/.

11 Ethiopian Theatre Professional Association, *Crossing Boundaries Performing Arts Festival-Conference* (Addis Ababa: Artet, 2015), 38.

12 Conversation with Chitra Vairavan, December 24, 2016. Chitra, a founding member of ADT who identifies herself as a Tamil (South Indian)-American contemporary dancer immersed in both Tamil culture and progressive brown politics in the United States, told me, "Story and knowledge sharing with East African diaspora have been through the lens of healing, justice and radical dreaming."

13 Gayatri Chakravorty Spivak, *Outside in the Teaching Machine* (New York: Routledge, 1993), 183. By taking translation as an analytic tool, Spivak says the following to show how women should not invoke sameness but attend to the differences among themselves in their attempt to build solidarity: "To surrender in translation is more erotic than ethical. In that situation the good-willing attitude 'she is just like me' is not very helpful." Hence, she suggests that learning the languages of the other(s) is important. Reducing language to linguistic competence would also cause violence. That sensibility of learning/knowing works against the imperialist desire that probes just to make profit at the expense of the other. In pushing back against those kinds of imperialist desires, the other would say, "Thou shalt not speak my language." See Abdelfattah Kilito, *Thou Shalt Not Speak My Language* (New York: Syracuse University Press, 2008).

14 Coloniality here refers to the raced, gendered, and sexed global capitalist system. See Aníbal Quijano, "Coloniality and Modernity/Rationality," in *Globalization and the Decolonial Option*, ed. Walter D. Mignolo and Arturo Escobar (New York: Taylor and Francis, 2010), 22–32; María Lugones, "The Coloniality of Gender," in *Globalization and the Decolonial Option*, ed. Walter D. Mignolo and Arturo Escobar (New York: Taylor and Francis, 2010), 369–90; Oyèrónkẹ́ Oyěwùmí, *The Invention of Women: Making an African Sense of Western Gender Discourses* (Minneapolis: University of Minnesota Press, 1997).

15 Surafel Wondimu Abebe, "Stage and State: Ethiopian Theatre and Political Ideology, 1942–2005," MA thesis, Addis Ababa University, Addis Ababa, 2010. A female performer, Firegenet Alemu, who performed at the opening night at CB, told me in 2016: "Theater betu ende eqa tetekmobin new yemiwerewiren" (The theater uses and discards us as if we were disposable objects). Romanticized and denigrated at once, the very profession of dancing at the state-owned theaters is aesthetically marginalized compared to theater and music. Living in this condition, the performing body, particularly queer performing bodies at the state-owned theaters, is doubly marginalized. Performers continue to challenge the status quo. To fight together, they formed the Ethiopian Dance Art Association on May 14, 2018. Surreptitious acts of dissidence have been staged using the traditional aesthetic safety valve called wax and gold, whereby artists would send messages with double entendre, the wax being the

obvious while the gold signifies the hidden meaning. The state would also censor art works on the premise that they might have deployed wax and gold while there was none. Hence wax and gold is a messy and dynamic institution. There are artists who collaborate with the state, a few have confronted it, and many live in a state of self-censorship.

16 See Vegard Mjelde Hanssen et al., "High Prevalence of Respiratory and Dermal Symptoms among Ethiopian Flower Farm Workers," *Archives of Environmental and Occupational Health* (2015), 204–13; Munir H. Idriss, Christopher Lovell, and Mihretu Woldeyes, "Occupational Irritant Contact Dermatitis Caused by Lobelia Richardii in an Ethiopian Flower Farm," *Contact Dermatitis* 67, no. 2 (August 2012): 112–14; Tekalign Admasu, "Female Workers in Flower Farm Industry: A Study of Socio-economic Impacts of the Job Opportunity, Case of Bishoftu City: Ethiopia," MA thesis, Norwegian University of Science and Technology, 2015.

17 Ngũgĩ wa Thiong'o, "Notes towards a Performance Theory of Orature," *Performance Research: A Journal of the Performing Arts* 12, no. 3 (March 2010).

18 Tibebeselassie Tigabu, "Crossing Boundaries," *The Reporter*, October 3, 2015, 38.

19 Mshai Mwangola, "Droplets of Dust, Particles of Water: Portraits of Survival from the Lake Turkana Desert," in *Crossing Boundaries Performing Arts Festival-Conference* (Addis Ababa: Ethiopian Theatre Professional Association, 2015), 43.

20 Mwangola, "Droplets of Dust," 43.

21 Ethiopian Theatre Professionals' Association, *Crossing Boundaries Festival-Conference. Video Documentary*, Addis Ababa, April 2, 2016, https://www.youtube.com/watch?v=aiEg2c8H_hk.

22 Conversation with Aklile Solomon, a member of Yellow Movement, April 21, 2016.

23 "In Ethiopia, a Safe House for Abused Girls Provides Shelter and Hopes for a Better Future," UN Women, accessed December 28, 2016, http://www.unwomen.org/en/news/stories/2012/10/in-ethiopia-a-safe-house-for-abused-girls-provides-shelter-and-hopes-for-a-better-future.

24 Meskel is an Ethiopian Orthodox festival that celebrates the discovery of the True Cross by Queen Helena.

25 Surafel Wondimu Abebe, "Message from the Organizing Team," in Ethiopian Theatre Professional Association, *Crossing Boundaries Performing Arts Festival-Conference* (Addis Ababa: Artet, 2015), 16.

26 Sebhat Nega, the person who ran this so-called Institute for Peace and who was considered the godfather of his party (TPLF), was captured by the state in a ravine where he had been hiding after the war between the federal government and his party broke out on November 4, 2020.

27 Michel Chossudovsky, "Monsanto and the Bio-Tech Conglomerates: Sowing the Seeds of Famine in Ethiopia," *Global Research* 1, no. 4 (May 2014).

11

SPECULATIVE CHOREOGRAPHY

Futures of Feminist Food Justice and Sovereignty

JIGNA DESAI

We were all there. Wearing masks. Protesting in the streets. Some getting shot at with tear gas and rubber bullets. Many patrolling neighborhoods against white supremacists at night. Donating bandages and antiseptic. Cleaning up in the morning. Everyone, giving. Scouring suburban supermarkets for dried beans, oil, onions, and other long-lasting perishable vegetables. Converting a hotel to a collective shelter, then transforming parks into refuges for the unhoused. Placing plywood again. Painting murals and portraits of solidarity. Taking responsibility and care of each other as a form of protest, resistance, and politics. Knowing that the police, the mayor, the national guard, electoral politics, and voting were never enough anyway.

ON MAY 25, 2020, GEORGE FLOYD WAS MURDERED BY MINNEAPO-lis Police Department officers outside of Cup Foods, a corner store, in South Minneapolis. During the Minneapolis uprisings that followed, the loss of key food stores exposed the economic instability accelerated by gentrification and the precarity of the food infrastructure in Minneapolis. The damage revealed the resentment against many of the corporate entities and businesses that extract capital within these neighborhoods and the deeper and long-standing rage about the great racial disparities in the Twin Cities, some of the largest in the nation. The closing of Cub Foods supermarket, Target, dollar stores, and numerous other venues disrupted the ability of tens of thousands of residents of South Minneapolis to procure food. The subsequent losses demonstrated how food apartheid and food injustice as well as housing, health, and water insecurities were grounded in and spatialized through racism.[1] Mutual aid efforts immediately created and organized elaborate networks of supplies and distribution throughout Minneapolis.

Mutual aid solidarity efforts and networks formed to meet the immediate needs, especially food needs, of people in these unstable conditions and to provide a way to mobilize and resist in the face of police and state violence. During June 2020, the overwhelming mutual aid response mobilized over social media received sustaining contributions, providing resources, especially to Black, Indigenous, and person of color (BIPOC) communities that were hit hard by the disruptions of COVID-19 and then the uprisings. The temporalities of the COVID-19 pandemic and the murder of George Floyd comingle, so that the subsequent uprisings are resistance movements not just against antiblackness and police violence, but also against health injustice, eugenics, racism, and settler colonialism. How then do we understand food security and sovereignty within the context of racial justice and liberation? The Twin Cities have long been the site of numerous food justice and food sovereignty movements. Ananya Dance Theatre, too, has contributed to these efforts. Furthermore, ADT opens up artistic and activist space to consider food insecurity and racial injustice by speculating on transformation through food sovereignty, healing justice, and probing of the relationship between corporeality and the human in a future grounded in radical collective care and interdependence.

ANANYA DANCE THEATRE

That a dance troupe is on the streets in protest. Visits farms. Cradles seeds in hands. Carries water from the source of the Mississippi River with Water Protectors. Dances with youth so they refind their bodies within the confines of public schools. Offers food to guests at the institute. Honors land and Native sovereignty. Practices in parks so that the public can join. Acts individually and collectively. Marches with Black and brown mamas to the sacred space of George Floyd Square. Has a commitment to make change. Again and again. To create what is not yet. Becoming. Present and future.

On stage and off, ADT is about praxis. They do. The company invests not only in storytelling and sharing within the ensemble, but also in research, community engagement, workshops, community-based performance and dialogue, and direct action. They speculate on the present that is to be unmade and made and the future that can be, together. They talk and work with activists, artists, community elders and leaders, academics, and youth while preparing works. They protest and take healing justice to the streets. Moreover, these relationships spill off the stage as members provide care and labor for each other, functioning through mutual aid and support in daily life and crisis. For *Roktim*, the company engaged Hmong American farmers, Frogtown Farmers, people of color co-ops, and Dream of Wild Health farmers (a Native organic and seed collection farm). These spaces place food justice in relation to other forms of healing praxis: Dream of Wild Health not only grows food and collects seeds but also provides space for Native peoples to come, stay, heal, and connect with the earth and ancestors.[2] ADT states that the "long research and creative process made sure that we all realized the deep link of seeds, earth, and food to culture, Indigenous knowledges, and self-determination of peoples."[3] At Dream of Wild Health, they experienced firsthand the embodied practice of planting seeds, tending plants, learning the healing and edible qualities of cultivated and wild plants, and cooking food. During the Minneapolis uprisings, ADT protested, patrolled neighborhoods to maintain safety, practiced deescalation, contributed to mutual aid, packaged food, created art, and nourished through healing justice. ADT enacts a praxis of radical engagement.

This praxis guides the speculative choreography and performance as well. What does it mean to dance speculatively for radical futures of collective care and food sovereignty as a feminist collective? For ADT, it means that the choreography, practice, and performance must also both sustain *and* enhance life for its individual and collective members. It means that the company postulates critical dystopias that engage and imagine what is already here and what futurities we may yet dream.[4] Speculative choreographies, like speculative fiction, imagine futures that examine past and present to proliferate branches, possibilities of futures that yet may be. Departing from perceived reality and the realism of dance, ADT's speculative choreographies engage, stage, and perform nonreal dystopic worlds that result from colonialism, capitalism, racism, and ableism, as well as heteropatriarchy, while simultaneously capturing and dancing feminist fragments of utopic possibility. In *Roktim*, they elaborate and extrapolate from feminist fabulations new forms of radical collective care and food sovereignty, and new individual and collective ways of knowing and being (figure 11.1).

These feminist fabulist futures must be as heterogeneous as the collectives that inhabit and dance them. An incredibly varied collection of

FIGURE 11.1. (From left) Ananya Chatterjea, Lela Pierce, Chitra Vairavan, and Renée Copeland in a moment of radical collectivity and resistance. *Roktim: Nurture Incarnadine* (2015). Photo by Paul Virtucio. Courtesy of Ananya Dance Theatre.

morphologies and movements, ADT is, nevertheless, a collective—one that must engage the different relationships that arise onstage among such different subjects, bodies, and the spaces that they occupy. To choreograph the integration of difference, rather than uniformity and similitude, requires negotiation, conversation, and harmonization without necessarily reverting to identical, synchronous motion. ADT performs these relationships onstage through its grouping of bodies, colors, spacing, and costumes. This also means that they adapt and transpose knowledge from one domain to another. ADT translates its knowledge about seed collection, farming, factory labor, and reproductive labor into collective spatialization, movement, and speculative choreography.

This praxis of radical care and speculative justice guides their broad geopolitical and racial solidarities. ADT confounds simple identity-based and geopolitical-based classification. While firmly grounded in the Twin Cities, ADT addresses experiences, struggles, and knowledge from the global North and South through the struggles and vision of BIPOC women and femmes. ADT intentionally forges solidarities by a border-crossing praxis that jumps scale and crosses geographies and ecologies. As a collective, members share their own individual experiences and geopolitical itineraries and learn from each other as well as other communities. They intertwine their geopolitical itineraries to create solidarities across physically discontinuous spaces and scales, choreographing imaginary topographical contour lines that enjamb and juxtapose spaces to imagine new and transformative feminist spatial imaginaries of solidarity. Both material and metaphorical, contour lines cross scale and borders, break down binaries and distinctions implicit in paradigms of global feminism, international feminism, and even transnational feminism. Deftly charting new topographies across global North and South through praxis and performance, ADT mobilizes speculative choreographies of justice to perform imagined and material worlds from the scale of the body to the scale of the planetary. ADT deploys movement and performance to reimagine economic, political, social, and cultural relations across space through choreographies of similarity, juxtaposition, and enjambment. These speculative choreographies make visible similar power structures and processes in various locations, enabling and creating social change imagined from radical futurities.

FEMINIST FOOD POLITICS

> I know she rises at dawn
> daily
> breathes in
> her dream of greening
> of returning to that intertwining
> of women, land, seeds,
> an ecology of connection
> and reciprocity.
> —ROKTIM, poem by Ananya Chatterjea,
> performed by Alessandra Williams.

Food politics cannot simply address problems of hunger and malnutrition as technical, political, or economic issues. In fact, discussing hunger and food without addressing structures of racism, empire, and capitalism leaves intact the larger systems that lead to food insecurity and inequality in the first place. Premiering September 2015 in Saint Paul, Minnesota, ADT's *Roktim: Nurture Incarnadine* imagines and performs, through form and content, transformative feminist and racial justice food politics through speculative choreography. *Roktim* is the Bengali word for "redden," and similarly, *Incarnadine* means to nurture a reddening, blood red, a fleshy pink-red, to enfleshen, to become of flesh (incarnate, carmine, carne, to color, to colorize). As conveyed by the title, the performance encompasses food politics in relation to racialized embodiment, care and labor, and cultivation and growth. In doing so, *Roktim* choreographs the material and metaphorical significance of seeds within feminist food politics. It considers how the meaning of food extends far beyond its nutritional and material value. *Roktim* takes seeds, food production, and gendered labor as critical to transformative justice and radical feminist futures grounded in racialized reproductive labor and racial food justice.

Feminist food work reconceptualizes the meaning and value of food itself. Carolyn Sachs and Anouk Patel-Campillo's expansive and encompassing essay "Feminist Food Justice: Crafting a New Vision" suggests that there are three major approaches to food politics: food security, food sovereignty, and food justice.[5] The United Nations' Food and Agriculture Organization (FAO) identifies food security through four priorities and needs: availability (addressing the issue of hunger through assessing the availability of food); access (ensuring that there are sufficient resources to produce food through aid, financing, etc.); stability (emphasizing that food supplies meet food demands through markets); and utilization (weighing the nutritional and dietary needs of populations).[6] For Sachs and Patel-Campillo, the food-security model is often a top-down global approach to food and hunger vis-à-vis a question of population, economy, and policy.[7] Moreover, a top-down technocratic state solution that takes food scarcity as its central problem participates in the very structures that have led to global food inequalities to begin with. In other words, food security frames hunger and food as a Malthusian-meets-market problem that can be addressed through techno-capital-state solutions involving increases in global agricultural production, international trade, development, and cooperation, as well as scientific and technical information. *Roktim* explicitly addresses these models of food security, proposing new ecologies of self-reliance and interdependence, rather than paradigms invested in the state, capitalism, and security.

Challenging this scarcity-requires-security model, food sovereignty proponents suggest that hunger and malnutrition need to be understood within power relations that result in and from global inequalities and oppressions. Hunger and malnutrition as well as overconsumption arise from unfavorable distributions of food and resources, including land, water, and seed. If food security raises the question of hunger, malnutrition, and food systems at the scale of the global, food sovereignty and food justice are often articulated as local solutions. It is positioned in contrast to the global top-down marketized control of food systems that is suggested by food security.

In contrast to food security, food sovereignty emphasizes local control of food systems as the mechanism for forging sustainability and equity. The global subsistence farmer network La Vía Campesina (LVC) articulates food sovereignty as "the right of peoples and governments to choose the way food is produced and consumed in order to respect our livelihoods, as well as the policies that support this choice."[8] LVC's food sovereignty model, for example, is a rights-based approach that emphasizes local control of the social, economic, and political dimensions of food and agro-systems. Arguing that food security is a neoliberal entrepreneurial effort that has negative impact, LVC seeks to connect people, communities, and places, as inextricably linked through food sovereignty. For LVC, self-determination in defining food and food systems at the local level is at the heart of food sovereignty.

Food sovereignty advocates in the global South seek the right of self-determination as enabling local communities to make food choices and decisions as well as set priorities and create sustainability. Hence, for them, food sovereignty challenges the global-system approach to food security and the erasure of social, economic, and geopolitical power relations in which food systems are embedded. For ADT, food sovereignty cannot be separated from other forms of sovereignty for Native people. Indigenous control and management of food ways and food knowledge guide the praxis of ADT and are at the foundation of *Roktim*. Within the context of settler colonialism in the global North, sovereignty, including food sovereignty, must always be linked to cultural and political sovereignty, self-determination, and land. Food sovereignty emphasizes local or Indigenous control and priorities within food systems, forwarding self-determination within uneven global development and settler colonialism, battling ecological degradation through sustainable valuing of knowledge, and promoting ecological preservation, diversification, and collaboration.

The center of gravity for food justice, like food sovereignty, is often self-reliance and local control of food systems. For Robert Gottlieb and Anupama Joshi, food justice represents "a transformation of the current food system, including but not limited to eliminating disparities and inequities."[9] For Black and other racialized communities in the global North, racial food justice, in contrast to food sovereignty, is often used to characterize a commitment to addressing the structural inequities that cause and impact hunger, malnutrition, and food insecurity. Within an intersectional framework, Kirsten Cadieux and Rachel Slocum broaden the meaning of food justice to consider transformative change at four key points of intervention: trauma/inequity, exchange, land, and labor.[10] Their vision of racial and feminist food justice acknowledges and confronts social, cultural, and historical processes of collective social trauma and persistent race, gender, caste, and class inequalities while emphasizing more economic and scientific concerns about land, labor, seed, and ecology. ADT's interdisciplinary artistic inquiry fuses food sovereignty and food justice politics in its performance of *Roktim*. Furthermore, it stages space-bending and geospatial-folding choreographies that conjure imaginary geopolitical terrains where Native, Black, immigrant, and refugee communities in the North are juxtaposed and continuous with those of the global South. Simply put, ADT speculates topologies that enjamb global North and South to forge new solidarities of food justice and food sovereignty.

Roktim bridges food sovereignty and food justice by choreographing solidarity across geographies of inequality, struggle, and reimaginings. Providing a resounding critique of inequality and food insecurity and security, and locating race, class, gender, sexuality, migration, nation, caste, and indigeneity squarely at the heart of food, *Roktim* forwards and imagines the need to have seed sovereignty and food justice. To understand local struggles for the production of food and meaning means to locate them within transnational struggles of self-reliance as well as memory, history, and practice. Deploying a border-crossing feminism that considers the geographies of food sovereignty and food justice, ADT choreographs BIPOC solidarity that addresses food politics across geographies of the global South and North.

PERFORMANCE

> yes, the time is upon us
> is it not?
> change is afoot.
> —*ROKTIM*, poem by Ananya Chatterjea,
> performed by Alessandra Williams.

Roktim stages feminist food politics through four movements performed through dystopic and speculative choreographies: (a) a feminist critique of global food security within late capital; (b) a feminist critique of the disproportionate impact of food security measures in terms of gender, race, caste, and indigeneity; (c) an endorsement of self-reliance, access, and autonomy through food justice and food sovereignty; and (d) finally, new imaginings of food liberation through futurities and biomythography.

The first act opens with a critique of food insecurity vis-à-vis the production of food and seeds (including genetically modified organisms) within industrial production by transnational corporations. Concurrent tours of the dystopic Pronto FeedzAll Corporation facilities given by ADT members lure the audience into the performance. The tours engage audience members by active participation through which they position themselves as consumers of food commodities within circuits of global capital in this dystopic world-making. The tours feature the narrative propounding the wonders of corporate-produced food, which the performers undermine and contradict through their revolting bodies, which vomit, become debilitated, and fall apart. Critical of commodity fetishism that offers bigger, brighter, more, *Roktim* satirizes the promises of these technocorporate futurities, demonstrating the damage done to racialized, colonized, and gendered bodies. Technocapital promises to feed the global North and South, albeit differently, through corporate and capitalist food securitization. Moreover, by positioning audience members merely as agents only through their acts of consumption, *Roktim* exposes how individuality, consumption, and liberal formations of choice shape neoliberal food politics. Within food security, food is merely a commodity, and we, merely consumers.

To choreograph food dystopias, *Roktim* physically displaces performances from the venerated performance auditorium and opens outside in a grassy plaza through which guides lead audience members in small groups. First feeling open and expansive, it quickly becomes clear that the paths appear to offer choices but are carefully managed, encouraging the participants to reflect on their own experience of food consumption as choice. The first act increasingly perturbs audience participants, who navigate from section to section and are exposed to the violent, sickening, and alienating impacts of Pronto FeedzAll Corporation food that is produced and consumed. Forced to move, gaze upon, and confront increasingly suffering people and bodies, this first act, while disturbing, is also pedagogical in that participants learn to read the unruliness and discomfort of their own and others' bodies within this dystopic space.

The technocapitalist control of food within food securitization minimizes agency, self-reliance, and self-determination, but also deepens the structural violence that furthers dispossession. "The work done under the auspices of food security has often reproduced the socially inequitable conditions and relations it nominally seeks to address."[11] Food as a global commodity within food security relies on the exploited labor of vulnerable workers and subjects, centralization of resources, and the separation of land, knowledge, and people. *Roktim* crafts a dystopia of necropolitical technocorporate food control across folded and enjambed spaces, citing newspaper headlines "about the farmer suicide epidemic in India ultimately traced back to the introduction of GMO seeds, about the death of workers from a late-detected gas leak in Texas, the harvesting of wombs from the global south, murders masquerading as suicides."[12] The laboring subjects of peasants, subsistence farmers, women of color, children, Indigenous, and the landless, whose increasing alienation, despondency, and death are felt in the field and the factory. *Roktim*'s world-making juxtaposes these various spaces—home, lab, factory, and field—as interrelated dystopic sites of contestation, trauma, and dispossession.

Performers and audience members alike are asked to witness the violence of the global corporate food system. Unsettled and ready to probe dominant narratives of food production and consumption, the audience is settled into their seats as the second act unfolds in a factory where the dancers engage in Fordist-like repetition and mechanical movements. Precise identical and mechanical movements are often associated, within mainstream dance, with the aesthetics of identical synchronization of line dancers such as the Rockettes or Riverdance. But *Roktim* deploys these precise straight lines and synchronized movements for an entirely different effect: to evoke rigidity, mechanization, coercion, and constraint. Audiences are again confronted by their expectations for ensemble dance as dancer Magnolia Yang Sao Yia begins to break down and diverge from the linear and mechanistic choreography. Her asynchronicity and lack of synergy take her out of alignment with the group. As her character unravels, so does the angular, tracked, and mechanical ensemble. Forced to recognize each other rather than operate next to each other, the dancers slowly shift from the long lines of Fordist dystopic production to the curved and rounded movements of a moving, breathing collective. This triggers new collective speculative choreography that unfolds over the next two acts.

Slowly, the ensemble builds an intersubjective and collective interdependence as they synchronize their breath and find a shared rhythm grounded in their integrated differences. They move as individuals, dyads, and small groups across the stage, re-creating new geopolitical and corporeal possibilities and solidarities. The juxtaposed narratives of the different scenes create paths of movement that trace topographies across the stage, linking new spaces, stories, and subjects. Arising from diligent and exhaustive rehearsing—and what is perhaps most required for collective performance— are the shared rhythm and breath. A breath that is collectively vocalized, heard, resonant, and repeating, like echolocation guiding each dancer to position herself within tightly coordinated and close spaces and movement. The speculative choreography pulls forth a fragment of feminist utopic collectivity embodied and performed through synchronized breathing.

As the group comes to consciousness and transforms from mechanistic ensemble to intersubjective collective, *Roktim* cracks open and nurtures the seeds of food justice and food sovereignty. Because of its work with Dream of Wild Health Farm, ADT is able to present food sovereignty as inextricably interwoven with Indigenous sovereignty and care, and integrally tied to broader questions of knowledge, subjectivity, and political and land sovereignty within radical futures. ADT reflects a broader understanding of decolonization and sovereignty as signifying "a multiplicity of legal and social rights to political, economic, and cultural self-determination. It was a term around which social movements formed and political agendas for decolonization and social justice were articulated. It has come to mark the complexities of global Indigenous efforts to reverse ongoing experiences of colonialism as well as to signify local efforts."[13] In configuring sovereignty as decolonization, *Roktim* undoes the equivalence of sovereignty as possession and the power of the sovereign over the object of governance for radical futures.

Food sovereignty is seed sovereignty is land sovereignty is political sovereignty is corporeal sovereignty is collective sovereignty. Indigenous food practices, seed collection, and land protection become the bases of the decolonizing food practices and seed sovereignty presented as a shared vision for the world. *Roktim* undoes the category of food as that which already has become, transforming it into the seed that is becoming. ADT emphasizes the need to collect, value, and nurture open-source seeds as living archives for collectivity. It views the gendered labor of collecting, caring for, and preserving seeds as a public and collective action. *Roktim* also decomposes the term "land" into "soil," shifting it from the economic and political aspects of sovereignty to the ontological, with soil as the essence of vitality and life. It marks the interdependency among soil, seed, sun, laborer, and meaning. *Roktim* expresses seeds and sovereignty as sites of interaction and interdependence rather than individualist self-determination. Self- and collective determination are choreographed through curvature and roundedness. As the relationship between the dancers intensifies, they interact with each other through arcs of movement and intertwinings. Individually, the body shape shifts from the straight limb movements of the factory to taller, feet-to-spine-based movements that open up the rib cage, gather energy and height from the power of jumps, and feature sweeping and bending arcs. The dancing bodies become enfleshed in movements of radical collective care and vitality.

This notion of seed is not just seed as non–genetically modified, not patented, genetically modified, or owned or controlled by emerging seed giants, but also seed itself as enfleshed—that which brings into being stories, memories, and histories, that which carries through the flesh the memory. In one scene, Chatterjea recounts the pleasure and the memory of eating ground poppy-seed paste with rice, salt, and green chilies. But the scene is not the simple enactment and performance of food nostalgia.[14] Instead, Chatterjea links her memory of the pleasure with the violence of opium. The seed not only holds the memory of the labor, belonging, and love between mother and daughter, but also the history of colonialism, heteropatriarchy, and capitalism that accompanies the seed. Moreover, ADT, in thinking of the seed archive and the seed *as* an archive, envisions the seed as more than the object of agricultural production, but as the splinter of speculation and world-making. The seed, in this case, is incarnadine carrying life and its stories and bringing into blood and flesh memory and history. Repeatedly throughout *Roktim*, ADT speculatively choreographs the simultaneity of being of woman and seed, human and food, labor and labored upon. Offering entanglement as a central paradigm of sovereignty and self-reliance in which food and body, seed and human, are mutually becoming, emergent, and provisional. Entanglement in radical feminist utopic futures suggests contestation, negotiation, impurity, and interdependence rather than power over.

CONCLUSION

> Human beings are magical. Bios and Logos. Words made flesh, muscle and bone animated by hope and desire, belief materialized in deeds, deeds which crystalize our actualities. . . . And the maps of spring always have to be redrawn again, in undared forms.
> —SYLVIA WYNTER, "The Pope Must Have Been Drunk, the King of Castile a Madman: Culture as Actuality and the Caribbean Rethinking of Modernity"

For ADT, research, praxis, activism, collaboration, and performance are worked through particular cultural formations that translate materialities, intimacies, and violences of the everyday and social movements into narrated and performed speculative choreographies. Indeed their speculations create and form, to use Audre Lorde's term, a biomythography, where the story of the self intersects with myth.[15] These stories of women's lives and work are refracted and interwoven through embodied practices, where the dancing body becomes the site of weaving together research, memory, and imagination to invoke and create new collective memories and stories. If biomythographies are the life of stories written and performed, where *bios*, *myth*, and *logos* come together, they evoke a *bios* that cognizantly moves against the dystopic necropolitics of Pronto FeedzAll. ADT identifies Indigenous and transnational feminist struggles of collective resistance and collective care as a form of speculation and mythmaking: the story of the Hawaiian queen Lili'uokalani, who called to her people to plant the garden as resistance; of Palestinian women claiming the land and its vegetation as their resistance; of the gifting and stewardship of seeds and leaves.

While food security typically emphasizes the global scale of production, food sovereignty and food justice privilege local self-determination and reliance. In challenging the global/local binary that characterizes food security and food sovereignty, *Roktim*'s speculative world-making juxtaposes places and spaces in noncontinuous geographies of trauma, struggle, and resistance in a vision of partial solidarities. ADT states, "We work through stories that are partly researched, partly remembered, and partly imagined."[16] This partiality never renders a story real and legible: "We are not interested in representation and rendering of the story."[17] Food justice in *Roktim* imagines not specific case studies through which we must find a local and pure politics, but a colonial and capitalist food dystopia that sullies, makes impure, and brings into being feminist fragments of utopic possibilities. In doing so, *Roktim* puts in question both the universalism of the global and the authenticity of the local, treating discontinuous juxtapositions of the transnational as a method of multivernacularism, of translation, of abstraction. ADT decolonizes and speculates new engagements and enjambments across time and space—for example, the conversation between Vandana Shiva and Wangari Maathai as it might have occurred. ADT produces new intimacies and socialities across spaces bringing together different histories.

It is in the final act that *Roktim* breaks from its previous style and mode, shifting from realism, angularity, and rhythm. Gone are the dystopic factory floor and its unbending, inflexible strength. Instead, *Roktim* offers arcs and bends, curving spines distributed in semicircles across the stage. The aesthetics and poetics of speculative choreography merge poetry, soft flows, shadows, and collectivity in which the line is broken and the body reaches toward sky and earth, becoming more fluid, elongated, and grounded. Stretching up and down. The body and word bridge air and earth as the groundedness arches into the back, and the torso reaches up and over. Each component of the spine's articulation is explored in the bending in different directions. The dancers anchored by their heels reach and extend through their spines to their palms and eyes.

As the scene continues, Heid Erdrich narrates the sky woman giving seeds. This time, seeds are given not within economies of agricultural corporate capitalism, but within ecologies of radical collective care and giving. Sky woman's gift is not transactional but mythical, beyond transactions of compensation and exchange. The biomythography conjures a prophecy for all—both performers and audience. This *bios* is one in which the human and the seed, the subject and object, myth and biography, become blurred in their making and unmaking. In the conjuring of stories of seed and struggle, ADT enfleshes, reddens, kills, and makes meat of, then returns to seed. The seed is, in the words of Kim Q. Hall, "the transformative potential of openness to the not yet."[18] *Roktim*'s speculative choreography offers us seeds: what has already been and is yet to be.

> Cradle in your hands
> His breath
> His Memory
> Cradle seeds of protest
> Tend plants of revolution
> Nourish each other

NOTES

1   For the notion of food apartheid, see Ashanté M. Reese, *Black Food Geographies: Race, Self-Reliance, and Food Access in Washington, D.C.* (Chapel Hill: University of North Carolina Press, 2019), 19.

2   Dream of Wild Health, "Peta Wakan Tipi," *Dream of Wild Health | Peta Wakan Tipi*, http://dreamofwildhealth.org/peta_wakan_tipi.html.

3   Ananya Chatterjea, "Roktim: Nurture Incarnadine," *Ananya Dance Theatre*, http://www.ananyadancetheatre.org/dance/roktim-nurture-incarnadine/.

4   Tom Moylan, *Scraps of the Untainted Sky: Science Fiction, Utopia, Dystopia* (Boulder, CO: Perseus, 2000), 195.

5   Carolyn Sachs and Anouk Campillo-Patel, "Feminist Food Justice: Crafting a New Vision Source," *Feminist Studies* 40, no. 2 (2014): 396.

6 Food and Agriculture Organization of the United Nations, *An Introduction to the Basic Concepts of Food Security*, http://www.fao.org/docrep/013/al936e/al936e00.pdf.

7 Sachs and Campillo-Patel, "Feminist Food Justice."

8 La Vía Campesina, *Food Sovereignty for Africa: A Challenge at Fingertips*, 2008, 57.

9 Robert Gottlieb and Anupama Joshi, *Food Justice* (Cambridge, MA: MIT Press, 2010), ix.

10 Kirsten Valentine Cadieux and Rachel Slocum, "What Does It Mean to Do Food Justice?," *Journal of Political Ecology* 22 (2015): 1–26.

11 Cadieux and Slocum, "What Does It Mean to Do Food Justice?," 4.

12 Chatterjea, "Roktim."

13 Joanne Barker, "For Whom Sovereignty Matters," in *Sovereignty Matters: Locations of Contestation and Possibility in Indigenous Struggles for Self-Determination* (Lincoln: University of Nebraska, 2005), 1.

14 Tracey Deutsch, "Memories of Mothers in the Kitchen: Local Foods, History, and Women's Work," *Radical History Review* 2011, no. 110 (2011): 167–68.

15 Audre Lorde, *Zami, a New Spelling of My Name: A Biomythography* (Freedom, CA: Crossing Press, 1996).

16 Ananya Chatterjea, "Creating a New, Contemporary American Dance," Ananya Dance Theatre, http://www.ananyadancetheatre.org/2015/10/creating-a-new-contemporary-american-dance/.

17 Chatterjea, "Creating a New, Contemporary American Dance."

18 Kim Q. Hall, "Toward a Queer Crip Feminist Politics of Food," *PhiloSOPHIA: A Journal in Continental Feminism* 14, no. 2 (2014): 203–25.

12

MUSINGS ON CROSSING

Ananya Dance Theatre in Addis Ababa

HUI NIU WILCOX

IN EARLY SEPTEMBER 2015, A FEW DAYS BEFORE OUR PREMIERE
of *Roktim* in Saint Paul, Minnesota, I received an elated phone call from
Ananya: "Hui, you are going to Ethiopia!" We wrapped up our performance
on Sunday, September 17, at about 10 p.m. At six the next morning, we
gathered at the Minneapolis–Saint Paul International Airport, departing
for Addis Ababa, to perform *Roktim* as the keynote of the Crossing Boundaries Festival. A key organizer of the festival, Surafel Wondimu, reflects on
and theorizes ADT's crossing as bodies of women of color from the North,
occupying positions that are both privileged and precarious. He sees Crossing Boundaries' invitation of ADT as a necessary intervention in gendered,
racialized neoliberal development in Ethiopia and Africa in general and
discusses the potential of mindful space making that mobilizes alliances
between artists across multiple borders.

Hoping for generative dialogues with Surafel Wondimu, I offer my own
reflection on border crossing and space making as a dancer of Ananya
Dance Theatre, based on my personal observation and experience in Addis
Ababa. I realize that even though the twelve of us traveled together (ten
performers and two supporting staff), we experienced Crossing Boundaries
and Addis Ababa each in our own ways, because of our different relationships with various nation-states and the ways in which our bodies are differentially marked: African American, Asian American, Arab American,

white American, ambiguous, female, male, and so on. I was born and grew up in China but have lived in Minnesota since 1996 and became an American citizen in 2012. In fact, American citizenship became a prickly point for me on this journey; so did my Chinese cultural identity and appearance. I learned much about my dual identities and was confronted with questions about home and homeland in many ways.

The moment I swore in as an American citizen was fraught with emotions, partly because I had to abdicate my Chinese citizenship, as the Chinese government does not allow dual citizenship. But I made a note to myself that I am still Chinese culturally: I will not forget my mother tongue, and I will not lose my deeply embodied connection with Chinese cultural practices. And of course, in the American racial landscape, I will always be read as Asian, not always as Chinese but definitely not white. There are many ways in which American citizenship sits in tension with my Asianness; the historical exclusion of the Chinese via immigration laws in 1882 has left its mark on American race consciousness.

There are other Asian bodies in the company, Ananya and Chitra as South Asian, Magnolia as Southeast Asian (Hmong), and Kealoha as Filipino-Hawaiian. I suspect that we were the primary reasons why the US State Department personnel who screened us for funding was puzzled: "Where is the American in the company?" But he must have also seen African American bodies in the company. They were also not sufficiently American for him. Our single white dancer, Renée Copeland, was perhaps read as ambiguous as well. In any case, there is just not enough whiteness in this company for it to be seen as American.

This story was relayed to us by an American diplomat working in the American Embassy in Addis Ababa. An African American himself, he was rightfully outraged by the questioning of our Americanness. He and his colleagues at this particular embassy were instrumental in securing State Department funding to support our travel to Addis Ababa, as an American dance company representing the United States in Ethiopia and participating in the commemoration of seventy-five years of diplomatic relations between the United States and Ethiopia—a critical strategic relationship for US national security interests.

Accustomed to being seen as an "alien," I considered the irony of my new responsibility of representing the United States. My daily burden in the United States is to represent Asianness, subtly or not so subtly pressed to respond to questions such as "Aren't you a tiger mom?" "Aren't you good at math?" "Aren't you a classical musician?" "Aren't you a terrible driver?"

And of course, "Do you speak English?" and "Where are you from?" My struggle to resist the stereotypes implied in these alienating questions is energized by my community, which is Ananya Dance Theatre, even though my comrades have different histories of injuries, healing, and resistance. We affirm to each other that, yes, we are Americans, in that we deserve the same kind of dignity and rights as anyone. But more than anything, through dance, we interrogate "America"—the nation-state built through slavery and colonization, imperial aggression, and racial, class, and gender violence. We interrogate how the contemporary consciousness, subconsciousness, or unconsciousness of "America" is shaped, embodied, and enacted through dance and dialogues. I never thought that traveling to Ethiopia with Ananya Dance Theatre would be equivalent to entering the belly of the beast that is the American empire, or to perhaps even becoming part of this beast, a possibility over which we must all be vigilant all the time.

What is the price of being included in the American empire? Asian American studies scholars have begun to question whether inclusion should be the end goal of our demand for social justice, as inclusion often depends on corollary processes of assimilation and acquiescence. To be funded by the US State Department is to be included, albeit temporarily. To uncritical ears, this connotes status: "Wow! Congratulations! How cool!" To critical ears, this provokes suspicion: "So, cultural diplomacy, eh?" It was definitely a compromise, considering how critically reflexive Ananya Dance Theatre's politics are. But given how poorly funded we are, and how desperately we wanted to meet our artistic counterparts in Africa, we took the money and made our journey a two-in-one: We would have to do the bidding of the US Embassy, but we were definitely more invested in our keynote performance at the Ethiopian National Theatre for the Crossing Boundaries Festival.

The relationship we had with the empire was one of exchange: we enjoyed the privileges that came as a result of our relationship with the American nation-state: funding, easier entry into Ethiopia (a company member who is an Indian national was not able to go on this trip because she lacked an American passport), being chauffeured in the conspicuously labeled American Embassy vehicle, staying in a nice four-star hotel. How apt it was that our material comforts were thanks to our affiliation with the empire.

Our end of the deal? We performed at the embassy event commemorating seventy-five years of US-Ethiopia diplomatic relations, and we conducted a workshop with the Yellow Movement—a local women's rights group—in the US Embassy. While we were not your typical representatives of the US women's movement, we were conscious of the ideological and discursive power of Western feminisms in global women's movements. We've made a collective decision to engage in active and compassionate listening and mutual learning. Regardless of what the embassy intended us to do, we could not assume the role of teachers, and definitely not "liberated women of the West." In fact, these young women had much more to teach us, as they told us about their courageous resistance against patriarchy on a day-to-day basis and about their dreams and visions as students of law working for human rights, climate justice, and so much more.

But I'm getting ahead of myself with the story. Echoing Surafel's theme of "mindful space-making," I want to talk about space for a moment. As we approached the perfectly manicured compound housing the American Embassy, some of us took pictures. A second later, a security guard walked over and told us to delete our pictures, "for security reasons." Security, of course, was also the reason why we went through a thorough screening before entering the compound and had to leave all bags and electronic devices at the checkpoint. We saw some young Ethiopian women going through the same procedures as we did. They were part of the Yellow Movement that we were to engage with for the next few hours. I remember being told that the ground an embassy sits on is considered territory of the nation it represents. If that is true, going through the security checkpoint is a border-crossing experience in itself. And we were certainly reminded in a very visceral way of how our bodies—no matter what nations have claimed us—are all considered suspect by the state apparatus of the United States.

Once we were inside the embassy and had been introduced to the young women of the Yellow Movement, we were more or less left alone, except that two female embassy employees, one white American and the other Ethiopian, stayed in the conference room as observers. There were brief introductions and a sharing of each other's work, one-on-one conversations, and movement exercises led by Ananya Chatterjea. We talked about the prevalence of gender violence in all of our social and geopolitical locations, and how we respond individually and collectively. At one point, Ananya instructed every single woman in that room to stand together and scream at the top of our lungs. I remember feeling the vibration of the powerful sound waves created by women of the North and the South. Did our consciousness-filled scream unsettle the people working in the embassy? Did our screaming penetrate the tightly secured walls and echo in the sky of Addis Ababa? What does it take for women to be heard and taken seriously? What happens when we cross the boundary between us and them, look each other in the eye, and say, "Let's scream together!"? I believe the performative act of screaming together drew intimate connections among women of different histories. We might have felt uncomfortable screaming in the American Embassy, but the lunch together afterward felt like sister-hood, filled with laughter and further learning about each other's work and life. A few days later, just walking on the streets of Addis Ababa, I was amazed to run into one of the Yellow Movement members. "Hi Rediet!" Oh, the beauty of seeing each other in unexpected places. During our lunch at the embassy, Rediet had asked me if I was informed about the upcoming Paris climate change conference. (And she has since become a friend I connect with on social media and visit when I go to Ethiopia for research.)

Although Ananya Dance Theatre was temporarily claimed by the American nation-state on this journey, we managed to stage an act of resistance through our artistic work. *Roktim*, after all, is a pointed critique of the domi-nation of global food production by US agribusinesses such as Monsanto. On one of the days we were in Addis Ababa, Monsanto was in the headlines of Ethiopian newspapers, having struck a deal with the Ethiopian government. We were reminded by the embassy personnel not to explicitly criticize US policies while we were there, but perhaps there was enough ambiguity in dance theater that the politics of our work did not become an issue. The local audiences, however, clearly recognized our message. They generously gave their energetic approval not just for our dedication to our art and aesthetics, but also for the critique we offered about the neoliberal system that inflicts injuries on raced and gendered bodies in both the North and the South.

As women and artists of color in the North, many of us have had lived experiences in the South. But we have also grown accustomed to being American, however marginalized. Just the possession of an American pass-port leads to taken-for-granted privileges, including mobility across borders and easier access to spaces. On the morning of our performance at the National Theatre, we had planned to do our technical rehearsal on stage. As we gathered outside our hotel to wait for our ride, we received the news that there was a prayer session for Ramadan in the stadium near the theater, and that all roads from our hotel to the theater were blocked. To us, giving a performance of multiple elements—dance, music, video projection, and so on—without ample rehearsal time was a nerve-wrecking thought. We must have expressed our distress and entitlement very well, because the Ethio-pian man who drove the American Embassy vehicle simply said, "I can take you there."

The next fifteen minutes or so of riding in the American Embassy van are forever etched in my memory. We went past barricades and checkpoints staffed by armed police without even being questioned. Slowly but surely, we went in the opposite direction of the peaceful crowd of Muslim families dispersing out of the stadium, where the prayer session was just ending. Ours was the only motor vehicle moving. I felt like an intruder, a voyeur, sitting behind tinted windows, witnessing the peace and contentment on sunlit faces that had just experienced something sacred, with their families, in community. Feeling ashamed, I was almost relieved that nobody paid much attention to us, American artists eager to get to work.

Many months later, I am able to see that moment as also one of encounter, fraught with power dynamics. The moment serves as a vivid reminder of what Surafel aptly named "precarious crossing." But for this jagged moment of crossing, I would have easily romanticized our weeklong experience in Addis Ababa, because there were so many heartwarming encounters with Ethiopian and other African artists with whom we shook hands, hugged, exchanged stories, sang and danced together, and felt human and loved together. The unsettling memory of sitting in that slow-moving van helps me remember that we had momentarily become part of an empire extending its tentacles across the globe, as we breached local norms and infringed upon sacred spaces. The real price we paid in this bargain with the empire was our inability to respect our hosts' norms because we felt compelled to put on a great performance. It was our way of paying respect to our hosts, of course, but our journey to the performance space betrayed our intention of mindful crossing.

Looking back, I think we need to recognize and take responsibility for that particular instance of failure if we are to align with critical transnational feminist praxis. The power and privilege of the empire were offered to us, but we did not have to accept them. There are, of course, ways in which we experience imperial power in more passive ways, and that power has also translated into confinement and constraints imposed on our movement as racialized and gendered American citizens in Addis Ababa. Even before our departure, we were given "advisories," including one about not going out after 8 p.m. We took that one to heart the first half of the week when we were under the care of the American Embassy. One day, we rehearsed in the hotel until 11 p.m., thinking the hotel restaurant would be open until midnight. But that was simply not the case. Following the government's guidelines, we did not venture out of our hotel, and went to bed with empty stomachs. Once the Crossing Boundaries Festival began, we quickly learned that Addis Ababa was perhaps one of the most alive cities on the planet at night. During the second half of our stay, each night after performances, we hopped on the festival buses and were welcomed into spirited spaces abundant with music, dance, food, and warm hospitality.

Even with the festival activities, I understand now, we were still sheltered from the multifaceted reality of everyday Ethiopia. We loved the grandeur of the National Theatre and were awed by the beautiful buildings of Addis Ababa University and other fine venues of the festival and conference. The young volunteers of the festival spoke perfect English, told us about their jobs as young attorneys or their plans to attend American universities. But there were glimpses of poverty when street children tapped on the windows of our American Embassy vans and pleaded for money, and when our generous volunteer Dawit took money out of his own pocket to give to an older woman begging on the sidewalk, so that we, the American visitors, would not be bothered. I also took note of the coexistence of partially paved, uneven roads and newly finished light rail, of older, one-level buildings and skyscrapers under construction. I felt instantly at home; this was the condition of my hometown in China when I left China in the late 1990s. I was eager to share my impression with a university student of the Yellow Movement, believing it to be my way of connecting with her. But she was a bit put off and coolly responded, "We'll get there someday." I realized that my sentiment was misplaced to say the least and condescending at worst, in a global context where all nations are measured and compared according to levels of development.

My connection to China and my American citizenship made my brief experience in Ethiopia doubly poignant. I saw large signs and logos of Chinese construction companies in many parts of Addis Ababa. I knew better than to rejoice at the familiar characters, as the deep voice that belonged to Mr. Yohannes, who worked for the American Embassy, commented, "The Chinese are building a lot here, but they use cheap materials." I could not refute him, as I had also observed broken floor tiles, peeling walls, and a faucet that sprayed water sideways in the recently built four-star hotel we stayed in. I had read about how China's economic development depends on its appropriation of resources and market on the African continent. But to experience that firsthand was something else to reckon with.

I knew I had a lot more to learn, from reading books about Ethiopian history, politics, and society, and from staying connected to people who live complicated globalized realities. One of the people I try to stay connected to is Dawit, our young volunteer guide. He is kind and has a great sense of humor, as well as strong opinions about Ethiopian politics. He also shared with us critiques of white supremacy and colonialism. Maybe that explained why he became close to us, Americans who were not white and were definitely antiracist. I checked in with him when the Ethiopian government declared a state of emergency in October 2016. He was angry with the Ethiopian government, "which is supported by your government." I was taken aback for a moment but then readily admitted that I was indeed implicated, as an American citizen, in the US government's action or inaction. After our conversation ended, however, I pondered, "Could he have meant the Chinese government?"

Despite all of the precariousness in our border crossing of many kinds, Ananya Dance Theatre had the good fortune to perform to the best audience in the world at the Ethiopian National Theatre. The house was full, and everyone was incredibly generous with the giving of their energy. We gave our best performance ever as a company—I can say this as a founding member of the company since 2004. Despite a frustrating technical rehearsal where we struggled through language barriers and equipment problems, the performance was perfect—everything fell into place, almost miraculously. Overwhelmed by the outpouring and converging of energy from both on and off stage, I was weeping backstage well before the performance was over. It is a cliché, but true, that I felt a part of something very big, bigger than myself, bigger than Ananya Dance Theatre. I was elated to be part of this inspiring moment of community building across borders and this moment of seeing and being seen.

Afterward the African American diplomat rushed onstage to congratulate us, and I will never forget what he said: "I have never been so proud of being American!" How should I unpack that one? Being American was not in the forefront of my consciousness that particular night. But I can't deny that we were yet again claimed by the American empire. We were introduced by the same diplomat at the Ethiopian National Theatre before the curtain opened for *Roktim*. His speech was formal during the introduction, but at the end of the show, there was something different in the emotional remark shared in a more personal setting. His eyes were glistening, as if there were tears in them. We saw each other as American subjects of color (albeit of different power and positions) in a space envisioned and created by artists and organizers of the South.

A couple of days later, I stood in a long line outside of the National Theatre, along with my ADT colleagues, waiting to see another festival performance. Magnolia, a fellow dancer from ADT, asked me a question about the history of socialism in Ethiopia. I mumbled something about Cold War politics, then quickly realized the paucity of my knowledge about Ethiopian history. I made a note to myself to go home and study.

At that moment I looked up into the night sky and saw a perfect full moon. It was the day of the Mid-Autumn Festival in China, a celebration of harvest, family, and community. In Ethiopia, it was the eve of Meskel for Orthodox Christians, who celebrate the finding of the true cross, also the coming together of community—at least it seemed to me as an outsider. I thought about my "homeland" for a moment (Where is it? What is it? Why do I feel so at home here?), but was pulled along by the energy of the great moving throng around me on the street of Addis Ababa outside the National Theatre. Minnesota seemed far away and distant. But it was the home I returned to just two days later, my heart and mind pulled in so many more directions than they used to be, before our crossing to Ethiopia.

January 3, 2017

13

ANANYA DANCE THEATRE AND THE TWIN CITIES

Community and Dance

DAVID MURA

SOMEONE ONCE ASKED MILES DAVIS HOW HE COULD BE SO FAR ahead of his time. Davis replied that no one could live ahead of their time; he was just living in the present while others were living in the past.

What is American culture? What is American dance? Why is it so difficult for so many to live in the present, to detect what is unprecedented and bears the seeds of the future? These questions arise when I contemplate Ananya Dance Theatre, its founder, Ananya Chatterjea, and the brilliant work these artists have produced in a little more than a decade in the Twin Cities. That a dance company of this multiracial makeup, with its aesthetic-cultural roots in Indian movement forms, should find its home in the heart of the Upper Midwest may puzzle some. But the story of this dance company makes sense to anyone who knows the Twin Cities and its artistic community. This company's existence and its work tell us that American culture is moving faster than the barriers erected by gatekeepers to keep those changes from occurring.

The popular image of the Twin Cities is as a very white place, dating back to cultural products like *The Mary Tyler Moore Show*, the movie *Fargo*, or Garrison Keillor's radio show and novels about Lake Wobegon. But since the 1970s waves of immigrant communities have come here—Southeast Asians, including the second largest Hmong population in the country;

African immigrants, including Somali, Ethiopian, and Liberian communities; a growing Chicano/Latinx community. There has always been a significant Native American population here and a well-established African American community. It is no mistake that August Wilson got his start here as a playwright working closely with Penumbra Theatre, the oldest African American theater company. Mu Performing Arts is the second-largest Asian American theater community in the country; there is also Pangea World Theater, headed by two South Asian theater artists and two Indian American dance companies, Ragamala Dance Company and Katha Dance Theatre.

More than 70 percent of the students in the Minneapolis and Saint Paul school systems are BIPOC students. And unlike, say, New York City, the geodemographic history of the Twin Cities and its relatively smaller population have created a very different version of a multiethnic, multiracial America. In cities like New York or Chicago, boundaries between ethnic neighborhoods are often rigid and sometimes deeply etched in the city's racial history. But in the Twin Cities the ethnic and racial populations are smaller, and they exist within neighborhoods where the boundaries between communities are more fluid in terms of geography and history.

Beyond this, there's a certain cast to the communities of BIPOC artists in the Twin Cities. Black, Indigenous, and artists of color from different ethnic and racial communities here see themselves as part of a larger community of BIPOC artists rather than as solely members of, say, the African American or Asian American artistic community. The local artists also tend to be more politically and activist minded. In part, this is also because of our relatively small populations. We don't have large geographic areas or concentrations of people from our own communities, so we tend to have more frequent encounters with various forms of "otherness," and we recognize that we live in a place which still wants to see itself as predominantly white. This sharpens issues of ethnicity and race here in ways that are different from, say, Asian Americans in the Bay Area or African Americans in Atlanta. Moreover, despite being politically liberal cities in a blue state, racial disparities in economics and education for BIPOC people here are among the highest in the country, and the white liberal veneer belies an entrenched systemic racism.

I'm a writer and vice president of the board at ADT, and I've been part of this artistic community of Asian Americans and BIPOC artists for several decades. In 1992, I helped start a community-based arts organization, the Asian American Renaissance (AAR). From the very beginning, we started AAR with a vision of developing Asian American artists through instruction, performances, community events, lectures/talks, and arts activism. In the 1990s, a seminal issue for many local Asian American artists and activists centered around the Saint Paul Ordway Theater's two presentations of the musical *Miss Saigon*. In organizing demonstrations against these presentations, we critiqued the yellow-face casting of the Broadway production and the Orientalism and racist stereotypes embedded in the musical—its glorification of sex trafficking and egregious sexual tropes of Asian women; its adaption of another racially problematic work, Puccini's *Madama Butterfly*, which assumed that all Asian cultures and people were the same and devalued life and celebrated suicide (Japanese, Vietnamese, who can tell the difference?); its depictions of Americans as well-intentioned innocents and Vietnamese men, whether Communist or not, as morally reprehensible, sexually depraved, patriarchal, and inferior in character to the American soldiers (the list of criticisms goes on). We in the Asian American community were particularly angered by the fact that the Ordway Theater had twice ignored the advice of its own Asian advisory committees not to present *Miss Saigon*.

All this is a way of saying that Ananya Dance Theatre and its focus on artistic excellence and activism has been in keeping with the BIPOC communities in the Twin Cities and the Asian American arts community in particular. ADT's vision is not confined to an ethnonationalist identity but has adopted one that is multiethnic and multiracial, reflecting the urban environment in which it operates. Just as pointedly, this intersectional stance would also make ADT's presentation of *Aahvaan: Invoking the Cities* an essential part of what happened in 2013 when the Ordway Theater again decided to bring back *Miss Saigon*.

Dancer Alessandra Williams's experience with ADT is an example of how the company's aesthetics and politics have emerged from the BIPOC communities in the Twin Cities. Williams was raised in the multiethnic sections of South Minneapolis, the Whittier and Phillips neighborhoods. Her father is Liberian; her mother is African American and was a community organizer. The causes of social justice and racial equity, and the bringing together of different communities and cultures were part of her mother's work, particularly between the African American and Native American communities. Williams grew up going to meetings and political gatherings as well as church activities centered on Liberian fellowship. She went to Southwest High, with an ethnically and racially mixed makeup similar to the high school my children and Ananya Chatterjea's daughter went to.

Williams then went to Macalester College in Saint Paul, where she majored in American studies and became involved with the Dance Department. In 2005, her professor Peter Rachleff took her to an ADT performance, *Bandh*. Williams had never seen anything like it—an ensemble composed entirely of BIPOC women, who danced with such "energy, emotion, strength" and used their gaze in connecting with the audience, almost as if they were "staring right through you." The piece, she says, "flipped anything I'd ever seen of dance."[1] It was unprecedented, absolutely new, and it "terrified" her. She didn't know what to make of it.

The next year she saw another ADT performance, *Duurbaar*, and this time the performance entered her in a very different way. She says she was struck by how, on stage, the dancers transformed and embodied their relationship to water, particularly the labor of women carrying the weight of water. At the end of the piece, Chatterjea danced and was drenched in water as other dancers scooped up the water onstage in gestures of libation, and Williams started to cry because "it was so beautiful."[2] Williams had never had an experience with Indian dance; at the time, she couldn't quite distinguish between classical Indian dance and Chatterjea's contemporary Indian movement. But she watched the African American dancers in the performance, Shannon Gibney and Kenna Cottman, and saw how their footwork connected them with the earth and the way they moved their bodies, and that told her there was a place for her in this work. Later, when Chatterjea came to Williams's history class, the two entered into a dialogue that took over the class. The discussion helped Williams see how Chatterjea's choreography worked across and through difference: "Ananya made it clear that the work was not about ethnonational identity."[3]

I asked Williams how the work of ADT fit with her sense of African American dance traditions. She said that while she later learned about the work of Alvin Ailey and its roots in the beauty and authenticity of African American history, she first approached African American dance through the intersectional work of Bill T. Jones and the ways it integrated political practice and activism and intertwined his identities as a gay African American. Through Jones she understood postmodern dance as a radical progressive practice rather than an experimental strain owned by European American dancers. Jones challenged ideas "about our African American bodies" rather than taking received ideas and validating them.[4] For *Still/ Here*, his work inspired by terminal illnesses, particularly AIDS, he had watched the movements of terminally ill patients and incorporated them metaphorically into dance. Jones's work then was not centered on an

African American cultural nationalism or essentialism, and in various ways it challenged cultural norms of the African American community. Williams could see a correlation between Jones's work and ADT more easily than, say, between Alvin Ailey and ADT.

Williams auditioned for and became a part of ADT in 2006 while still in college. She worked with the company from the beginning of the trilogy on environmental justice. The fact that the company would make a lengthy concerted effort in studying, discussing, and creating work from the issues of environmental justice made her realize that they were not simply touching on a subject and then hopping on to something new. The company reached out to members of the community working on environmental justice, including the Women's Environmental Institute, and other organizations located in the Phillips neighborhoods that Williams had grown up in. One of the issues these organizations were dealing with was the presence of arsenic in the neighborhood soil. For Williams, then, the issues of environmental justice and the company's work with the community were not abstract or distant but alarmingly close, visceral, and vital.

Williams says that her further training in West African dance during her graduate studies at UCLA deepened her connection with ADT's work: there was a similar groundedness and a preference for horizontal over vertically oriented movement, where dancers "take time to appreciate and honor the earth."[5] Williams's sustained yoga training also aided her transition back into the company after grad school, even as she struggled with the aftereffects of spending a lot of time sitting alone as she did her research and writing. The traditional Indian dance form Odissi calls for flexibility in the hips, and Chatterjea could tell from Williams's movements and her breathing that Williams's body had changed, that it now bore evidence of the type of work she had been doing in relative isolation and also the emotional work she had not been able to make time for. Chatterjea's sensitivity to Williams's body and her movements are part of her view of dance as holistic and healing, as ecologically framed to the body's nature.

Ananya Dance Theatre brings together dancers from a number of widely different backgrounds, ethnicities, races, communities: Chinese American, South Asian American, African American, Palestinian American, Filipino/Hawaiian/Chinese/Portuguese American, Nigerian American, Black/Creole/Black Creek Indian/Croatian/Rusyn American, Hmong American, and mixed race. As Chatterjea observes, "A community of Black and brown women and femmes is a possibility in America."[6] And yet the company

FIGURE 13.1. (From left) Sherie C. M. Apungu, Rose Huey, Chitra Vairavan, Ananya Chatterjea, Hui Niu Wilcox, Renée Copeland, and Lela Pierce in a nightmare sequence, with puppets manipulated by Alessandra Lebea Williams, in *Moreechika: Season of Mirage* (2012). Photo by Paul Virtucio. Courtesy of Ananya Dance Theatre.

clearly doesn't fit in with the ways those back in India or in the rest of Asia, and elsewhere in the globe, view America. Nor does the company yet represent the image America has of itself. And yet the company and its aesthetic could not have emerged anywhere else but in America, in the Twin Cities (figure 13.1).

ADT's 2015 piece *Aahvaan: Invoking the Cities* was commissioned for the grand opening of the Ordway Center Concert Hall in Saint Paul. The piece "weaves together images inspired by the rich history of the Indigenous communities on this land, the diversity of communities who now call the Twin Cities home, our rich legacy of water, the vicissitudes of urban life, and artistic innovation."[7] As is their practice, *Aahvaan* emerged through conversation between choreographer Chatterjea and the company members, who study and discuss the issues of the upcoming piece and meet with experts and community members who can speak to the issues in the piece. As the company begins to work on their movements, this discussion continues and informs the piece. Rather than passive vessels for the choreography, the dancers in the company are active participants in shaping both the movements and the aesthetic and political vision of the piece.

At the same time, ADT's pieces are created in collaboration with a wide variety of artists. With *Aahvaan*, the company worked with Chinese American director and behavioral and social practice artist Marcus Young. Recorded scores were composed and arranged by Greg Schutte in collaboration with Mankwe Ndosi, Laurie Carlos, Pooja Goswami Pavan, Dorene Waubanewquay Day, and Michelle Kinney. These artists brought music from the African American, Native American, and South Asian traditions. For me, a highlight of the piece occurred when Chatterjea performed a solo dance to Schutte's guitar work as both Pavan and Ndosi sang, interweaving a contemporary American strain of music with vocals from Hindustani classical and African American soul/jazz traditions. In her movements, Chatterjea seemed to reach for a freer and more lyrical movement, spurred on by a combination of music that created an unprecedented cultural space and yet, at the same time, was distinctly of that moment—2015—in our history. Yes, Pavan's singing fit in with the Indian traditions that form the basis of Chatterjea's choreography, but Chatterjea's movements were also responding to the rhythms of Schutte's guitar and Ndosi's blues- and gospel-inflected jazz improvisations—a combination that was Indian-based but contemporary American, in that constant mixing of cultures that takes place uniquely here.

But *Aahvaan* was not only a concert piece performed on a stage. Before the dancers performed onstage, the company used the spaces in the lobby of the Ordway to construct the type of installation and audience participation piece that ADT often performs in addition to its concert pieces. In this way, *Aahvaan* presented the full range of ADT's aesthetic and practices. In a portion of the lobby near the entrance, Hui Wilcox stood propped up fifteen feet in the air, adorned by a huge gown made in part of newspapers painted red, presenting herself as "the Empress of Fortune and Whimsy," a figure meant to question the audience about "Fortune, karma, whimsy, consequence." There was a wishing well with running water, where audience members were asked to write down wishes and blessings, and which was "inspired by the tremendous work of the Anishinaabe leader, Sharon Day, who has led 'Nibi walks' for several years now, walking for many days along the lengths of rivers in this country, praying for their well-being and resuscitation."[8] As the Twin Cities have long been a center for Native American culture and political resistance and were the birthplace of the American Indian Movement, another space paid tribute to the Dakota homeland origins of Minnesota and asked audience members to meditate on the forced march of 1,700 Dakota men, women, and children to Fort

Snelling, which resulted in the death of a large number of Dakota. "Please tie a tear on the Cord of History that connects us all and walk with us," said one of the signs, asking participants to join hands and follow the dancers in their movement in a circle. This breaking down of the wall between dancers and audience members is a key component of ADT's work in spaces outside the concert hall and reflects its aims to respond to and create a sense of community.[9]

But there was also a hidden aspect of ADT's work in social justice that was part of *Aahvaan*. As mentioned earlier, the Ordway Theater had presented the Broadway musical *Miss Saigon* two times before restaging it again in 2013. Each time, the presentation was met with protests by the Asian American community; each time, the Ordway convened Asian American advisory committees, which also protested these presentations and urged the Ordway not to go through with them. The last presentation instigated the formation of a local activist organization, the Don't Buy *Miss Saigon* Coalition, of which I myself was a member. The Coalition created a website with essays, a Tumblr page of testimonies by Asian Americans across the country criticizing *Miss Saigon* under the heading *"Miss Saigon* Lies," a national petition, and statements against *Miss Saigon* by Asian Americans and local community leaders. The Coalition also organized a protest in Rice Park in front of the Ordway on the opening night of *Miss Saigon*, with Asian American, African American, Latinx American, and Native American participants and speakers. The dancers of Ananya Dance Theatre performed as part of that protest. Prior to the opening, the local Asian American theater company, Mu Performing Arts, held three forums to discuss *Miss Saigon*, one with Asian Americans, one with the theater community, and an open forum at Minnesota Public Radio (the Ordway had asked Mu to conduct joint activities, but Mu, citing its objections to *Miss Saigon*, refused to do this). In this protest work, we activists employed many of the lessons of Sun Tzu's *The Art of War*. Though Mu was working with the Coalition, we never revealed this. We did reconnaissance; we had contacts with the Ordway; we knew more about the enemy than our enemy knew about us; we let them underestimate us. When local arts foundation personnel showed up at Theater Mu's public gathering, the Ordway freaked out (and rightly so—one of the foundations later turned down a substantial grant request from the Ordway).

The Ordway's position was simply that the organization had the artistic freedom to present whatever work it desired, and if controversy ensued, that was part of the purpose of art. The Ordway administration was ignorant of the history of protest against *Miss Saigon* by the local and national Asian American communities and of the numerous critiques by Asian American artists, activists, and scholars, who have critiqued the musical's racism, ethnocentrism, sexism, promotion of sex trafficking, and numerous inaccuracies about Vietnamese culture (including the fact that in a portrayal of a Vietnamese religious ceremony, the actors do not actually speak Vietnamese but make up nonsense syllables).

When the Ordway approached ADT to commission a piece for its opening, ADT first consulted with the Don't Buy *Miss Saigon* Coalition. ADT proposed building into its contract a clause mandating another meeting between the Ordway and the Coalition to discuss the issues of the Ordway's lack of institutional memory and its ignorance of Asian American activist and artistic history. Before the meeting occurred, there were tense negotiations with the Ordway because ADT had invited members of the community to the meeting, including local funders. The Ordway was already aware that the Coalition's work had evoked widespread criticism of the Ordway from the general public, local arts critics, and the funding community, and there was some evidence that this had had at least a small effect on its funding. But through negotiations and patience, ADT ensured that the meeting occurred.

Previously, Patricia Mitchell, the president of the Ordway, had said she was surprised by the vehemence of the negative reaction from the community, thus revealing that she was unaware of the Ordway's own history in regard to the musical and the Asian American community. At the meeting arranged by ADT, I cited Mitchell's remarks and then held up a textbook, *Asian American Resistance in the 1990's*, with its cover photo of Asian Americans protesting the original Broadway production of *Miss Saigon*. "So what you're saying," I told her and the Ordway board, "is that you are ignorant of our political cultural history. You don't realize that our most famous Asian American playwright, David Henry Hwang—our August Wilson— wrote two plays concerning the controversy of *Miss Saigon*. So you don't know our political and cultural history, you don't know our theater, and you don't even know the history of your own organization's relationship with our community, and yet you presume to present us with this awful musical to 'help spark conversations in our community' [one of the Ordway's purported defenses of their presentation of the musical]." One white-haired white board member admitted, "I think he has a point there."

Afterward, representing the Coalition, I met with Patricia Mitchell and continued the discussion of issues raised in the meeting. The eventual result was an unprecedented letter of apology from Mitchell and the Ordway, acknowledging the hurt the presentation of *Miss Saigon* had caused in the Asian American community and the failure of the Ordway's institutional memory. Mitchell and the Ordway promised never to bring back *Miss Saigon*. (The letter, though, did not address the Ordway's huge gap in its knowledge of Asian American activism, scholarship, and theater.)

The Ordway's apology marked a victory for local Asian American activists. Subsequently, this protest emboldened all involved to speak up on social and racial issues and challenge hierarchies of authority. Our efforts highlighted multiracial and multiethnic artistic and activist collaborations between artistic organizations and different ethnic and racial communities and how such collaborations can make previously marginalized voices not only heard but a force for racial equity. This victory would not have been accomplished without the coordinated efforts of many individuals and organizations in the Asian American community, and Ananya Dance Theatre played a prominent part in this effort.

Overall, ADT's work in relationship to *Miss Saigon* and its production of *Aahvaan* represent a prime example of the company's melding of dance, social activism, and community organizing, and how ADT is forging a new model for dance companies and other arts organizations. Artistic excellence and arts activism are not mutually exclusive but indeed can be mutually reinforcing and a benefit both to the art world and the greater community.

NOTES

1   Interview with Alessandra Williams, July 30, 2015.
2   Interview with Alessandra Williams, July 30, 2015.
3   Interview with Alessandra Williams, July 30, 2015.
4   Interview with Alessandra Williams, July 30, 2015.
5   Interview with Alessandra Williams, July 30, 2015.
6   Interview with Ananya Chatterjea, July 12, 2015.
7   This description is from the Ananya Dance Theatre webpage: http://www .ananyadancetheatre.org/dance/aahvaan-invoking-the-cities/.
8   This description is from the Ananya Dance Theatre webpage: http://www .ananyadancetheatre.org/dance/aahvaan-invoking-the-cities/.
9   This is articulated on the Ananya Dance Theatre website, http://www.ananya dancetheatre.org/philosophy/daak/: "In our recent work, Daak [call to action] has been strongly influenced by Ananya Chatterjea's concept of #Occupy-Dance! Influenced by the conceptual frame of the Occupy Movement, she has crafted recent iterations of Daak by saying to audiences: Let this company of

women of color occupy your imaginations as we etch the possibility of a different world through our dancing. Then, come occupy dance: dance with us, and let the stage become the space where you explore metaphoric gestures that remain lodged in your muscle memory and translate into practices toward justice in daily life."

14

FORECAST

MANKWE NDOSI

Written and performed for the 2013 *Mohona: Estuaries of Desire*
production's exploration of global water depletion and access.

What we gonna do
Now I'm askin' you?
How we gonna roll
When water's worth more than gold?
More scarce than oil?

Stated with only one of a hundred droplets
Fresh water for our tongues.
What we gonna do?
Why can't we pay attention to the water?

Ain't got time to think about it
Ain't got a mind to talk about it
Ain't got room to act on it
Think about the water

Ain't got time to think about it
Ain't got a mind to talk about it
Ain't got room to act on it
Actin' on the water

(V1—WHAT GETS IN THE WAY)

There's the bills and the job
The kids the stress

179

the transportation
Long flowing hair
The green green lawn
Fresh fresh toilet
Wiping it all so clean
The long hot showers to wash it all away
The Mangoes, Avocados
Loved ones overseas we want to see them so bad
Technology that needs the water so pristine
There's so many reasons we can't pay attention
Is it taking it for granted or our insecurity
Ain't got time to think about it
Think about the water

But Now
Forecast is **dry dry dry**
And the ripple effect
Lasts for all time and
while we're sleeping the poison is leaking
And turning our freshwater gray

Gotta make time to talk about it
Talk about the water

Why?

(V2—WHY WE HAVE TO TALK AND ACT AND PAY ATTENTION)

Fukushima waves unchecked for three years now
Corporations meltin' down mountains, stealing from underneath the
    farmers
Politicians selling the right to poison us some more
Pumpin' frackin' chemicals that kill the water for good
Not too far away
Can't even take a dip in the old Mississippi

Gotta Make up our mind to act on it
Acting for the water

But Now
Forecast is **dry dry dry**
And the ripple effect
Lasts for all time and
while we're sleeping the poison is leaking
And turning our freshwater gray

I said
Forecast is **dry dry dry**
And the ripple effect
Lasts for all time and
while we're sleeping the poison is leaking
Stealing our fresh water away

What you want your ripple effect to be?
What you want your ripple effect to be?

IV

AGAINST CATEGORIES OF TIME

History, Tradition, Contemporary Dance

15

THIS STAGE IS NOT A SAFE SPACE

THOMAS F. DEFRANTZ

IN 2017, I ATTENDED THE PERFORMANCE OF *SHYAMALI* BY ANANYA
Dance Theatre at the O'Shaughnessy Theater in Saint Paul, Minnesota.
Pleasure. In this remarkable work, a dozen artists move through a three-act
fantasia concerned with the ways that "dissent against oppression fuels life
force." In ninety full minutes, the artists reveal connections among the
valiance of women who reject silence to work together against injustice.
Many elements of this work command attention. We in the audience note
ADT's mature physical technique, which combines strengthening methods
from martial arts with Odissi dance movements based in advanced deploy-
ments of rhythmic structures, in meditation and transcendental techniques, and in breathtakingly coherent compositional devices. We note how
the performance builds out from Ananya's core company and those who
have gathered to perform in this particular work, alongside the astonishing
guest artistry of Mankwe Ndosi. We note that the first portion of the performance includes participants from ADT workshops seated on the floor
of the very stage where the dancing happens, creating an intimacy of connection among them and, indeed, all of us in the theater. We note the
mature musical, costume, lighting, and visual coordination of the work,
which confirm shared concerns across material environments in the service
of this storytelling. And we note how the work feels confident, full, surpris-
ing, and moving in its engagement of theatrical dance within histories of
social justice activism.

The experience reveals relationships of affiliation. By being in the presence of the performance, we claim relation to its possibilities; we claim

FIGURE 15.1. (From left, foreground) Kealoha Ferreira, Renée Copeland, Ananya Chatterjea, and (background) Alessandra Lebea Williams as Ahiwa / Seer in *Sutrajāl: Revelations of Gossamer* (2019). Ahiwa witnesses the intimate trio of Ua / Rain-Spirit-woman, Izzicatapir / Mad Musician, and Siyaah / Shadow Dancer. Photo by Paul Virtucio. Courtesy of Ananya Dance Theatre.

responsibility to participate in its process. We gather in the theater to join in the challenge of joining; of agreeing to participate in a questioning toward shared care and a potential crafting of safety of expression, emotion, affection, action. In presence of the theatrical invention, and in knowledge of the ways that the experience represents an aspect of a larger activist-feminist-of-color-artist intervention, we work with the questioning of safety as a scarce resource, one necessary to the enlargement of social exchange. Pleasure. Affiliation. Safety. (figure 15.1)

Safety, in this encounter in the theater, as we consider the performance and its terms, and its extensions into the world and from the world. The theatrical event encapsulates our willingness to vibrate together in a shared stuttering toward understanding. Its architecture allows us a safety of assembly, for the moment.

ADT continues as a beacon of creative artistry that brings out the best in its collaborators and audiences in the contexts of contemporary performance. The company engages a range of artistic activity that includes dancing, staging symposia, participating in activist actions, facilitating meetings among diverse leaders, including organic intellectuals and PhD faculty members. Most importantly, ADT values the place of artistry as participation in social justice movements, as a crucial connective site that can inspire necessary shifts in shared awareness.

Shyamali arrives as part of a multiyear sequence of creative explorations, destined to move to *Shaatranga* in 2018. Reflecting on the performance, I consider how the artists of ADT model ways that women artists of many ethnic, sexual, gender identities and presentations can work together to create unimaginable, inspirational worlds of possibility, bringing us all forward in the space of crucial creative encounter. I begin to consider a context for recognizing this particular artistry, and the ways that it connects to social justice, yes, but also to global flows of contemporary dance theater.

Contemporary dance theater tends to depict physical vistas of change and mutability suited to the theatrical moment. In the work of Pina Bausch, Ohad Naharin, and Bill T. Jones, for example, exquisite physical gesture comments upon its own invention and disappearance as capacities of the moment. But dance theater concerned with fomenting and inspiring social change materializes infrequently in global contexts. The pointed ambition of ADT is to create performance that comments upon the theatrical moment in response to events and circulations of the social outside of the theater. ADT works well beyond the decorative spaces that might inspire other works by other artists, which might reflect rather innocently on a historical occurrence or the character of a cityscape. ADT works to inspire social activity by delving into the challenges of contemporary living in relation to research conducted by its collaborating artists. Moving us toward concerns that are decidedly "unsafe" for far too many outside and even those gathered inside the theater.

Ultimately, ADT proves that the rhetorics of "safety" inside theatrical dance circumstances can be disrupted by choreographic and activist work that intends to straddle possibilities among these modes. While the space of the theater may have allowed for a moment of meditative confluence, the themes of ADT works and their fierce, evanescent remainders push us toward action that might jar the floor and shake loose oppressive social convention. Theatrical seclusion may have held contemporary dance at arm's length from general considerations of social crises, and especially antiracist, antimisogynistic, protofeminist possibilities. ADT works to bring light to values of communal resistance, demonstrated by physical gestures deployed for the theatrical moment—and also toward activist dissent in the world. Reflecting on the 2017 performance and its relationships to other modes of contemporary dance theater in circulation, I realize that the stage that ADT dances on is *not* safe.

DIASPORIC ENCOUNTERS

I've been fortunate enough to collaborate with Ananya herself, in an invention we constructed to consider an encounter through difference. In March 2001, we met in the rehearsal hall to develop dance theater that allowed us to explore questions around coalition-building and shared political struggle among diasporic populations. Over many years we had asked these questions of each other, particularly about how we engage conversations outside of Europe. How do diasporic populations of color encounter each other outside of the specific gazes and lenses put in place by white hegemonic structures? We wondered: What are some of the ways in which performing bodies of color negotiate considerations of identity in their creative processes? How do mainstream cultures racialize Black and Asian performing bodies differently depending upon their nationalities and passports, their individuated social histories, or the particular economic and geographic locations that surround the material circumstances of performance? How does the performance of specific cultural forms rise in importance within shifting grounds of white mediation? How can theatrical bodies insist on a redefinition of assumptions and resist the stereotypical representations that overdetermine the reception of cultural forms in the spaces of a globalized popular imaginary?

We created a small dance theater work with a dynamic, open structure that can absorb ongoing conversations and questions that concerned us in the shifting terrain of world situations. A movement texture that is porous, and an open structure that can accommodate injury, travel, distance, musician availability, differing performance circumstances, and available technological possibilities. The work, *Diasporic Encounters*, premiered in Boston at Kresge Little Theatre in 2002 and has been shown in Minneapolis at Intermedia Arts, at the India International Centre in Delhi, and at the Centre National de la Danse near Paris.

Our creative process was rich with questions, and our conversations interlaced movement improvisations and our arrivals at structural and compositional moments. As we worked to stage the politics of this encounter, we found that we couldn't make do with the given models of choreography—as in "the well-made modern dance" or the expressional abhinaya of Odissi. We had to create hybrid models of performance and process, to make a dance that embodied the politics and the physical techniques we each brought to our encounter. Our questions pushed us to arrive at a place where the elements of performance invention had to be realigned to account for our positions in diaspora and our need to meet outside the colonizing gaze of Europe. We realized that performance is not an isolated moment; rather, it offers a nugget of condensation, heightened by the saturated ideas within our body that we had been exchanging. Years of conversations allowed us to enact the liveliness of space that embraced the intersections of these ideas and constantly changed the piece.

Here I share some of the conversations and concerns that emerged as we developed this work. To begin, we wondered at possibilities of relation across and through race, without having to privilege white supremacy as the beginning point of our collaboration.

BEGINNINGS

ANANYA: It is impossible not to recognize that peoples of color, while lumped together as an undifferentiated mass of people when needed, are also racialized very differently in the United States. While all of these communities have very different histories in this country, this also disrupts the possibilities of creating a politics of solidarity and consolidates our positions in a pecking order where we turn back on each other as competitors for precious morsels.

We need to shift the focus from always having to talk through Europe. It seems that we remain so entrenched in the hegemony of Eurocentric conversations that our concerns cannot move away from the locus of whiteness. Attention to our relationships with one another is always deferred by the need to deal with the larger oppositional force.

THOMAS: I want to talk about Black culture as a text that is mis/read all over the world as a strange cipher of resistance and coolness. As in hip-hop, of course, which stands as a convenient dissident pop culture mélange for youth around the world. This becomes annoying because (at least) the political—and material—history of Black people in the United States is minimized/erased from this depiction.

ANANYA: See, this is why I want to be around you; you make me see things differently. Now I'm in Java. And it is like what I see in India, in Singapore, in other places in Asia. Once again, when I turn on the television, I see the very image that the capitalist culture machine wants to reproduce. It seems that for most of the young rap artists on TV, English offers little—they're not so comfortable speaking the language when they are being interviewed, for instance. But when they rap, every gesture, every musical intonation, is about being Black, and especially American Black. But do they know what being Black in the United States has meant? I mean, I understand the power of rap and hip-hop, but is there a way of loving the music and the dance while appreciating the underground whence it came?

THOMAS: This is why I want to engage a materialist analysis of dance and corporeal presence. It's not enough to think of hip-hop as a way to dance resistance, or a way to express cool, all of it wrapped up in an innocent sort of detachable style. Cultural theorist Richard Wright gestured toward the inherent tension in dancing through the desires of others in his report on the Bandung Conference: "There is a nervous kind of dependence bred by imperialism: not only are the people taught Western law, ethics, and finance; but they are encouraged to develop a taste, yea, a need, for goods which are only to be had from the European mother country. . . . [H]ow can they have the cooperation of the West and at the same time fend off what they feel to be the desire of the West to dominate?"[1] How, indeed, can we be attracted to modes of expressive performance born in the crucible of disavowal as a means to engage contemporary theatrical thought? Hip-hop contains the evidence of resistance and cool in its very structures, but the need to replicate its contents throughout the world is born from models of capitalist dependency. Yes, hip-hop offers so much information as a form of resistant creativity, but there are other sources of resistance as art available in other contexts. Your work in ADT, for example, models an urgent physical chronicle of hegemonic refusal.

American studies theorist Roderick Ferguson, in his exquisite articulation of a queer of color critique, calls on us to "reju-

venate our understanding of intersectional analysis to address
a moment in which capital must negotiate with differences of
race and class as well as gender and sexuality to achieve itself."[2]
He suggests that our too-easy capitulation to normative expressions of gender and sexuality places us in systems of racial formation controlled by the states that we are called upon to represent.
How do we dance against expectations? Is there any safety to be
had in this nonnormative relationship?

———————

ANANYA: I'm caught in the high contrasts of cultural production here, so much like when I am in India. I see the sassy
hip-swinging of the young women pop culture stars. . . . I've
never seen anything like it. It could more than compete with
Lil' Kim or Nicki Minaj. And then my gaze is torn away by the
perfect balance and contemplative inward focus of the Bedoyo.
Simultaneously. . . .
    Keep talking to me. Tell me more what you mean when you
say "material analyses of dance."

———————

THOMAS: We must return to the materialist narrative. In this,
I mean a materialist historical narrative, as opposed to a textual narrative that might be created through an analysis of
performance. I don't want to create a sort of Judith Butlerish
rendering of a "performance of gender and class in dance." This
reading can defuse real-world circumstances of class and economy, and render all performances as equivalent "performative
acts." But all is not equal. I mean to consider dance as a practice
that may have class effects through performance—by its very
existence. I follow Ferguson here, who reminds us again and
again that canonical sociology "attempts to discursively sup-
press an actual material heterogeneity," to force us into identities far too narrow to be creatively useful in our shifting
varieties of intention and relationship. Material heterogeneity
"critically exposes the gender and sexual diversity within racial
formations"; this might be exactly what we hope to do in our
creative invention.[3] We wonder at a Marxist analysis of theatrical performance. This becomes hard to do because Marx didn't

consider performance as practice. Meanwhile, Butler and many of the textual critics want us to consider all practices as performance. In this model, in awkward shorthand, I "perform" being a Black queer academic, artist. Well, we know in dance there is a practice of dance that precedes and in effect supersedes any performance—this practice is what I'm trying to uncover. How can concert dance make a material difference in the world through its very performance? The early moderns believed this to be possible, and some Black Americans like Katherine Dunham and Alvin Ailey have proved this to be true. And of course there are professional dance artists who achieve class mobility through their practice of performance. Ailey started life dirt poor, and now his company has built a huge complex on 55th Street, the largest dance center in the United States. I'm not sure, but I'm trying to unpack some ideas around this.

LOCATIONS

Ferguson propels us to consider how state formations and minority nationalisms must be simultaneously critiqued, as "investments in gender and sexual regulation [are] the linchpin between state, cultural, and revolutionary nationalisms."[4] We struggle to find our footing in critique within and across Black and brown communities, all the while surrounded by whiteness that intends to collapse our possibilities and narrow our points of view. As we critique nationalist proscriptions of gender and sexual normativity, our queer meetings in dance *matter* as actions of resistance. We stretch "classical" forms toward experimental distensions, to queer tap dancing or so-called modern dance partnering, amplifying our disidentifications with spoken text in the performance. Still, performing the work in different parts of the world, we realize how critique moves; that state formations are slippery, that resistance can resemble titillation depending on the context. We push each other toward a vigilance of exploration, reminding ourselves that "staying safe" was never part of how we decided to collaborate.

————

THOMAS: How do you think it's going?

ANANYA: Well, I'm a little bit anxious about how this piece is going to be read because it seems that whenever a "man" and a "woman" dance together, there's a way in which the piece gets read in specifically gendered terms, so that it's either about a romantic relationship or about the fact that they're engaged in a battle of the sexes. As if people exist only on that plane.

THOMAS: That's true, but there is also a place where men and women seem to have different responsibilities to each other, or to society at large, and then we ask questions such as, "What kind of action is appropriate for a man that is political? What kind of actions are appropriate or preferred for a woman?" And we have to be willing to try to resist that as well. I think that's something that you and I are trying to think through: how we can move toward something where the power dynamic isn't preset or predetermined.

ANANYA: Don't like surface multiculturalism . . . machinery for producing diversity? Naaah.

THOMAS: My difference from you—nonimmigrant, forced migration. . . . I *want* to look back.

ANANYA: But looking back not through nostalgia . . . to find cultural specificity.

THOMAS: We support each other, share power, share weight, build a coalition.

ANANYA: A politics of commitment, staying committed to the process of working together, building solidarity.

THOMAS: Work through it, past misunderstandings, through the misdirections, work through it.

ANANYA: Through our dancing and through our performing, and see how our bodies get scripted in terms of these politics that I can only describe as radical.

THOMAS: I think the most radical part is how messy it is and it has to be. It's not neat to think deeply and intently about our differences and our shared struggles. But we have to. We have to find ways to look toward something that is progressive and ultimately, we hope, liberatory. We have to.

REDIRECTING

We dance together. Gestures emerge. We collaborate with an amazing musician, Akili Jamal Haynes. Akili conjures music through an astonishing, endless array of musical instruments and approaches to sound. He works as a trombonist, bassist, keyboardist, beatboxer, and most regularly as a percussionist. He composes across genre, constructing sound as it might be found, crafted, revised, reheard, and remixed. Ananya's daughter Srija, a child at the time, plays through our research rehearsals, singing a melody that she makes up as she runs and skips. Akili incorporates the spontaneous song into the soundscape of our work, playing it on a flute. The room is potent with questioning, even as the room expands across the globe through our travels, physical, intellectual, spiritual.

> ANANYA: Resistance might also mean deflecting. It often takes the path of insisting on beauty and working toward coalitions even when war is the order of the day.

> THOMAS: In *The Color Curtain* Richard Wright details his personal experiences at the 1955 Bandung Conference, where leaders of Asian and African nations met to discuss issues including colonialism, racism, international economic and social cooperation, and world peace. What came of that gesture toward collaboration by people of color? How do artists of color collaborate across geographies and cultural traditions? Is Europe always figured as the centerpiece for collaboration?
> Reading *The Color Curtain*, I wonder who Wright imagines as its audience. Yes, it is written to the magazine that commissioned it, but who else? Who is getting to hear Wright be critical from his own perspective as a Black American? And what is the point here? Also amazing is the degree to which he reproduces racial stereotypes about Asians and how he doesn't locate his own paternalistic impulses in all of it.
> The volume reads like an insider's travel narrative, which places it in a strange context among other texts that we might

now call cosmopolitanism. For example, he relates how he read about the conference in the newspaper and decided to go on the spot, just having returned to Paris from a "long, tiring trip in Spain." All of us should be so exhausted. But the guest list of the event was extraordinary—Sastroamidjojo of Indonesia, Nehru of India, Nkrumah of Gold Coast, Zhou Enlai of China, Ho Chi Minh of Vietnam, and on and on. Wright calls it "this meeting of the rejected [that] was in itself a kind of judgment upon that Western world!"[5] The event was sponsored by Burma, India, Indonesia, Ceylon, and Pakistan. At the conference, twenty-nine nations convened with the following stated aims:

> to promote good will and co-operation among the nations of Asia and Africa,
> to consider social, economic, and cultural problems,
> to consider problems of special interest to Asian and African peoples,
> to view the position of Asia and Africa and their people in the world of today.

In his commentary on the conference itself, Wright stressed the "potential unity among the participant nations based on their shared distrust of the West . . . the hostility of Asia and Africa to the West based on how they had been constructed by the West as the racial Other."[6]

This was such an important event, and yet it is not taught in many Black studies departments.

ANANYA: That's because Black studies was conceptualized narrowly within area studies and its white lens. It makes me think of Trinh T. Minh-Ha and her comments on access to the other in ethnographic research. How it seems to mandate that all others stay within their racially prescribed areas so that Indians should study Indians, and Taiwanese should do Taiwanese, and Ghanaians can do Ghanaians, but white researchers can do anything. I so appreciate being able to work on Sardono Kusumo and Nora Chipaumire, artists and thinkers with whom I find a solid political and artistic resonance.

TRANSNATIONALISMS

Jigna Desai, Danielle Bouchard, and Diane Detournay write toward "an epis-temological and political economy of queerness that questions and decenters the United States and places queer studies into question in relation to trans-national feminism, postcolonial feminism, and women of color feminism."[7] We wonder toward this formation and its affordances, and how we can enliven our creative projects without resorting to a US-centrism that depends on white scaffoldings for understanding experimental dance. Following Desai et al., we have taken up the task of "theorizing 'epistemic violence,' 'thievery,' and other such concepts—attending to their connections and discrepancies— as a means of forwarding responsibility as a persistent question without resolution."[8] We look for allies but don't fret when few come forward.

ANANYA: Where are you? We should talk.

THOMAS: I'm at a dance conference in Ireland, writing, sending you strength. I wish you were here. Is this a new cosmopolitan-ism? Our travels around the world seeking strategies to better enliven discourse as well as creative address with each other, students we work with, communities who gather around our performances. But traveling matters here: in moving through, we begin to imagine how to hone our awarenesses in diaspora.

In Ireland things are different—Ireland is a "first" world sort of—but you know they too are a "postcolonial" people in a way, having only achieved independence from that same British Empire in 1923. The people are friendly, but their spirits seem really beaten up. Out in the countryside, I met a young woman who had never thought of college or been to the big city— Limerick—that is only sixty kilometers away from her home. Her access to the privilege of mobility is cut off in a way that seems familiar to me. But of course, it is different, as she is Irish in her homeland, not in diaspora.

ANANYA: I wish you were here and we could think about Ireland and Indonesia side by side—what a profound contrast. So much dance here. The anxiety around time—something I have learned from rushing around all day in our crazy schedules—cuts into my ability to appreciate classical Javanese dance. My hurried blood is responding jerkily to the steady, slow stream of movement. I can't get it to still. Sitting in the court yesterday, watching the dancers perform the Bedoyo under that hugely vaulted roof, painted so beautifully, I thought, "How can I dance of angst here?" I listened to the finely crafted yet complex harmony of the gamelan and reflected on the different kind of dance possible here, one that lives and breathes outside the global political unrest and mainstream American-influenced pop culture trends that inhabit the street right outside.

THOMAS: Why am I not there with you? I'm thinking about the idea of the beauty of the roof coming from the acknowledgment of all the time and effort, energy and patience that have gone into producing it. Patience and focus as being part of what can clear the way for beauty, and with so much concentrated effort, how can we imagine a future violence? Beauty is often created in response to a violent past. Think of the beautiful spirituals that grew as resistant creativity—and hidden messages for escape—out of the crucible of slavery and lynchings of Black people in the US South. But when we make beauty, can we imagine something that subverts the need for making violence? Misogyny, abusing children, race crimes, ethnic cleansing. Maybe there is less time for this because of the effort, the desire and passion, that goes into making outrageous beauty. A relationship with beauty might preclude some of the dispersals of violence.

There is a gamelan at MIT; I made a kecak for them once. I thought it was a violent form, crafted to express human response to epistemic violence. Its hybrid arrangement of voice and interlocking rhythm surprised me. Rhythms fit together in a jangle there, and the human voice amplifies the sense of striving toward something as much as achieving it. Its form revealed striving as a condition of its creation in a palpable, breath-filled manner.

Where are the dances about the social violence in Java? Does Sardono create dances about political unrest? How does he do

this? Are other choreographers working to express social and
political violence?

ANANYA: I talk about the politics in dance making here with
Sardono a lot. The conversations flow freely from multiplicity
in the interpretation of Islam, to class and gender violence, to
xenophobia and the dangers of nationalism. His work pulls me
into the heart of these issues, into their intersection, and sometimes collision, with each other. We talk about the necessity of
holding complexity, so even as we critique organized religion,
we push back against violent stereotypes of Islam. On the
streets outside, I see the women in hijab riding their scooters
and going about their day. Their performance of daily feminini-
ties overturns the proclamations of many Western feminists
about how the scarf has impeded a notion of "feminist progress" for Muslim women. Through rehearsals, at regular inter-
vals, we hear the *azan* (calls to prayer) over the loudspeaker,
from neighborhood mosques, and they heighten the soundscape for the artistic work. Conversations about the political
unrest, about the bombing in Aceh, are like a murmur, constantly present, part of life and the artistic process.

WORKING TOGETHER

Ferguson reminds us that "we need modes of analysis that can address
normativity as an object of inquiry and critique."[9] Toward this, we meet in
dance, as a formation that resists normativity in terms of its unwieldy
unpredictability as we imagine it together. We honestly don't know how any
audience might take in our inventions, even as we hope that its oddities and
specificities inspire reflection and, possibly, a resistant stance. Working
together, we hold each other up in some ways, and leave each other out to
dry in some ways, allowing each other to do as we will in the invention. This
formal organization seems crucial: each of us, including Akili Haynes,
could discover ideas and reveal performance as we would in each iteration
of the work. Above all, we know that we will not arrive in normative, rec-
ognizable formations in this work together. We will arrive unpredictably,
to each other, the experience, and the various audiences we encounter. Our
performance is not a place of safety; rather it offers an urgent site of working
through and toward our ever-emerging relationships.

THOMAS: But how does dance fit into the political unrest? Is it altered—as a practice—by the world situation and the place that individuals feel in the ever-changing world? Are the interruptions for prayer that we now endure new or continuations from before 9/11?

ANANYA: To my outsider's eye, the political unrest seems to move outside of the classical dance; like in India, the historic violence has been folded into the normalness of life. There are discussions constantly, of course, so it's in the air, and much talk on TV; I see Megawati Sukarnoputri doing powerful campaign speeches. I find myself very frustrated by my lack of knowledge of the language. The Bedoyo sits in the midst of all of these life streams.

THOMAS: Richard Wright settled some scores with an observation that many journalists "seemed to have forgotten that for centuries Asian and African nations had watched in helpless silence while white powers had 'disposed of' their 'destinies.'"[10]
    We mustn't let this happen again and again.

ANANYA: I think there's a problem—how folks of color get racialized differently—because I constantly wonder why white folks try hard to delegitimize my work in a different way from that of Black Americans . . . and I think it's because subconsciously (because you will argue that they're not so evil) at least they don't want us to talk across them, only through them and with their permission.

THOMAS: I don't think the white folks care enough to try to stop our conversations across them, or for us to only be allowed to meet each other through them and with their permission. I *do* think they want access to all information and conversations. But then it's up to us to grant that or not. So for me, many of the conferences we attend re/present *their* turf, *their* conception of the possibilities of academic debate. So when we want a group of international scholars working through ideas or concepts that interest us, we've got to arrange it all from scratch. Well, we've started to do this through our collaborations. But you know, I'm not interested in restructuring their group; it's actually fascinating to me to witness how they work and think.

I do wonder, though, how we have these conversations in English, and often in the high theoretical literary language of the academy.

Back to Richard Wright, who offered, "Thus, the strident moral strictures against the Western world preached at Bandung were uttered in the language of the cultures that the delegates were denouncing. . . . [B]y this means English was coming to contain a new extension of feeling, of moral knowledge."[11]

ANANYA: But this is why we dance! When we dance we reach to communicate through the realm of the body, beyond words, beyond concepts bound by the West. Remember the ending of our dance piece *Diasporic Encounters*; we kept counting it "wrong." The "one" was in different places—we never could get round to where the "one" really was. We decided to listen to each other's without altering our own "one." We had to create an alternative listening in order to achieve the final bit of the piece and work together. This is the possibility of our encounter.

THOMAS: The possibility to not know together and discover by doing and building out from our differences. Performing the piece, I always feel a need to stay entirely attuned to the choices that you and Akili make in the moment; that my preparation for the work is allowing myself to be available to our encounter and its complexity. And it is complex trying to imagine diaspora as movements that distend and diverge, even with some similarities, but more disparities than agreements. What we share cannot only be our discomfort with Western hegemonies and US-centric global popular cultures. It must be something about the knowing through moving alongside, the making together that encourages us each to bring so many ways of understanding into the process and resist narrowing our vision to a single step or a balance. Sharing weight in our dance amplifies how I understand social possibilities for ancestors and great-grandchildren to come. Now as part of a continuum.

ANANYA: I wonder how we can hold on to these solidarities
that we have built over time when everything seems to be
crumbling. It would seem these unwavering friendships and
alliances are in fact what keep us grounded through these
times. We must question so much of what we have learned.
Thank goodness I can call you. . . .

———————

Dancing with Ananya opens space and time toward possibility. Unantici-
pated spaces—spaces of diaspora, in the case of our collaboration many
years ago. Spaces for women of color, and those intentionally identifying
alongside them, in the case of *Shyamali*. Spaces for all of us to reconsider
how we come into relationship. And openings of time: a daughter singing
a tune half-remembered that becomes the material of a musician's invention; imagining dance through historical events that predict future alignments. The creative process is unstable in its searching through and toward.
Unstable, and unpredictable, the stage crafted through this urgent artistry
surprises, confronts, demands, and remains emphatically not *safe. Axe!*

NOTES

1   Richard Wright, *The Color Curtain: A Report on the Bandung Conference* (Cleve-
land: World, 1956), 112–13.
2   Roderick A. Ferguson, *Aberrations in Black: Toward a Queer of Color Critique*
(Minneapolis: University of Minnesota Press, 2004), 144.
3   Ferguson, *Aberrations in Black*, 21.
4   Ferguson, *Aberrations in Black*, 146.
5   Wright, *The Color Curtain*, 12.
6   Wright, *The Color Curtain*, 241.
7   Jigna Desai, Danielle Bouchard, and Diane Detournay, "Disavowed Legacies and
Honorable Thievery: The Work of the 'Transnational' in *Feminist and LGBTQ
Studies*," in *Critical Transnational Feminist Praxis*, ed. Amanda Lock Swarr and
Richa Nagar (Albany: State University of New York Press, 2010), 46–62, 50.
8   Desai, Bouchard, and Detournay, "Disavowed Legacies and Honorable Thievery," 61.
9   Ferguson, *Aberrations in Black,* 148.
10   Wright, *The Color Curtain*, 238.
11   Wright, *The Color Curtain*, 200.

16

MY WORK IS WORTH THE STRUGGLE

SHERIE C. M. APUNGU

Exhausted, I plead for sweet rest.
Falling alone, I fall apart. I surrender and let go.
Instead of bitter embers and ash, calm and stillness enter.
No longer bothered by the thought of being left behind.

I VIVIDLY REMEMBER A-DI'S VOICE DURING REHEARSALS CHISELING technique onto my body. Ananya often also made remarks that would speak to our inner spirit. "Sherie, why is your dancing not the full manifestation of the goddess inside you?" At the time, I did not see the powerful affirmation hidden in her question. Six years later, I finally realized what A-di recognized many years back while performing in the production of *Kshoy!* My solo begins with Pooja Goswami's ethereal voice lifting the theater. I am on stage, lying on the floor facing the majestic brick wall of the Southern Theater. I can feel my breath bounce from the marley floor and graze my lips. I wake up expecting to see the stage lights above me. But I was transported into a landfill. I feel the caustic mud on my skin, burning as it dries on my skin. Rubbing the mud off my skin brings little relief. I jump up and kick my legs up into a semihandstand to avoid going deeper into the mud. Unfortunately, there is no way to avoid the mud, and I look up to see pools of mud everywhere around me, and I am alone. I lift up my arms and see my hands completely burned. I scream, but no one hears me. Then, just as I had rehearsed over 150 times prior to opening night, I lie on the stage flat on my belly with legs stretched and toes flexed, and immediately start rolling down to stage front. I see my mark, and a few revolutions later, I abruptly stop at her feet. Koko is sitting front-center on the floor with her legs crossed at her ankles. My grandmother. I do not know how, but there she was smiling at me years after her departure. It took me six years to reach her. Although there may never be another time in my life when technique and understanding of self are manifested in a performance with my grandmother, my work is to try. As a nontraditional dancer, my energy stayed lifted through intense dance rehearsals because I believed working with a community of like-minded men and women is where change will happen. As a leader, I know the aforementioned is true.

17

ANANYA DANCE THEATRE IN THE GENEALOGY OF WOMEN OF COLOR FEMINISM

RODERICK A. FERGUSON

IN HER ARTICLE "CREATING A NEW, CONTEMPORARY AMERICAN Dance," Ananya Dance Theatre founder and artistic director Ananya Chatterjea grounds her vision of what a "new, contemporary American dance" could look like in the memories of the Kolkata streets that were—once upon a time—her home. She writes, "Like those streets where a multinational bank stands beside a small, broken-down shrine and women's groups perform street theatre at the bus stop outside my guru's classical dance studio, my urban aesthetic is imbued with spiritual possibilities, and my work is in dialogue with the secular and the political."[1] In this memory—where the national, the multinational, the local, the spiritual, and the artistic negotiate one another—we find the cultural and material bases for the Ananya Dance Theatre. Discussing the material conditions out of which her company arose, she writes, "My commitment to choreographing women's stories and themes of social justice took form as I walked the protest-rich streets of Kolkata, hearing, in memory, my mother's songs about the dreams she longed to have fulfilled."[2]

Chatterjea's framing of ADT is telling in that it evokes theoretical developments that are particular to the genealogies of women of color feminism—the changes that occasioned postcolonial and neoliberal state and economic formations as well as the emergence of women of color cultural productions as social practices that have historically born witness to those changes. All the elements of Chatterjea's and ADT's version of "American dance" are captured in that scene on the street and have made their way into the intellectual and choreographic components of her company. It is important to understand, though, that while this is a vision that comes from Chatterjea, the grammar for that vision comes from formations that preceded and—it might be argued—occasioned her and her company.

To that end, I would like to use this chapter to briefly demonstrate the critical genealogies that have given birth to ADT and its particular intersection of performance and politics and to argue that the company represents the choreographic embodiment and elaboration of theoretical insights from women of color feminist formations. Specifically, I would like to spend some time briefly detailing some of the ways in which the company mobilizes women of color feminism's investments in historiography as a mode of intervention. In addition, the company exercises that formation's experiments with difference and distance as principles for making political and intellectual associations. Lastly, ADT provides a model of art that attempts to radically attend to the exigencies of the present day.

REVISION OF TRADITIONAL INDIAN DANCE

ADT is a dance company that bends the "classical" into a contemporary dance form, and one of the aspects of the dance company's practice is a sophisticated rebuttal to nationalist assumptions about "traditional" Indian dance. ADT's aesthetic, in fact, draws "on Classical Odissi, the martial art Chhau, and Vinyasa Yoga, to explore feminine energy and celebrate a feminist aesthetic."[3] Indeed, in ADT's extending of "classical" Indian dance, the company critiques and subverts ideologies that claim "classical" dance for the promotion of Hindu nationalism. Instead, ADT reclaims Indian dance to address issues and circumstances that exceed the prescriptions of state and cultural nationalism (figure 17.1).

To begin with, members of Ananya Dance Theatre hail from everyday communities, working as students, activists, teachers, artists, and so on. Upon joining, members are trained in the company's signature contemporary movement form and Indian dance styles and use those styles to learn about and interpret present-day concerns around immigration, rape, environmental racism, sex work, land rights, genocide, and so on. As a theater that deploys contemporary dance to address issues that exceed the usual

FIGURE 17.1. (From left) Renée Copeland, Kealoha Ferreira, Sophia Hill, Alessandra Lebea Williams, Hui Niu Wilcox, Alexandra Eady, Ananya Chatterjea, and Lizzette Chapa reclaim sculpturesque elements of traditional Odissi in a moment of "Ritual Thickening" in *Shyamali: Sprouting Words* (2017). Photo by Paul Virtucio. Courtesy of Ananya Dance Theatre.

parameters of that dance form, the company is an example of the convergence of social justice with liberatory art and education.

Indeed, we can think of ADT as the performative embodiment of what Chatterjea argues in *Butting Out: Reading Resistive Choreographies through Works by Jawole Willa Jo Zollar and Chandralekha*.[4] In that book, Chatterjea critiques and subverts ideologies that claim dance and women's bodies for the promotion of various forms of nationalism. Using the works of African American choreographer Jawole Willa Jo Zollar and Indian choreographer Chandralekha, Chatterjea reclaims vernacular choreographies to critique cultural and state nationalism, demonstrating the ways in which those performances speak to histories of gendered and racialized violence. As an expression of her theorizations in that book, ADT mobilizes tradition to meditate on the historical conditions for racial, gender, sexual, as well as environmental regulation and emancipation. The company thus represents an ironic use and reversal of traditional dance, using traditional dances to interrogate and encounter the very modes of difference that national traditions have typically suppressed and regulated. This rearticulation of "classical" dance away from its nationalist rendering is part of women of color feminist interventions into culture and historiography.

To fully appreciate the genealogical conditions compelling that convergence, we have to turn to the history of women of color feminism, particularly its investments in cultural production and historiography. In "Cartographies of Struggle: Third World Women and the Politics of Feminism," Chandra Mohanty's classic introduction to the equally authoritative 1991 anthology *Third World Women and the Politics of Feminism*, Mohanty argues that writing, as a mode of cultural production, has been central to women of color feminist praxis. As she states, "Writing often becomes the context through which new political identities are forged. It becomes a space for struggle and contestation about reality itself."[5] For Mohanty, writing emerges from particular historical exigencies: "If the everyday world is not transparent and its relations of rule, its organizations and institutional frameworks, work to obscure and make invisible hierarchies of power . . . , it becomes imperative that we rethink, remember, and utilize our lived relations as a basis of knowledge."[6] Mohanty's investment in writing's capacity for activating the cultural and rearticulating the social is definitive for women of color feminism. As she puts it, "Writing (discursive production) is one site for the production of this knowledge and this consciousness."[7]

One way of understanding ADT is to say that it uses dance rather than writing as a way to forge new political identities and create new spaces to contest reality. Take, for instance, the company's inaugural 2005 performance, *Bandh: Meditation on Dream*. That performance used the goddess images of Bengal and Odisha, known as *chalaman brigaha*, to explore and celebrate feminine sensuality. In that performance the company used traditional divinities to imagine a world grounded in the social autonomy of women. Or consider its 2007 performance of *Pipaashaa: Extreme Thirst*, in which the company used classical and contemporary modalities to address environmental devastation. To create that performance, the company researched environmental toxins and their effects in Côte d'Ivoire and Minneapolis.

Throughout the company's performances, we can see a conversation between Chatterjea's choreography and her work as a theorist. For instance, *Butting Out* discusses dance's ability to rewrite the dominant and underline performance's potential for intellectual engagement. She writes, for instance, that performance "offers possibilities of using bodies in certain ways to either reaffirm sociocultural expectations or to subvert them in the context of such expectations."[8] In *Bandh* and *Pipaashaa*, we see the ways in which dance becomes the process for and the end point of ADT's research commitment as the company uses each performance to examine such issues as environmental devastation, feminine sensuality, land dispossession, climate justice, the injustices caused by resource extraction, or the politics of oil. Rather than see these issues as beyond the interests of dance, ADT insists that they and other issues are well within the aesthetic and critical universes of dance. In doing so, the company demonstrates precisely what Chatterjea theorized in her book, that is, how the body can be used to "subvert sociocultural expectations" around what can and should be tolerated in our world.

Part of the genius behind ADT's performances is the deliberate way in which the company attempts to demonstrate how dance—as a cultural form—can become a political force. Describing the conditions by which culture gains political momentum, Lisa Lowe and David Lloyd write in the introduction to their anthology *The Politics of Culture in the Shadow of Capital*, "We suggest that 'culture' obtains a 'political force' when a cultural formation comes into contradiction with economic or political logics that try to refunction it for exploitation or domination."[9] Part of what ADT attempts to do is to put dance in contradiction with the political logics of cultural and state nationalisms. In relation to traditional Indian dance, this effort grants dance a political force at odds with the state's deployment of dance as an emblem of national unity and distinction. Moreover, Indian "classical" dance becomes a formation dispersed among various sites and social issues, dispersed in such a way that it refuses to be the domain upon which the state's unity is established.

Revising notions of the traditional for women of color feminism has always been understood as a historiographical intervention. Discussing the relationship that critical formations have had to historiography, Mohanty argues, "Third world feminists have argued for the rewriting of history based on the specific locations and histories of struggle of people of color and postcolonial peoples, and on the day to day survival utilized by such peoples."[10] As a cultural production arising out of women of color feminism, ADT rewrites historical exigencies based on its movement across a wide area of constituencies and concerns, areas made up of various folks disenfranchised by race, empire, capital, nationalism, and heteropatriarchy. In this way, the company reveals the limits of grounding Indian dance within the parochial confines of national belonging. As Lowe and Lloyd argue, a crucial characteristic of feminist historiography is the refusal of that parochialism. They write, "Feminist historiography . . . reveals that women's practices are only partially grasped when reduced to the horizon of the national state, and that implicitly those practices demand alternatives to the formations prescribed by the modern state, whose emancipatory promise is contradicted by the persistent subordinations."[11] Through its revision of traditional dance forms, ADT works to demonstrate that nationalist formations never have the last word where culture is concerned. The company also demonstrates that Indian culture—through dance—can be the site of "alternatives to the formations prescribed by the modern state."[12]

ADT AND THE CRITICAL ASSOCIATIONS OF WOMEN OF COLOR FEMINISM

As the company's artistic, political, and intellectual interest in environmental, economic, political, and social urgencies suggest, ADT's programming emerges in response to the transformations between nation-state and capital, transformations obtained in the moments of postcolonial, neoimperial, and neoliberal state formation. Discussing the relationship between those transformations and women of color feminist work, Mohanty writes, "World market factories relocate in search of cheap labor, and find a home in countries with unstable (or dependent) political regimes, low level of unionization, and high unemployment."[13] This economic configuration implicates the lives and livelihood of postcolonial women, in particular. As she argues, "What is significant about this particular situation is that it is young third world women who overwhelmingly constitute the labor force. And it is these women who embody and personify the intersection of sexual, class, and racial ideologies."[14] The company's performances emanate from these circumstances, in which the lives of women of color internationally are made more precarious by global capital's search for cheaper forms of labor and by its quest to expand the range of natural resources that it might exploit.

For instance, in 2014, the company premiered *Moreechika: Season of Mirage*, a performance that grapples with the vernacular and corporate meanings associated with oil. In the company's description, *Moreechika* encompasses a variety of meanings attached to oil, vernacular meanings having to do with "the belief of the U'wa people of Colombia, who think of oil as *ruiria*, blood of the earth, which must be respected as part of the natural world."[15] *Moreechika* also connotes "the protests of the Indigenous Kichwa women of Ecuador to Chevron oil; the debates in North America about the Keystone XL Pipeline through Native American lands." The term signifies as well "the fight and martyrdom of Nigerian activist Ken Saro-Wiwa against Shell Oil, responsible for the destruction of the land and ecosystem of the Ogoni people." The performance therefore pondered the question of what happens when a natural resource, in one context, is respected for its social and cosmological place and, in another context, is disfigured into the alienating commodity of global capital. As a performance that tries to connect political resistance in South America, the disruption of Indigenous territories in North America, and activism in Africa against multinational corporations, *Moreechika* connects a variety of movements and struggles that span national and regional boundaries. Through this performance, the company uses dance to produce various "cartographies of struggle" that reconceptualize "ideas of resistance, community, and agency in daily life."[16]

ADT's ability to use dance as a way to map out struggles that are geographically dispersed is to a large degree derived from the ways women of color feminism understands both difference and distance as principles by which to build connections rather than as alibis for dismissal and rejection. The philosopher David Hume threw difference and distance into the dustbin of analysis when he theorized resemblance and contiguity as the real basis of the mind's associations, as "the only bonds that unite our thoughts together, and beget that regular train of reflection or discourse, which, in a greater or lesser degree, takes place among mankind."[17] For him, our impressions of things and our passion for them are connected only by resemblance. About contiguity he stated, "It is certain that distance diminishes the force of every idea, and that, upon our approach to any object; though it does not discover itself to our senses; it operates upon the mind with an influence, which imitates an immediate impression."[18] For Hume, distance is an intellectual and social liability. In Hume's philosophy, "we are able to sympathize more easily and strongly with individuals with whom we have strong associative ties. The stronger the associative relations, the stronger our sympathetic responses."[19] Hence, contiguity and resemblance help to engender clarity and connection. Hume's formulation therefore helped to construct difference and distance as the signs of an inaccessible foreignness.

Women of color feminism helped disrupt the presumption that distance and difference could not be the basis for political and affective identification. One of the first articulations of difference and distance as principles of association rather than disconnection and isolation can be found in Audre Lorde's essay "Age, Race, Class and Sex: Women Redefining

Difference." In that essay Lorde argues, "Certainly there are very real differences between us of race, age, and sex. But it is not those differences between us that are separating us. It is rather our refusal to recognize those differences, and to examine the distortions which result from our misnaming them and their effects upon human behavior and expectation."[20]

As Lorde suggests, under women of color feminism difference becomes the basis of producing critical associations out of which comparative analytics and coalitional politics might emerge. Mohanty invokes this mode of association when she writes, "What I want to emphasize . . . is the urgent need for us to appreciate and understand the complex relationality that shapes our social and political lives."[21] For Mohanty, the work of third world feminism involved imagining communities of international coalition in contemporary capitalist societies, coalitions that would link "ideologies of gender and sexuality that would affect women's daily lives, whether it be in Brazil . . . , Lebanon . . . , Iran . . . , China . . . , Trinidad and Tobago . . . , or the U.S."[22] As the passage suggests, we might say that women of color feminism is an attempt to redirect social thought toward the possibilities of difference and distance as the point of political and social connections. Difference and distance, in this instance, do not hinder intellection and politicization but activate them for the good of antiracist and anticapitalist feminist struggles.

In the preface to *This Bridge Called My Back*, Cherríe Moraga, writing against parochial and separatist notions of feminist practice, also yearns for a feminism that can see what society constructs as the distant worlds of the other as a basis of identification and coalition-building. This feminism would take Moraga from the white Boston suburbs of Watertown, through Harvard Square, to the Black neighborhood of Roxbury. Writing against exclusive articulations of feminism, she states, "Take Boston alone, I think to myself and the so-called feminism my sisters have constructed does nothing to help me make the trip from one end of town to another."[23] In her reading of Moraga's preface, theorist Grace Hong has argued, "Moraga's analysis secures an understanding that different racial and gender formations are not produced in isolation, but relationally."[24] ADT galvanizes this aspect of women of color feminism to produce a relational understanding of differing and distant forms of injustice and struggle. Like the feminism that Moraga yearns for in the preface, ADT produces a feminist praxis that attempts to help viewers make the trip from one end of the world to the other.

It is important to note as well that ADT's performances represent a constant attempt to determine the stakes of antiracist and postcolonial feminism. In this way, the company represents one of the core principles of all critical formations: the need to base one's actions on the delineation and clarification of political and social stakes. Discussing this in relation to the founding of the Birmingham School of cultural studies, Stuart Hall wrote, "Not that there's one politics already inscribed in it. But there is something at stake in cultural studies, in a way, that I think, and hope, is not exactly true of many other very important intellectual and cultural practices."[25] Women of color feminism and ADT both show that our stakes cannot be limited to the people and communities that look like us or that are near us. The well-being of the peoples, communities, and worlds that are foreign to us and distant from us is part of our stakes. Our broad political, intellectual, and ethical mandate must reach the different and the distant.

This attention to the multiple stakes that deserve attention and activation coheres with Mohanty's understanding of one of the functions of third world feminism. As she states, "Third world feminists have argued for the rewriting of history based on the *specific* locations and histories of struggle of people of color and postcolonial peoples, on the day to day strategies of survival utilized by such peoples."[26] In the spirit of these interventions, Ananya Dance Theatre—as a dance company, a research entity, and an activist organization—demonstrates an open-ended feminist politics but one where the stakes are constantly renewed and clarified, where history is always reimagined and rewritten, and where distant struggles are always theorized and choreographed as within reach.

NOTES

1 "About," Ananya Dance Theatre, accessed December 31, 2020, http://www.ananyadancetheatre.org/2015/10/creating-a-new-contemporary-american-dance/.

2 "Dances," Ananya Dance Theatre, accessed December 31, 2020, http://www.ananyadancetheatre.org/2015/10/creating-a-new-contemporary-american-dance/

3 "About," Ananya Dance Theatre, accessed December 31, 2020, https://www.ananyadancetheatre.org/about.

4 Ananya Chatterjea, *Butting Out: Reading Resistive Choreographies through Works by Jawole Willa Jo Zollar and Chandralekha* (Middletown, CT: Wesleyan University Press, 2004).

5 Chandra Mohanty, "Introduction: Cartographies of Struggle," in *Third World Women and the Politics of Feminism*, ed. Chandra T. Mohanty, Ann Russo, and Lourdes Torres (Bloomington: Indiana University Press, 1991), 34.

6 Mohanty, "Introduction," 34.

7 Mohanty, "Introduction," 35.

8   Chatterjea, *Butting Out*, 23.
9   Lisa Lowe and David Lloyd, *The Politics of Culture in the Shadow of Capital* (Durham: Duke University Press, 1997), 1.
10 Mohanty, "Introduction," 10.
11 Lowe and Lloyd, *The Politics of Culture*, 19.
12 Lowe and Lloyd, *The Politics of Culture*, 19.
13 Mohanty, "Introduction," 28.
14 Mohanty, "Introduction," 28.
15 "Moreechika: Season of Mirage," Ananya Dance Theatre, accessed December 31, 2020, https://ananyadancetheatre.org/dance/moreechika.
16 Mohanty, "Introduction," 3.
17 David Hume, *An Enquiry Concerning Human Understanding* (Cambridge: Cambridge University Press, 2007), 49.
18 Hume, *An Enquiry Concerning Human Understanding*, 50.
19 "David Hume," *Stanford Encyclopedia of Philosophy*, https://plato.stanford.edu/entries/hume/.
20 Audre Lorde, *Sister Outsider: Essays and Speeches by Audre Lorde* (Berkeley: Crossing Press, 2007), 115.
21 Mohanty, "Introduction," 10.
22 Mohanty, "Introduction," 5.
23 Cherríe Moraga, "Preface," in *This Bridge Called My Back: Writings by Radical Women of Color*, ed. Cherríe Moraga and Gloria Anzaldúa (New York: Kitchen Table/Women of Color Press, 1983), xiii.
24 Grace K. Hong, *The Ruptures of American Capital: Women of Color Feminism and the Culture of Immigrant Labor* (Minneapolis: University of Minnesota Press, 2006), viii.
25 Stuart Hall, "Cultural Studies and Its Theoretical Legacies," in *Stuart Hall: Critical Dialogues in Cultural Studies*, ed. Kuan-Hsing Chen and David Morley (London: Routledge, 1996), 263.
26 Mohanty, "Introduction," 10.

18

ABSENCE/PRESENCE/ SILENCE/NOISE

TONI SHAPIRO-PHIM

SEA CALM

How still,
How strangely still
The water is today.
It is not good
For water
To be so still that way.
—LANGSTON HUGHES

ANANYA DANCE THEATRE'S WORK TAKES FLIGHT AT THE NEXUS of art and social justice efforts, where it riles the waters. It disturbs an apparent calm, what may be an already uneasy hush surrounding inequities and suffering, especially as endured by women of color across the globe. It shatters silences and brings visibility to lives and experiences that have been ignored or erased through omission in documentation, policy debates and enactment, and corporate exploits. Ananya Dance Theatre, part of an international movement of artists committed to seeking justice, also works in consonance with people who might not identify themselves as artists, but who are nonetheless engaging with aspects of their own valued expressive practices to turn the world of the powerful on its head.

This chapter conveys the essence of two conversations with and among artists of movement, including Ananya Chatterjea, all of whom demonstrate brilliance and courage as they navigate memory, historical and contemporary power imbalances and abuses, and the fostering of empathy, understanding, and action through exquisite creativity. I was present at both, facilitating one and participating in the other. And though Chatterjea and members of ADT took part in only the first, the centrality of Chatterjea's characterization of the stage as "a space for action and for historicizing" in the creative lives of all involved in both of these conversations became manifest, and remains so.[1]

What follows are stories of events in two cities. In each site, artists spoke of their commitment to intentional embodied engagement with injustices, whether present-day or those whose legacies still impact the world. Through movement and sonic artistry, these dancers, choreographers, and vocalists inscribe experiences in our consciousness that might otherwise go unrecognized by the broader public. Placing contemporary lives on the radar of others counters that absence. In addition, foregrounding the implications of systemic, structural, and physical violence, and creative resistance to them, the artists, sometimes at risk of harm, use their bodies and voices to shatter the silence that underpins insidious complicity with a status quo that denies dignity, safety, beauty, and joy to so many.

PHILADELPHIA, OCTOBER 2012

In 2012, Philadelphia-based Germaine Ingram and Leah Stein copiloted a "professional learning community" composed of dance artists from diverse styles and traditions, including contemporary Western, contact improvisation, tap, classical Indian, traditional Chinese, and hip-hop.[2] These dozen dancer-choreographers share an affinity, according to Ingram, in that they all "use percussion and/or improvisation in their work, and are interested in history, memory and social justice as content or inspiration. We use those threads to stimulate . . . new processes for unpacking all the talent and imagination there is in the group."[3] When Ingram learned that Ananya Dance Theatre would be visiting Philadelphia, she organized two days of programming through which she and her community of dancers could meet with Ananya Chatterjea and her ensemble members to explore their aesthetic, intellectual, ethical, and emotional commitments to social justice work and uncompromising artistry. The first day provided for a private exchange between the two groups, focused on Chatterjea and her company's long-standing / always evolving holistic, inclusive, and transparent creative process.[4] The richly textured conversation among all these artists illuminated the reasons why Chatterjea is so highly distinguished as a performing artist committed to transforming the world through a social justice lens.

Chatterjea prioritizes the contemporary moment for women of color by recording and interpreting their complex positionality and potency. She confronts absences of justice, safety, dignity, and divergent voices. She exposes and counters silences surrounding those realities. Performed by an ensemble that moves with compelling urgency and precision, her work celebrates collaboration, compassion, and meaningful reflection. It rejoices in beauty, difference, wonder, and what might just be possible. In ADT's 2014 *Neel: Blutopias of Radical Dreaming*, for example, dancers evoke women's dreams: dreams that frighten, dreams that have been shattered, and dreams that carry the kernels of transformation.

Chatterjea and her ensemble train rigorously in "classical" Indian Odissi, vinyasa yoga, and Chhau, a martial arts-inspired Indian movement tradition,[5] so as to begin to envision and embody the complexities, nuances, and sensitivities of their themes. They use vocal and instrumental soundscapes layered with the syncopated clap of feet against the floor. Sustained energy that reaches to the body's extremities and beyond, stunning angularity in tension with serpentine curvilinearity, exacting rhythmic footwork, as well as flexibility and strength are some elements of their technique that contribute to the evocative metaphoric and abstract representation of story—whether historical, current, or mythical.

In partnership with that technical prowess is the establishment of collaborative relationships with community organizations, activists, and scholars, the conducting of their own research, participation in story-sharing circles with members of the broader community, and work in dialogue with audiences. In 2015, for example, ADT artists undertook a field trip to investigate agricultural practices at Dream of Wild Health, an organic farm in Minnesota that encourages traditional Native ways of growing food and medicine and supports the health and well-being of Indigenous communities. The dancers did this as part of their development of *Roktim: Nurture Incarnadine*, a piece honoring women's cultivation of the land. Chatterjea explains how even though her ensemble's research leads to amassing numerous facts, it is not the compiling of those facts that constructs the truths she and her company seek to reveal. Rather, she shares, "the truth for us is in the stories we [hear] and imagine, and that we embody. In embodying them we reimagine them, and that becomes a part of our history and the history of women's movements."[6] Ingram, too, addresses the idea of "truth" and representation: "My job [when I was] a lawyer was to create *a* truth, given myriad facts. For my choreography, [I ask myself,] What can I take from here and from there to create something that is valid as a truth that has resonance for me and for others, that speaks with some meaning about something of substance?"

During the 2012 public presentation in Philadelphia (part of Ingram's project), titled "Defining Ourselves: Performance at the Intersection of Art and Social Change," Chatterjea spoke to the audience after she and the other dancers performed an excerpt from *Tushaanal: Fires of Dry Grass* (2011), her piece about how human beings have interacted with gold and other conflict minerals, and again between performances of an excerpt from *Moreechika: Season of Mirage*. After eliciting responses to questions about what viewers saw and understood, and even how they might retitle what they had just seen, Chatterjea and her artists took to the stage once again, incorporating elements of audience input into a repeat performance. They would, Chatterjea explained, work selected feedback into future performances.

ADT's approach to working where dance and social justice intersect acknowledges the resonances between those two fields.[7] Chatterjea explains that "there's not a material 'thing' inside social justice movements. You carry a certain experience or resonance of a struggle within you, and that's exactly what [happens in] dance. Hopefully, what we are left with in the moment of performing and in the moment of witnessing resonates within, to shift things inside of us. Just like what happens as part of a [social change] movement."

ADT might be uniquely positioned in terms of this work, given its composition of diverse women of color from varied ethnic and cultural backgrounds, with a range of dance experience and expertise and body types. The company's process of art making represents a model or metaphor for honoring difference and making the differences within an entity a source of social power. The kinds of negotiations that the ensemble undertakes, in conversation and movement—to develop a performance about a pressing issue, a performance reflective of experiences they've witnessed, experienced, or researched—are the kinds of negotiations at the heart of policy development and enactment. Their artistry is a form of activism, paralleling the community organizing and policy formulation and implementation undertaken by others. "Our job as artists is to provoke questions all the time," adds Chatterjea, while creating alliances with community groups, policy makers, and even political activists. "It's important to not isolate ourselves. We have to do what we do best. We know best how to work as artists.

We know how to harness [art] to shift people's minds. Then, [we can] let the next group/organization run with that," as a means of inspiring further dialogue and action. ADT founding dancer Hui Wilcox explains that they aim to "evoke and provoke a paradigm shift."[8]

As a platform for global communities of women of color, ADT meshes counternarratives and diverse perspectives with superb artistry, disrupting systems and the assumptions they provoke, placing those who are usually off the radar now front and center in public discourse.[9] "No seed is ever planted in vain," Chatterjea adds, in particular when it involves the lives of women taking risks to protect and encourage their families in circumstances of scarcity or danger, the lives we too rarely hear about in history texts or the news. Those seeds, thus planted, promote the presence of women's subjectivities where they might have been otherwise ignored, "so that questions of gender difference [ultimately] become fundamental to all policy planning."[10]

SAN FRANCISCO, AUGUST 2013

At the 2013 Performing Diaspora symposium hosted by CounterPulse in San Francisco, three choreographer-performers spoke as part of a panel on the body as a vivid carrier of histories lost and "re-membered."[11] Each explored what happens when a dance artist's sense of body is problematized through birth into a society or community that has both endured and perpetrated unspeakable acts of violence. Byb Chanel Bibene of the Republic of Congo, Chey Chankethya of Cambodia, and Germaine Ingram of the United States articulated relationships between histories and legacies of brutality and inhumanity, and the ways in which they imagine, create, and share their art. Poignant themes coursing through their varied stories included the power and complexity of silence and of absence.

Bibene was a teenager when, in 1997, war erupted in the Republic of Congo. He became separated from his family in the ensuing chaos. Searching for them, making his way from one camp for the internally displaced to another, being beaten, and never knowing what danger was around the corner framed his immediate reality. Bibene explains that eventually, when war was behind him, he and the other people in Brazzaville, his hometown, continued to live as if they might have to run for safety at any moment. His work addresses this legacy of trauma and ongoing fear. It also puts audiences face-to-face with violence, beseeching them to pay attention to injustice around the world, as such stories reflect the contemporary experience of many.

Cambodian dancer Chey was born in Phnom Penh, Cambodia's capital, in 1985, six years after the fall of the genocidal Khmer Rouge regime, headed by the infamous Pol Pot. While Pol Pot was in power, from 1975 to early 1979, between a quarter and a third of the country's *entire* population perished from starvation, illness, torture, overwork, and execution. Before the Khmer Rouge era, Cambodian classical dance, long associated with spirituality and royalty, was believed to serve as a bridge between the everyday world and the heavens. The Khmer Rouge allowed no practice of dance and music as Cambodians had known them. Instead, they imposed new, formulaic songs and dances on the populace—pieces extolling the greatness of the revolution and hatred toward previous regimes. Once liberated from the Khmer Rouge, surviving professional artists from around the country took stock. They estimated that between 80 and 90 percent of the country's fine, literary, and performing artists had died in the previous three-plus years.

Thus Chey came of age in a country trying to put itself back together after all markets, schools, and most major roads had been destroyed, in an impoverished nation with ongoing violence, including against women, in the wake of genocide and a legacy of impunity. In her choreography, Chey addresses both the situation of women and the pressures of being a culture bearer with the weight of responsibility for not letting any more traditional knowledge get lost.

Germaine Ingram's work engages social justice and historical narratives, as well as various aspects of the African American experience. The trans-Atlantic slave trade brought millions of Africans to the Americas. Slavery ripped mothers from their children and wives from their husbands; it put human beings on the auction block and left hundreds of thousands of individuals subject to exploitation and physical violation, with no recourse. Olaudah Equiano, formerly enslaved in the United States, says in his memoir: "Is not the slave trade entirely at war with the heart of man? And surely that which is begun by breaking down the barriers of virtue, involves in its continuance, destruction to every principle, and buries all sentiments in ruin! When you make men slaves, you . . . compel them to live with you in a state of war."[12] Ingram choreographs at a temporal distance from her subject matter that is greater than that of both Bibene, who experienced civil war firsthand, and Chey, whose immediate family members and mentors survived a genocide. Yet the legacies for each community are visceral and inescapable. Whatever the relationship between now and the atrocity, these artists create and shape aspects of the remembering, reimagining, and reinscribing of recent and distant histories and unreconciled pasts.

As part of the panel in San Francisco, Bibene spoke of his work in relationship to his life as a survivor of war, during which silence along city
streets—avenues that were in peaceful times usually bustling with com-
muters, markets, and music—screamed of impending chaos. Chey focused
on her work in relationship to life as a child, sibling, and student of survivors
of genocide. The absence of so many culture bearers who had perished led
Cambodian classical dance teachers to push young students (literally,
through physical manipulation and pressure) to the limits of their capacity,
frightened that they would never be able to re-create repertoire and rituals
if they didn't repopulate the ranks of accomplished artists. In addition, her
mother would, for no apparent reason, fall into silences that scared and confused Chey, only to reemerge unwilling to share the distance she had traveled
moments before in her mind, to those years of deprivation. Ingram touched
on dance and song in relationship to her life as an African American in a
country in which the enslavement of Africans was institutionalized for more
than two hundred years. In conducting research for her work *The Spirits
Break to Freedom*, about historical individuals enslaved by the first president
of the United States, George Washington, she discovered that there were
scarcely any firsthand accounts by or about their thoughts, traumas, and
joys—especially in relation to their placement at the physical heart of power
in a supposed democracy, in a city (Philadelphia, which was the US capital
before Washington, DC) with the nation's largest free Black population at
the time, while news of (and people who had experienced) the Haitian revolution were filtering in. Absence and silence sat in subjective memory's place.

Each of the atrocities that these artists address in their dance work (work
that blurs boundaries between tradition and innovation) is characterized
by violence: physical, symbolic, or psychological force that results in violations of body, soul, and spirit; violations of place, the earth, and community.
The horrors they reference involve trauma—a word that, in fact, comes from
a Greek word for "wound," an *injury inflicted on a body*. These histories also
involve both forced migration and confinement—displacement (of bodies)
within or just over national borders; or migration across waters, from one
continent to another. And confinement in camps or on plantations or in
secret locations along the Underground Railroad.

Distressing and sorrowful histories, if left unattended, sap communities' emotional and spiritual reserves. They eat away at the sinews that
bind, impacting contemporary and future possibilities. The sensations,
memories, and stories imprinted in these artists' movements, gestures,

rhythms, songs, and choreographies make absences visible and call forth noise to fill voids: "literal and imagined space[s] of justice" appear.[13] As do the dancers of ADT, they create new histories—of themselves, of their forebears—as they weave multidimensional tales that capture imagination and reinterpret legacies. Hope and celebration emerge. Their dances express caution, too: war, oppression, and systemic cruelty remain operative, often insidiously, around the globe and right under our noses, and demand our active opposition. This is akin to ADT's concept of Daak: dance as radical practice; dance as a call to action.

Writer Edwidge Danticat, who calls on artists to "create dangerously," reminds us that among the interpretations of what that means, "Albert Camus . . . suggests that it is creating as a revolt against silence, creating when both the creation and the reception, the writing and the reading, are dangerous undertakings, disobedience to a directive."[14] Indeed, members of a vocal performance ensemble I initially wrote about in a now-deleted section of this chapter requested, at the last minute, that mention of them and their work be removed from the text. They've been a thorn in the side of political authorities in their Asian nation for years, with a noted presence on the streets, and worry that international exposure of this sort, at this time, might put them and their collaborators in a situation of even greater risk of harm.

While making final edits to this chapter in mid-2020, thousands rise in outrage and exhaustion to demand rehumanization of Black individuals and communities, and an end to white supremacy and its attendant systemic and direct violence targeting dignity and possibilities, and indeed, lives, in the United States and elsewhere. I write as Black and brown women, in particular, in roles as frontline workers during a pandemic, are shouldering greater risks and losses than others, and seeing their families and neighborhoods disproportionately decimated.

Writer Arundhati Roy, in a May 2020 conversation with Kimberlé Crenshaw, speaks of this moment of crisis. Answering a question about her use of the term "portal" in an essay about the COVID-19 pandemic, Roy beckons us to acknowledge this as a time of "rupture." "It's almost like there's a past and there's a future," she says, asking us to consider how we might, eventually, "stitch this together." Being in a liminal space, between the known of before, with all its burdens, and something not yet formed, the creative envisioning of that future—or even an openness to questioning, to deep and active listening and risk taking, all as part of not-knowing—will make all the difference.

Of course you have to first imagine [another world] before you fight for
it. . . . But what is that imagination? That imagination involves looking
at a mountain with minerals in it and saying, Can we leave the minerals
in the mountain? Can we leave the bauxite in the mountain? Because that
bauxite in the mountain serves a purpose. . . . In nature bauxite holds water
and irrigates the plains. . . . To the people who live there it means everything. But to the capitalist world it only means anything when it's extracted
[for use in manufacturing aluminum]. [The question becomes:] Can you
leave the bauxite in the mountain as you walk through the portal?[15]

The choreography of disavowal of and alternatives to injustice, greed, and
danger, on streets across the globe and in the aesthetic constructions and
ethical practice of artistic ensembles such as Ananya Dance Theatre, remains
an essential source of and inspiration for the imagining and enacting of
relationships (among humankind, between humanity and the natural
world) that are just and reciprocal. The water ripples, heaves, and swells.

NOTES

1 Ananya Chatterjea, during conversation at the Community Education Center,
Philadelphia, October 6, 2012.
2 Germaine Ingram is a jazz tap dancer, choreographer and vocalist, and Leah Stein
is a dancer and choreographer who makes site-inspired collaborative dance
works.
3 The professional learning community initiative was supported by grants from
the Pew Center for Arts and Heritage and the Leeway Foundation, and by the
Asian Arts Initiative. The quotations of Ingram's words in this section are
from that conversation between Ananya Dance Theatre members and Ingram
and Stein's professional learning community, which I recorded at the Community Education Center on October 6, 2012.
4 The second day involved a public demonstration and discussion of their respective approaches.
5 One particular style of Chhau is from Bengal, where Chatterjea was born. Chhau
was inscribed on UNESCO's list of the Intangible Cultural Heritage of Humanity in 2010. "Chhau Dance," UNESCO website, https://ich.unesco.org/en/RL
/chhau-dance-00337.
6 The quotations of Chatterjea's words (here and throughout the chapter) are from
the conversation between ADT and Ingram and Stein's professional learning
community that I recorded at Philadelphia's Community Education Center on
October 6, 2012.
7 Chatterjea thinks about and carries out each aspect of her practice, whether
the establishment of relationships, thematic and choreographic development,

costume design and construction, or ensemble member selection and training, with an exceptional commitment to equity, social consciousness, and respect for the environment.

8   Statement by dancer Hui Wilcox following the *Defining Ourselves* performance by Ananya Dance Theatre at the Performance Garage, Philadelphia, October 7, 2012.

9   Those comfortable with things as they are often don't recognize or acknowledge systems that set and maintain oppressions. They don't have to. As one example of this willful or blind denial, which ADT brings to the fore, in "I, Racist," John Metta writes, "Racism is the fact that 'White' means 'normal' and that anything else is different. Racism is our acceptance of an all white *Lord of the Rings* cast because of 'historical accuracy,' ignoring the fact that this is a world with an entirely fictionalized history. Even when we make shit up, we want it to be white. And racism is the fact that we all accept that it is white. The system was made for White people, so White people don't have to think about living in it." "I, Racist," in *Those People*, podcast, 2017, https://www.thsppl.com /thsppl-articles/2017/4/14/i-racist.

10 Sally Engle Merry, *Human Rights and Gender Violence: Translating International Law into Local Justice* (Chicago: University of Chicago Press, 2006), 66.

11 The panel, "Body Destroyed/Body Remembered," was curated by dancer/writer Roko Kawai, then based in California at the Yerba Buena Center for the Arts. Byb Chanel Bibene is a choreographer and performer working in theater and contemporary dance, with technical and aesthetic sensibilities rooted in the culture and dances of his native Republic of Congo. Chey Chankethya is both an accomplished classical Cambodian dancer and an award-winning contemporary choreographer and performer, and was, at the time when this panel convened, artistic director of Amrita Performing Arts in Phnom Penh, Cambodia. Germaine Ingram, mentioned earlier in this chapter, is a renowned jazz-tap dancer, vocalist, artistic director, and writer. All three artists have done extensive international work.

12 Olaudah Equiano, *The Interesting Narrative of the Life of Olaudah Equiano, Or Gustavus Vassa, The African, Written By Himself* (1789), https://www.guten berg.org/files/15399/15399-h/15399-h.htm.

13 Cathy J. Schlund-Vials, *War, Genocide, and Justice: Cambodian American Memory Work* (Minneapolis: University of Minnesota Press, 2012), 25.

14 Edwidge Danticat, *Create Dangerously: The Immigrant Artist at Work* (New York: Vintage Books, 2011), 11.

15 Arundhati Roy, "Under the Blacklight: Narrating the Nightmare and (Re)imagining the Possible," May 26, 2020, in *Intersectionality Matters with Kimberlé Crenshaw*, podcast, https://soundcloud.com/intersectionality-matters/18-under -the-blacklight-narrating-the-nightmare-and-reimagining-the-possible. Roy's article to which reference was made is "The Pandemic as a Portal," *Financial Times*, April 3, 2020, https://www.ft.com/content/10d8f5e8-74eb-11ea-95fe -fcd274e920ca.

V

IMAGINING RESISTANCE AND HOPE

19

A POLITICS OF HOPE

Letters, Dance, and Dreams

PATRICIA DEROCHER, SIMI KANG, AND RICHA NAGAR

March 10, 2013

Dear Simi and Richa,

I was recently at a meeting to organize for the local May Day events in Albany, New York, in which people were voicing the need to do something other than teach-ins for the event. They were specifically calling for exercises to be more intersectional in approach and to build community in a dynamic way. So I heard myself say, "Why not focus on the arts? Creative resistance can be a powerful way to build dialogue and community through the artistic process."

I'm not sure this was a welcome suggestion, but it does, I think, closely resonate with the Ananya Dance Theatre project, which seeks to create "an active citizenry for dance."[1] As documented in "So Much to Remind Us We Are Dancing on Other People's Blood," the company labors in discussions and dance productions to forge solidarities among BIWOC (Black, Indigenous, women of color) as an important project for addressing structural racism, specifically within the United States. This coalitional effort provides a tangible example of a social justice project that does not insist on erasing differences to confront larger power imbalances. Rather, as the authors/dancers suggest, the project is both enriched and strengthened by a "differential approach," to reference Chela Sandoval, which is voiced by the writers in terms of their differing motivations, subject positionings, and accompanying experiential knowledge.

I am drawn to the fragmented, polyvocal structure employed by the chapter and how it representationally signals this differential approach. The at times uneasy alliance of the dance troupe is not seamless—as made visible by the breaks between the authors' otherwise interweaving voices— and it is not the purpose of the company or project to gloss over these differences. Rather, within the ethos of the project, dance is employed as a methodology that requires flexibility, fluidity, and continual movement to creatively work through social difference: "this troupe of multicolored women showed how with rhythm and flow instead of rigidness, with all cinnamon bark feminine suppleness, you can move around things that otherwise could cage you."[2] Even as differences are highlighted and negotiated within and between members of the dance collective—and as members recognize the false assumptions of the other members—this shared commitment to working through difference and fostering connections forms the malleable ethos of the collective, always pivoting around an imagined, unstable center. I found myself thinking about this when I recently reread June Jordan's "A Report from the Bahamas," where she states, "It occurs to me that much organizational grief could be avoided if people understood that partnership in misery does not necessarily provide for partnership for change."[3]

The members of ADT seem profoundly aware of the dangers in surface-level assumptions of "sameness," even as they continue to uncover their own false assumptions about what unites them. And so ADT instead presents itself as a "community of singularities" in which "the solution can only be no solution, can only be maintaining tension between what rushes us together and what flows us apart, returning endlessly to negotiate this balancing act and then renegotiate it and renegotiate it again."[4] And yet, even with this ethos, there remains a central question: how to create a lasting, meaningful connection among BIWOC within the Minnesotan social landscape in a way that actively forges connections *across* communities of color, instead of just relying on a discursive flick of the wrist to signal an imagined, mythic community? In looking for a "common current," the metaphor of water—as manifested by the Mississippi River—remains one constant point of connection even as the singularities of each ADT member's social location and differing investment in the project are expressed. How did we all end up in this space—this "great white north"—the dancers ask, and how does our presence here testify to our interconnecting racialized histories?

The company's creation of a dialogic space that attends to the silenced racialized, colonial histories within the United States is also extended to the audience, and yet the type of relationship invited between the audience and the performance also depends upon the social locations of the audience members. For me as a white-bodied person in the United States, the chapter's discussion on the much-needed coalition building across BIPOC communities reminds me that while I am invited to attend the staged productions and to understand the political methodology that underpins the BIWOC dance troupe, I am asked to listen—to witness—and not to assume the role of white interlocutor. This is what the figure of the "white paunchy man" comes to signal to me within the chapter, symbolically reminding me how far I am allowed entry into the ADT project. This figure also reinforces how the dancers self-consciously highlight in this piece what Shank and Nagar term "backstage preparations,"[5] the political discussions and interventions that might not explicitly come through during the performance. In a sense, ADT seems to recognize dance as an excavation device to extract lingering colonial residues that inhibit communities from overcoming the legacies of divide-and-conquer strategies. By mixing forms and histories, ADT sets the stage for a hybrid set of politics and strategies (figure 19.1).

In connecting the ADT project to the May Day meeting, I find myself replaying one of the author/dancers' final questions over and over again in my mind: "How to suggest the power of performance as a mode of organizing communities?"[6] How can creative resistance serve to organize communities? And what specifically about dance as an *embodied art* lends itself as an adept organizing tool for citizens whose bodies bear the weight of racialized and colonial legacies? My own mind quickly moves to bell hooks's insistence on the political imagination as our most potent transformative tool. She suggests that we must harness our abilities to think, imagine, and be differently to effectively bring a more just order into existence; that while political analysis is needed to call attention to what *is*, we need the arts to usher in a politics of hope with suggestions for *what could be*.

Dance also productively disrupts this linear chronological model. If to perform, and to consider how we are always already performing, enables

FIGURE 19.1. Hui Niu Wilcox (foreground), (L-R) Alessandra Lebea Williams, Johnathan Van Arneman, Julia Gay, Felicia Perry, Sophia Hill, and Lizzette Chapa in a furious moment from "Tiger Protest" in *Shyamali: Sprouting Words* (2017). Photo by Paul Virtucio. Courtesy of Ananya Dance Theatre.

us to realize how we might also perform differently, then the performance of dance—and/as identities—would seem to allow a citizenry of dancers to reinhabit their bodies anew, creating more self-conscious performances on and off stage the more they revisit intersecting histories.

What are your thoughts on this, Simi and Richa?

Warmly,
Trish

April 11, 2013

Dear Trish and Richa,

Thank you for beginning this exchange, Trish. I think the questions you raised, particularly in the interest of understanding self- and community-making projects like ADT, offer rich points of entry into "So Much to Remind Us We Are Dancing on Other People's Blood." What I found most compelling in your letter were the questions: "How can creative resistance serve to organize communities? And what specifically about dance as an embodied art lends itself as an adept organizing tool for citizens whose bodies bear the weight of racialized and colonial legacies?" I trained as a dancer for many years and am particularly interested in trying to understand embodiment's role in resistance and practices of recentering ourselves in larger cultural narratives of belonging as BIWOC.

I have danced sporadically and sometimes not at all over the past five years, but I know the feeling of practicing a combination, of forcing my fingertips, toes, hips just a little farther than they would go. There is something bright, beautiful, about learning the boundaries and curvatures of our bodies—it allows us to reevaluate the possibilities and risks of pushing against them. I think this is what Tinsley, Chatterjea, Wilcox, and Gibney touch on when they invoke the fluidity of sweat and blood as a metaphor for their embodiment of and resistance to the racializing experiences they encounter. This fluidity snakes between each author's contribution to the text. It is animated in their collaboration, their choreography, their bodies, and their presence, onstage. I feel that "So Much to Remind Us" allows BIWOC artists to reevaluate the possibilities of our bodies as they exist in space; not only can we tell stories as we speak, sweat, and move, but in doing so, we can recognize our experiences as vital to tell. In trying to articulate our experiences through our bodies, we must realize that "the solution can only be no solution, can only be maintaining tension between what rushes us together and what flows us apart, returning endlessly to negotiate this balancing act and then renegotiate it and renegotiate it again."[7]

In a way, the authors of "So Much to Remind Us" are creating what Lila Abu-Lughod calls an "ethnography of the particular," or producing "the effects of extralocal and long-term processes" locally in "the actions of individuals living their particular lives, inscribed in their bodies and their words."[8] By writing from an intra- rather than intersocietal perspective, the authors use their bodily experiences to dissolve the societal markers of "other" produced by structural violence. One author says, "There have been several moments in my life when I saw my own body for the first time," asserting her claim to her body while at once marking it as a part of larger histories that allow her to see that body as both particular and universal.[9] These encounters with the self trace a particular life story. In this tracing, the author's body and her experiences of embodiment create new ways of knowing, at once refusing canonical histories and allowing BIWOC to see ourselves in the past, present, and future.

The creative resistance of the artists of ADT is animated through and against the histories that have foreclosed their experiences and disciplined them through racializing and gendered language. As Gibney says, "My body belonged, not to myself, but to a particular history—a history of economic, political, and social oppression based on American conceptions of 'race.'"[10]

As an ethnographer and community advocate, I rely on the knowledge that the stories we create can incite people to action, make meaning differently, and answer the questions we carry about our past, present, and future. Tinsley, Chatterjea, Wilcox, and Gibney do this work in "So Much to Remind Us," asking questions about how our experiences as women of color allow us to make our own lives and bodies more legible, more true, by intervening in histories produced for but without us. This piece allowed me to assess how the work we do as scholars of color can challenge hegemonic discourses about our communities and those we labor for. As my personal project is to cocreate ethnographic knowledge with Vietnamese American commercial fisherfolk in Southeast Louisiana— folks I care about deeply but whose communities I am not part of—I am constantly forced to question my own ability to initiate an effective dialogue with pasts and presents that are not mine.

For this reason, I would like to know more about how, as a collective body that acknowledges singularity and difference while recognizing the intertwining threads of their lives, do these artists craft stories that resonate with each dancer, the audience, and their broader goals of collaborative life making? How do we use our lives as opportunities to teach and articulate new ways of understanding self, community, and ultimately, how art makes this storytelling possible?

Thank you both again for this opportunity to collaboratively explore this piece and our own ability to coauthor new histories.

My best,
Simi

April 19, 2013

Dear Simi and Trish,

Questions of location, difference, and power surround me and push me in the context of the many intimacies that I live, dream, and write about in multiple worlds and genres, between and across oceans. Sometimes, I see endless possibilities with languages that can speak with and to one another. At other times, the only available translations and energies emerge in the form of stillness and silence—meanings that cannot be fully understood, uttered, or repeated. . . . However, the same questions of location, power, and difference also drown me, paralyze me, confuse me. And in those hard moments I find myself returning to "So Much to Remind Us" to find hope and to feel the beauty and sheer power of words that emerge from movements—from moving and snaking bodies that are individual streams but bodies that also rise together in massive waves to act upon dreams they have made a collective commitment to sweat for, despite the slipperiness of the terrains on which they flow. This was the main reason why I suggested this piece by four members of ADT as a focal point for our epistolary exchange. In engaging and reengaging the dreams, motions, and reflections of Omise'eke Natasha Tinsley, Ananya Chatterjea, Hui Niu Wilcox, and Shannon Gibney, however, your letters generate so many more possibilities of conversations and connections that are inspired by the political and artistic vision of the dancers but also stretch beyond it. You offer concrete entry points for connecting the dancers' motions and reflections with the dance of social movements— where dance is not solely a metaphor but also an embodied reality of living and sustaining collectivities and hopes—a choreography, a methodology, a vision that involves forging ahead, stepping behind, leaving, returning, withdrawing, and rising again, in configurations that cannot be entirely predicted before the dance begins . . . or ends.

> Ultimately, I moved away from the performance of these classical forms to re-embody them in ways that could resonate with contemporary life experience, and to choreograph pieces about issues that move me or change my life in different ways.[11]

> figurative fluidity is hard, and i know this as materially as i know the heaviness of a bucket of water . . . always, always when there's a little

water it makes it easier to fall when you step on the dry spots . . . but
the solution to this unevenness can't be eliminating fluidity, can't be
throwing over attempts to organize in multicolored, multigendered
ways in favor of organizing (yet again, the eighties returning like bush)
around a single identity.[12]

Trish, you summarize exquisitely ADT's shared commitment to working through difference and fostering connections as "the malleable ethos
of the collective, always pivoting around an imagined, unstable center."
This shared commitment finds strong resonances with the alliance work
that I have participated in since 1996, especially with Saathis or members
of the Sangtin Kisan Mazdoor Sangathan, or SKMS, an organization of
mostly Dalit farmers and laborers in Sitapur District of Uttar Pradesh. I
feel that it is precisely through the unending process of learning how to
pivot around imagined, unstable *centers* that those working in solidarity
can learn why "the solution can only be no solution, can only be maintaining tension between what rushes us together and what flows us apart,
returning endlessly to negotiate this balancing act and then renegotiate it
and renegotiate it again."

Simi, the critical questions you pose toward the end of your letter are,
for me, intimately related to this continuous grappling with what rushes
"us" together and what flows us apart. They remind me of the ever-present
and necessary agony of who counts as "us" and who must step back, when,
and how, in the crafting of histories and solutions that are created—only
to be renegotiated and renegotiated again—forever attentive to the ways
in which those who constitute the provisional "we"s are differentially
written out of histories and geographies. In other words, an engagement
with your questions about collaborative life making must emerge from
the singularities that roil and clash. However, in defining the aesthetics
and ethics of how these roiling and clashing singularities must be represented or narrated, each one of us must also learn to account—however
partially and provisionally—for that which is written, silent, and silenced.
We must learn to account for that which counts as movement without
ever forgetting that which remains still, paralyzed, or unknown.

I have been reading *Writing Out Loud*, the diary of Faeza Meyer, a resident organizer in a shack dwellers campaign in the township of Mitchells
Plain near Cape Town. Faeza, along with five thousand backyard shack
dwellers, occupied land in Tafelsig in May 2011. In conversation with Koni

Benson, a feminist life historian who has been active in movements against eviction in that area, Faeza has been writing a diary of what she is seeing, remembering, and becoming as she lives through and emerges as one of the leaders of this struggle. Last month, Faeza and Koni shared this diary with members of SKMS after reading parts of SKMS's collective dairy, *Ek Aur Neemsaar*, in translation. As someone who has accepted the responsibility of translating across continents these two diaries (however partially and imperfectly) to those who are immersed in the struggles that the diaries represent, I cannot separate the words and thoughts of Faeza and Sangtins from this conversation we are having on the aesthetics, ethics, and politics of singularities in collective organizing and movement. Let me share with you some glimpses of these accounts.

EXCERPTS FROM FAEZA MEYER'S DIARY

I don't know what to say about our kids anymore, because sadly as the fights go on, the struggle gets harder and they, "our kids," they suffer the most. . . . Can somebody at least attempt to save their lives? . . . Doesn't the so-called beautiful Constitution of our country protect our children at all cost? No. . . . It is ok to turn a blind eye when someone is worth nothing? The poor is of no use to anyone. No one is making a profit when we have nowhere to go. When we [are] illegally occupying land, when we do not have water and sanitation. When where we come from has a stench. . . . (Entry titled "Our Kids," July 1, 2012)

Yesterday I was at my aunt's [fiftieth] birthday. I was very close with her. She was at all my births. . . . But everyone had to . . . be careful not to knock over the champagne glasses and sit and wait to . . . queue up to wish her happy birthday. Very bourgeois. . . . All high heels, so uncomfortable. It wasn't like that when I was little. [Then] it was about people and having fun. Not about sitting proper. My uncle gave a speech and it was all about making our children capitalists. I can't blame him because I used to do that, wanting to be up there and get somewhere in life. Have a better car. Be better than the next person. I don't want to compete with anyone anymore. . . . I would rather wear my broken tekkies and broken pants, and see me for me. . . . I don't want my kids exposed to that either. . . . (Entry titled "Contagious Disease," October 9, 2012)

Writing is not that easy, especially when you think someone else will read it. But when you are writing it as if speaking to someone it makes it easier. Having written to Koni, even in sms on the phone, when I send a message as part of this project of recording my history, it's like having a conversation. . . . So often I would not have written had I not been talking to her, . . . so we can't take her name out of the diary entries like she suggested, because people must see that that is one way to write, one way to put your history down, one way to feel you can go on when you are not sure you can. (Entry titled "Closing a Chapter," October 23, 2012)

TRANSLATED EXCERPT FROM SANGTIN KISAN MAZDOOR SANGATHAN'S DIARY, *EK AUR NEEMSAAR*

Saathis dream the big dreams of changing all of this [ending forever the state violence in multiple forms that kills, displaces, and disempowers the rural and Dalit poor] but they also have their little dreams—of claiming their housing, pensions, wages. . . . In these fights for big and small dreams, there is always hope; sometimes we win hope and at others we lose hope. The movement becomes strong with every little victory, with the arrival of every new Saathi who bring her hopes and energies to the struggle. But failures, too, can make us strong. A young woman is killed by her own relatives for their "honor" far away from Sitapur, and we are unable to do anything because of our own limitations. At the same time, our failure in one place makes us more determined than ever to stand up against every such killing wherever it happens again. Every defeat gives us the strength to continue the fight a little longer.

Many supporters of SKMS, a number of them far away from Sitapur, are deeply critical of what we have been calling "the system" while also enjoying some privileges that are bestowed upon them by the same system. They, too, become sources of hope and strength and allow us the space to think more critically, to dream more daringly.

We also pause and turn around to see what we are doing, to examine the absences and faults in what we have done, and to reflect on what we could have done differently. We are reminded of a story from our childhood—a story called "Abbu Khan ki Bakri," written by Dr. Zakir Hussain during India's war of independence. Abbu Khan's mountain goat, Chaandni, knows that it is dangerous for her to step out of the security of Abbu Khan's fenced yard because there are wolves on the other side; she knows that she can lose her life if she jumps over the fence. Yet Chaandni cannot resist her only chance to know liberation. When Abbu Khan lovingly calls out for Chaandni and asks her to come back, she hears him; she even turns around to let him know that she knows how much he cares. But then she moves forward toward the mountains even as she can feel the wolf's eyes staring at her. The love for one's freedom, the love for the core of one's identity and integrity drive our journeys of struggle. They give us the same strength and hope that they gave Chaandni.

There are huge risks and dangers in jumping over the fence—in writing, singing, and speaking together for transformative justice. The biggest danger emanates from the ever-present possibility of epistemic violence that we cannot grasp or know, especially as translators or narrators who retell struggles across difficult and unequal borders. Faeza and the Sangtins know this well and yet they/we must carry on believing in the possibilities inspired by the very commitment to dream together. Faeza does not agree with Koni's suggestion about removing Koni's voice from her story; she refuses familiar narratives of voice and privilege because she does not want to give up what she has found: "A way to feel that you can go on when you are not sure you can." Faeza's faith in cocreation of energies and stories opens up hope for all of us, in the same way that a decade of collective struggle against the violence of Development machinery allows members of SKMS to celebrate Chaandni's courage as nonnegotiable love for one's freedom and dignity. The collective struggle makes Saathis believe in situated solidarities that are grounded in geopolitical, institutional, material, and affective specificities—a belief that enables them to trust me with the writing of their stories in Hindustani as well as with partial translations of those stories for potential allies. Faith, trust, solidarity, commitment—are these at odds with critique? No. Marginalization and violence necessitate all of these, for they bring hope. As the dancers of ADT articulate so powerfully,

> We cannot afford to give up hope. Is that specific to the experience of marginalization? Possibly. Hope is what pushes us to resist and fight against forces so much bigger than us. If we rationalized hope, it is about survival, it generates energy and passion. All our projects are about hope ultimately. . . . What enables us to dance? To dance, really?

There is so much to remind us we are dancing on other people's blood. It takes work to be able to create that beauty as a healing force and to enjoy creating it. Building that community and ensemble is about finding a way to let hope materialize into energy.[13]

I wonder if, through our letters, we can offer some open-ended reflections on what a politics of hope might look like? And how that politics necessarily implies risks. Risks that come with loving and trusting, with letting ourselves flow with the stories we have inherited and disinherited. Risks that must be embraced in order to find new rhythms and movements that give us life, joy, and community as we continuously renew and reinvigorate our struggles for justice.

I am grateful for your inspired letters that have allowed us to connect our hopes with the creative and political energies of the dancers of ADT.

Richa

May 20, 2013

Dear Simi and Richa,

To pick up on Richa's final thread: What does a politics of hope entail? And what does ADT mean by their suggestion that "building . . . community and ensemble is about finding a way to let hope materialize into energy"?[14] That it "takes work to be able to create that beauty as a healing force and to enjoy creating it"? That is, what is the difference between passive, idle hope and deliberately utilizing hope as a political tool?

Richa, your closing questions bring me to a Frida Kahlo quote: "Nothing is worth more than laughter. It is strength to laugh and to abandon oneself, to be light. Tragedy is the most ridiculous thing." I've considered and reconsidered this quote, because the materialist in me immediately wants to contest it—to insist that tragedy does exist, and that to laugh in the face of it is to stage an unethical response, to turn one's back on it. To not fully look at the world head on. And yet, over and over I reconstruct this quote in my head to read: "It is strength . . . to be light." I am compelled by the notion that lightness is an intentional posture, a daring choice to look the world in the face, trauma, oppression, and all, and to refuse to buckle under its weight.

A politics of hope, for me then, fiercely insists that it takes strength to be light. How fitting this idea seems in the context of dancing bodies that bear the weight of social marginalization—of bodies that through their conscious choreography and movement refuse to reduce themselves to the functional drudgery of daily life, of bodies to be worked upon. And then I hear another voice—Lorde's this time—suggesting that it is not enough to survive. That to live a life, fully lived, one must create the conditions that will allow oneself to thrive within one's environment. To open to the possibility of joy in the midst of suffering, without depending on things being different to access joy in the now.

Such adages, like the phrase "a politics of hope" itself, seem all very well and good. They are comforting, uplifting. But they also threaten to be interpreted in reductive, narrow ways that filter out their radical potential. Richa, you ask what a politics of hope might look like. I wonder what it *feels* like. For hope, like dance, is connected to rhythm. A rhythm of thoughts and actions lining up with the intentions and actions of other people and events that allow one to move beyond the cynicism of seeing what *is*, into the generative realm of what *could be*.

Simi, you ask what it might look like as knowledge producers to do justice to communities we find ourselves a part of, communities we love, and communities with which we are aligned. You suggest that dance might be one possibility for moving behind the suffocating confines of the rational in such academic efforts. I find this to be an incredibly bold, powerful, and necessary proposition. Too often rigidly academic paradigms close down where they are meant to open. Creative resistance, by willfully breaking the rules of what counts as rational critique, establishes its own terms of engagement. It fluidly moves from the realm of critique to reconstruction. Of ushering in what could be and what is already on its way. It creates an opening and a disruption of the status quo. The "dance" of social movements does the same.

There is nothing rational about hope. Statistics and history and daily experiences all attest to this by measuring the current moment. Hope requires a looking differently. A looking, seeing, and being beyond the surface. A future making in the present. It's a queer existence. A way of resignifying received legacies and reengaging with the what is from a defiant posture. In relation to ADT, how to measure the political success of a staged dance piece? In creative resistance more generally, how to measure the effectiveness of a political poem? Of a street theater production? And does—or should—it matter? How do we measure a dream? A possibility? A world that has yet to materialize but that we can *feel* is on its way? That already exists beyond what is seen?

There is something ineffable about the very notion of hope. Idealists are dismissed as being out of touch with reality. We are told we must accept what is. And yet, clearly, there is political power in hope. President Obama built an extremely successful rhetorical campaign premised on it. And it is widely recognized that squelching hope is one surefire way to cultivate acquiescence. To ensure that the populace is surviving rather than thriving.

As an engaged scholar turned somatic worker, I used to wish that my work efforts had more quantifiable outcomes. In a previous relationship with an engineer, I would playfully suggest that while he built actual bridges, I built metaphorical ones. But behind closed doors, I used to wonder if those metaphorical bridges really counted for anything; I belittled my contributions of building interpretive avenues of connection across social differences. But lately, *real* bridges have been crumbling left and right. People have died from structural miscalculations and brittle materials. Rationality, that prized Western concept, continues to fail people. It has asked people to trust it with a blinding devotion, and like all human concepts, proven itself fallible. And so, I have been rethinking how privileged I am to be doing the intangible work of interpretive bridge building—of forging *possibilities* for connection, discussion, focused thoughts and actions where none existed before—rather than being in the domain of the merely functional. When my attempts at bridge building fail, they spark—at the very least—new opportunities in place of lives lost. Even failed attempts render visible the social and material chasms that already exist and allow for focused, more careful future attempts.

And so it is with the dance of social movements. I used to wonder how it could be that those who regularly contemplate the existence and manifestation of structural inequities and oppressions are also the most joyful people I know. I no longer wonder. Hope may be a choice, but it is also *the only choice* we have in imagining, and ushering in, a more just social order. Idealists, activists, creatives, people living in material poverty who refuse to accept a deadened existence—that is, anyone actively living a politics of hope—are brave for staring the odds stacked against them straight in the face and not being deterred. For erring on the side of possibility anyway.

What does a politics of hope entail? For one, it means that success, while strived for, cannot be the motivating factor. It cannot be strictly outcome based. And our very view of success must dramatically alter as we dance. ADT's suggestion that community building through dance is a "way to let hope materialize into energy" is one way of letting go of externally defined "successful" outcomes by refocusing on the *process* of community building itself.[14]

In connection with ADT's collaborative model, for me, a politics of hope must move coalitional organizing efforts beyond an understanding of cross-border connections as merely useful to recognize that actively bridging social actors from a multiplicity of social locations is also epistemically *valuable*. The cultivation of communities of meaning, of building interpretive communities rooted in trust, vulnerability, courage, and shared commitment—these are the ineffable, intractable conditions that I see as constituting an (imperfect?) politics of hope.

Warmly,
Trish

June 20, 2013

Dear Trish and Richa,

The questions we have formulated thus far have been incredibly provocative for me. Richa, your question about how we can collectively articulate one (or many) entry points into a politics of hope has made me think more about what we might mean when we identify hope as a practical and bodily political possibility. The question you pose about collaborative life making, asking how we account for what is silent, still, unspoken, has given me a valuable way to think about the silences that, I believe, galvanize us into moving, creating, and speaking our collective and individual hopes and pain. Silences (by this, I mean the absences we ourselves grapple with as an everyday process as well as those that have been culturally and historically created for us and the communities that we identify ourselves as a part of), particularly those imposed upon us, force us to do different kinds of work than if we did not feel or recognize the absences they create. In this way, I see silences not just as oppressive forces but as concrete absences that incite us to speak, move, and be more present.

In your letter, Richa, you say: "Sometimes, I see endless possibilities with languages that can 'speak' with/to one another. At other times, the only available translations emerge in the form of stillness and silence ... meanings that cannot be fully understood, uttered, or conveyed. . . . But the same questions of location, power, and difference also drown me, paralyze me." I have been similarly immobilized at times; I often wonder how much my singular voice can act on and tell the kinds of stories we are grappling with here just as you have, Trish. I think the work we are doing in this exchange is a kind of storytelling—about our own positionalities, experiences, (in)disciplines, and the kinds of privileges and silences we endure differently. This movement, this telling, alone gives me hope.

As global and hyperlocal movements for recognition and justice continue to grow and reframe both their needs and their approaches to meeting those needs, I think the collaboration you gesture to, Trish, is imperative. I feel that to begin establishing a politics of hope, we must first recognize our own voices and, in so doing, must subsequently acknowledge their ability to speak not only for ourselves but for, "before," and with others. More and more, social science and humanities scholarship calls for us to self-reflexively identify our own positionality as a part of our academic labor; I believe that this "naming" of the self is a viable first step in collaborative work—would my words do the same type of work if I did not first identify myself as an often white-passing queer woman of color, an artist, an ethnographer, or with any other name that I might give to my life, my body, my experiences? Ultimately, however, this labor is not nearly enough. This is not to say that we should, or even can, move toward a politics of hope without this process, however.

Richa, I believe the chapter from *Muddying the Waters* that you recently shared with me about the necessity of vulnerability in collaborative work revitalizes and reorients the problem of speaking the self. Richa, you say, "It is in the acknowledgment, recognition, and sharing of [our most tender and fragile] moments, memories, and mistakes that we live our trust and faith, and where we often encounter our deepest courage and insights."[15] Following this, in an exchange of letters with Piya Chatterjee, you write:

> The promise of this continued dialogue, this patching and quilting between us—and between fragments of our multiple worlds that haunt us *and* make us—is precisely what makes me hopeful about ... the process of finding faith, meaning, *and* languages together so that we

can make ourselves radically vulnerable as we create an honest dialectic between our "internal" struggles—of making sense of our souls, our intimate silences, betrayals, nightmares (the uttering of which has been permanently postponed at times)—and our "external" struggles that involve our associations with other souls, their silences, hopes, fears, and sufferings.[16]

I feel this way about our exchange, Richa and Trish. Not only are we "uttering" our souls in some ways, but we are grappling with how we might better connect with the souls of others. This in itself is a politics of hope.

For me, the work of calling out to and reimagining with other souls is, following Veena Das, an act of inhabiting "the same space now marked as a space of destruction in which you must live again."[17] What I mean by this is that when we connect with others to create new possibilities, we are at once given the opportunity to learn anew and asked to return to the deepest pain we have known. Turning our silences, hopes, fears, and sufferings into the compost of never-before-dreamed-of possibilities allows us to reinhabit our spaces of destruction, from ancestral trauma to personal failure, and imagine alongside that pain rather than in spite of it. I say this because I think our hurt is generative when brought into conversation with the hurt of others. We learn the most when we can hope together and when our hope can be predicated on doing less harm than has been done to us—and doing less harm than we have done—in the past.

However, I want to clarify that our pain should never be the precondition for our future survival. In my work, I reject the notion of resilience because resilience is often used by policy makers and politicians in Louisiana to identify people who can withstand more harm more often and, as such, do not need support. Rather than resilience, what I want for us is possibility. Rather than bracing for the next storm, I want us to create networks of care that allow us to see the storm coming and work together to mitigate its effects. I want us to look at the storm after it has passed and ask how we can prevent it in the future rather than building a tolerance to storms. Ultimately, I believe that is what hope looks like: starting from Richa's radical vulnerability and cultivating Trish's communities of meaning, we are already building communal futures predicated on care.[18]

In terms of identifying our artistic and bodily stakes in this work, I keep returning to a line from the ADT text: "There have been several moments

in my life when I saw my own body for the first time."[19] I wonder if this
moment of self-recognition and realization could itself be a useful place
to begin establishing a politics of hope. To see ourselves—as women, people of color, queer, kin, artists, scholars—not only as bodies occupying
space but as selves moving through it, affecting and, ultimately, effecting
it, is powerful.

To return to the work of this exchange between us, then, I believe that
in committing our own approaches to analysis, labor, and writing to text,
we offer pieces of what we might call our personal hopes. I thank you both
deeply for this opportunity to share, learn, and create stories together.

My best,
Simi

NOTES

1   Omise'eke Natasha Tinsley, Ananya Chatterjea, Hui Niu Wilcox, and Shannon
    Gibney, "So Much to Remind Us We Are Dancing on Other People's Blood:
    Moving toward Artistic Excellence, Moving from Silence to Speech, Moving
    in Water, with Ananya Dance Theatre," in *Critical Transnational Feminist
    Praxis*, ed. Amanda Lock Swarr and Richa Nagar (Albany: SUNY Press, 2010),
    147–65, 149.
2   Tinsley et al., "So Much to Remind Us," 151.
3   June Jordan, "Report from the Bahamas," *On Call: Political Essays* (London: Pluto
    Press, 1985), 46–47.
4   Tinsley et al., "So Much to Remind Us," 163–64.
5   Sofia Shank and Richa Nagar, "Retelling Stories, Resisting Dichotomies: Stag-
    ing Identity, Marginalization and Activism in Minneapolis and Sitapur," in
    Rethinking Feminist Interventions into the Urban, ed. Linda Peake and Mar-
    tina Rieker (Oxford: Routledge, 2013), 90–107.
6   Tinsley et al., "So Much to Remind Us'," 165.
7   Tinsley et al., "So Much to Remind Us," 163.
8   Lila Abu-Lughod, "Writing Against Culture," in *Recapturing Anthropology:
    Working in the Present*, ed. Richard G. Fox (University of Washington: School
    of American Research Press, 1991), 474.
9   Tinsley et al., "So Much to Remind Us," 156.
10 Tinsley et al., "So Much to Remind Us," 156.
11 Tinsley et al., "So Much to Remind Us," 156.
12 Tinsley et al., "So Much to Remind Us," 163.
13 Tinsley et al., "So Much to Remind Us," 164.
14 Tinsley et al., "So Much to Remind Us," 164.
15 Richa Nagar, *Muddying the Waters: Co-Authoring Feminism across Scholarship
    and Activism* (Champaign: University of Illinois Press, 2014), 23.

16   Nagar, *Muddying the Waters*, 41.

17   Veena Das, "The Act of Witnessing: Violence, Poisonous Knowledge and Subjectivity," *Cadernos Pagu* 37 (2011): 9–41.

18   Nagar, *Muddying the Waters*, chapter 1.

19   Tinsley et al., "So Much to Remind Us," 156.

20

A PERSONAL RECKONING

Reflections from *Duurbaar* to *Mohona*

BRENDA DIXON-GOTTSCHILD

I wrote this reflection on ADT in the middle of the second decade of the new millennium. Now, at the end of this time marker and with cosmic shifts in individual, communal, national, and global lives, the past is receding at warp speed. Rereading this essay took me back to a rare moment of calm in what was already a tumultuous era. It stands as a memory of an ever-evolving canon of work by Ananya Chatterjea—a verbal snapshot that I wish for the reader to see with the mind's eye.

Open your eyes
Let the tears fall,
Reach from your heart
And touch your forehead

I open the Ananya Dance Theatre website, click on the link for *Mohona*, and find Ananya and one of her dancers simultaneously repeating these words and demonstrating the movements that accompany each line to a group of people who will participate in the *Dance of a Thousand Water Dreams*, a public performance/procession done in consort with indigenous activists for the Northern Spark 2013 project in Minneapolis.

For me not only do the words represent this dance, an ingenious way of teaching movement by using words and images rather than counting, but also they represent "the essential Ananya." Who is she? Like the refrain, she is eyes and heart, full of compassion—and her head is overflowing with ideas. She and I are Librans, lovers of peace, loyal friends, seekers of balance (and often that's the point: not that we *are* balanced, but that we *quest after* balance, sometimes teetering from one pole to another), and obsessed with the ideal of justice. As Bertolt Brecht said, "All art forms are in the service of the greatest of all arts: the art of living."[1] In Ananya's case, her art is in the service of living righteously and fairly.

My Ananya stories begin at Temple University, exactly how many years ago I cannot recall. But there is an immediate attraction (by the entire Dance Department faculty) to this diminutive, fast-talking, clear-thinking, *gorgeous* human being who, unlike so many of our students, approaches us with authority and dignity but also with respect. Obviously, she wasn't brought up in the United States! And though she is slight in size, she is a powerhouse intellectually and as a dancing body. Just as teaching my signature course, "Black Performance from Africa to the Americas," galvanized, mobilized, and revolutionized my modus operandi, so also the experience of taking this course may have had something to do with Ananya's journey and her wise decision to be a dancer-choreographer-scholar—to do it all and show that there are paths to follow beyond the either-or. I like to believe that the course also strengthened her rationale for writing and dancing gender, race, and ecology. She makes a strong political statement by (a) having an ensemble predominantly composed of women of color, (b) taking on an activist agenda with choreography as the lens through which she focuses her ideas for social change, and (c) using non-Europeanist movement forms as her fundamental dance vocabulary. She builds on the path struck by Jawole Willa Jo Zollar's Urban Bush Women, also women of color, and Rennie Harris, who made urban vernacular hip-hop and breakdancing idioms his equivalent of Modern Dance 101. It was a bold move for these artists to embrace movement genres other than ballet, modern, postmodern, and contact improvisation and bring them to mainstream concert dance venues. Their starting point was based on revising the traditional canon from its core.

Looking at Ananya's work, what do I see? My recollections are flashpoints, illuminations, sparked by viewing the performances discussed in these notes and musing on how they resonate in my own experience. As such, these comments are neither right nor wrong, but merely the way in which these dances spoke to me. And that's what I love about dance: it is a language that carries multiple meanings and cannot be translated literally. (If it could be, there'd be no need to dance.) My view is simply my view—a lesson I wish I could teach the anointed pundits and review writers who think they are objective and know it all.

Ananya's dances are dramatic movement narratives—*gesamptkunst-werks*—bringing to bear dance, music, costume, sets, props, verbal language, and vocal syllables in creating a multidimensional, near-sacred event in the intensity of its sensory effect. Once, in a letter to me, she said that she was "no *god* person," yet her works exude a spiritual ethos. But this is my spin on them, based on my own backstory in yoga, devotion, and traditional forms of Indian dance, all of which communicate the spirit through the senses. I had seen early Chatterjea performances in Philadelphia, but I didn't know how far she'd traveled from those beginnings until I was at the opening of *Duurbaar* in Minneapolis in September 2006.

DUURBAAR (UNSTOPPABLE)

I remember the excitement rippling through the audience at the Southern Theater as the premiere of this work was about to begin. Climaxing in a spectacular water ceremony, it is, in Ananya's words on the website, "an exploration of histories and pathways, of loss and femininity through the metaphor of water." And now in 2013, as I write these words, Ananya Dance Theatre is about to premiere *Mohona*, whose guiding principle is once again women's relationship to water—subtitled *Estuaries of Desire*. Water: a primary impulse and life symbol in her work—and I'm laughing at myself for the multiple messages involved in choosing to bookend this essay in water by focusing on these two dances.

I am moved by the way *Duurbaar* is organized. The music, like the dance, is spacious, allowing me, the spectator, to roam through the work in the chambers of my own experience. It's not a polemic shoved down my throat, nor is it an a-b-c, beginning-middle-end type of tale. It travels internal pathways and lends itself to my interventions. I am impressed that this group of women, perhaps eighteen in all, have all mastered Odissi, yoga, and Chhau well enough to be comfortable in their own skin while telling the unstoppable story. They are *all* beautiful! Having said that, I see that the movement and the intention are most clearly and precisely manifested in Ananya. The figure eights that she initiates in her chest, articulating her arms, are just one example. But this is to be expected: Ananya Dance Theatre is Ananya's vision. True to her sense of humility and respect for the Elders, Ananya gives her one senior dancer a solo moment—exquisite, touching—allowing this woman, who looks to be in her sixties, the time and space to find her own rhythm in the life of the piece. Also very touching: in this piece every performer has her hair in braids or locks of some kind. It's an incredibly unifying decision, and regardless of differences in hair length, color, or texture, it confers sisterhood upon the group.

In locked arm poses—arms aloft, locked behind their head, or low and held behind the back—the women lunge their way across stage in the opening moments. Then one woman enters, racing through on a diagonal, her energy contrasting with this slow surge; then another woman is running, holding a child in her arms. I feel the entrance as an exodus. Tension fills the air. Threat hangs over them, thick with foreboding. When Ananya enters, holding two small water pitchers, one in each hand, another dancer joins her, mirroring her movements, and then another, in counterpoint. Consonance gives way to conflict as another woman enters, whose presence and power drive Ananya to the ground. This interloper feels like a deity, demanding obeisance or prophesying doom. She is dressed in yellow. She exits and Srija, Ananya's daughter, dances with her mother in a sequence on the floor, mother and daughter curling around each other in yogic slow motion, suggesting to me that for some of us the umbilical cord is never truly broken, and we mothers are always as peaceful or strong or joyful as our daughters.

This duet is followed by an Ananya solo. With hand gestures she makes movements evocative of scooping up water and letting it run over her face. Then a powerful group of dancers, fourteen in all, move in unison with rhythmically stamping steps that cover the entire stage space. They are ubiquitous, moving north, south, east, and west with assertive affirmation. They generate an inexorable energy force—palpable, almost tangible. Aah, the power of moving in unison: what a statement it makes about teamwork, about women for women! And regeneration reigns when other dancers enter in a slow walk, each carrying a pitcher or pot on the hip, shoulder, or head. In another emsemble section, thirteen women make their way across the stage by crawling in cross-legged poses, inching their way along the ground, and ending center stage. There they progress from the yogic goddess pose (lying on the back, legs bent, soles of feet together, knees falling to either side, so that the crotch and the entire front of the body are open). The posture itself suggests giving and receiving, earth mother and sun daughter. From this they deftly get those bent legs underneath the torso, stamping the feet to get themselves standing in a deep squat, more or less moving the goddess pose from supine to upright.

Meanwhile Ananya, upstage left, moves toward Srija, downstage right, where the two meet on the floor. The thirteen-woman formation then breaks and exits, with just one left onstage with Ananya—the dancer who mirrored her movements in the opening vignette. They seem entranced, shadowing and reflecting each other. Other themes reenter as well: the older woman has another short solo, which precedes a lively sextet with Ananya, her shadow dancer, the goddess-like figure in yellow, and three others. Another group enters from downstage left with a movement combination that takes them sliding onstage, crossing over their legs, rolling forward to progress across the floor. Here I'm seeing women's labor, though the dancers are not overlaying the movement with an emotional tone. They are detached, but the movement itself speaks of labor.

What is compelling in all this activity is that a cast of less than twenty dancers is deployed in such a way that it feels like a world populated by women, searching, challenging, soothing, loving, aiding, and abetting one another. Twenty feels like hundreds, in power and presence (figure 20.1).

Little Srija is the dancer who initiates the final section: water. She tosses and dribbles water on the one woman left onstage and exits, while the woman remains. (She is one of those who entered carrying a vessel.) With the pot on the floor in front of her, she bends her head forward and drops her waist-length locks into the bowl, then in one sustained movement deliberately whips the braids back to make a droplet spray in the air; she then empties her vessel across the stage. Others enter, pouring water from jugs, pots, and pitchers, totally immersing the stage. Srija and the one other girl child in the cast romp and play in the wet medium.

The performance concludes on the saturated stage. Some dancers move slowly, ground level, in the water. Others take their time and leisurely cross the stage, bringing in more water and pouring it on the floor. Rather than the water taking on a life of its own, the women *shape* the water, giving it *their* life by their particular paths of cupping, tossing, pouring. In the final minute, water pours from the rafters, so that the performers and the stage are totally wet—drenched—with Ananya dancing and smiling in a solo spotlight downstage while the ensemble continues dancing as the lights dim.

Program notes for *Duurbaar* give us the names of sections: "Loss," "Letting Go," "Regeneration," "Connection," "Working to Transcend," and "Joy"—which was the water section. That was 2006, when ADT was just starting to come together as an ensemble in style, aesthetic, and philosophy. Fast-forward to 2013: *Mohona: Estuaries of Desire* takes the water motif on a path of righteousness, with that element central to this ninety-four-minute work. This is the seventh dance Ananya has choreographed since *Duurbaar*, having created a full-length ensemble work each year, beginning

FIGURE 20.1. (From left, foreground) Ananya Chatterjea, Chitra Vairavan, Alexandra Eady, (from left, background) Renée Copeland, Hui Niu Wilcox, Brittany Radke, Orlando Zane Hunter Jr., and Katie Haynes in a final moment of collectivity in *Mohona: Estuaries of Desire* (2013). Photo by Paul Virtucio. Courtesy of Ananya Dance Theatre.

in 2005—an amazing achievement for a full-time, tenured professor. But it makes sense for an artist who is consumed by a passion for dance and who utilizes movement as a medium for consciousness raising. In the interim years she collaborated with the Women's Environmental Institute (*Pipaashaa*, 2007; *Daak*, 2008; and *Ashesh Barsha*, 2009) and worked on themes dealing with women and systemic violence (*Kshoy!Decay!*, 2010; *Tushaanal*, 2011; and *Moreechika*, 2012); *Mohona* is the final work in this series. About this work Ananya says in her website blog, "*Mohona* has emerged from and embodies just such an estuary—one where stories of assault and appropriation, violation and devastation, loss and despair, rage and depression mix and alter course with those of cleansing and reclaiming, remembering and rebuilding, revealing and forgiving, hoping and loving—to reflect the emotional life of water and of life dependent upon water." From *Duurbaar* to *Mohona*, the score and movement vocabulary have evolved, matured, and expanded to embrace an enticing brew of Africanist flavors inbred with the choreographer's signature dance technique and music. The unison work in ensemble dancing, always outstanding in her previous choreographies, has complexified: at times the full ensemble breaks off to regroup in different formations while still performing unison movement, or echoes movement in canon form, or expands (stretching out) and contracts (pulling together in tight formation) as they cross the stage. Several wonderful solos by different dancers are embedded in the piece and demonstrate how thoroughly particular artists have now mastered and internalized the "Ananya technique." A noteworthy new addition to the company: one male, of African lineage, dancing with the ensemble and seamlessly integrated in the collective. There's now also a European American woman who, in the group, doesn't register as noncolored. It is evident that Ananya has continued to study by dancing and teaching in studios (as far afield as West Africa and Indonesia) and through discourse, reading, and her own scholarly writing. As she grows, so does the work. I'm not talking in Europeanist *cognitive/comparative* terms, not implying that 2013 is better than 2006; *affectively*, I'm addressing the place, the space, where this artist is mindfully present, right now.

Vocalist Mankwe Ndosi, one of the collaborators on this project, is the first performer to emerge from the theater's semidarkness. Clad in a silky, loosely flowing, ankle-length dress of colors shading from sea-foam to blue-green, she scat-sings a blues-like riff, approaching us on a runway extending from the center of the proscenium stage into the house. She is Griot, pointing the way while weaving her song-story. Her *vocalise* is definitively Africanist. As she moves onto the stage and lifts her arms with a whooping sound, a black screen covering the scrim magically rises to the rafters to reveal Ananya, crouched inside a large transparent dome. Like Ndosi, she is costumed in flowing sea-blue multitones (as will be the soon-to-emerge ensemble): sleeveless top and wraparound soft trousers with splits from heel to hip, allowing freedom for leg gestures. Is she captive? Imprisoned? Voluntarily isolated? Is this see-through enclosure a bubble? An aquarium? Slowly Ananya shifts into an asymmetrical headstand, bended legs nearly touching the sides of her bubble, which gently rocks when she moves. The soundscape is now gurgling water. Rainbow-specked flecks of light reflect off the round surface. Already, in these first few minutes, I feel sea, ocean, water—estuaries, indeed. Ananya rises to standing. Her poetry begins in torso articulation, fanning out to arms making liquid, fluid arabesques of sustained, caressing, embracing movements that attract outsiders, as the ensemble dancers alone or in twos slowly slide (on their bellies) or glide toward this transparent enclosure and its caged bird. Curiosity soon changes to conflict, and they push on the dome, punch at it, finally puncturing it so that it deflates, with Ananya crumbled inside. Are they trying to join her, free her, destroy her? Metaphorically, is our love always laced with hate? Are we humans simply bundles of contradictions? They exit, and Ndosi reappears, with an enhanced costume: turquoise chiffon scarves attached to her shoulders and a swath of fishnet as a cape, her hair coiled like seaweed. She could be a mermaid goddess emerging from the sea to enchant us beleaguered humans and direct us to some knowledge. She is both goddess and the *principle* of water itself, as told in some of the words in her chant: "Put me on your head . . . anoint yourself . . . carried to pipelines . . . we'll find our future . . . we are not tame . . . estuaries of life . . . I can heal, I can kill . . . feel my vibration . . . no matter what you do to me, I will flow . . . we're made of ancient waters of the world." With this incantation she "saves" Ananya, the two dancing briefly together before exiting.

Soon
I'll take you to the ocean
And we'll take off our shoes
Into the blue, steady and true
Running deep, I'm running too
I'm water inside like my blue[2]

Hui Wilcox dances a solo, with two children seated at the side of the stage as her witnesses. We hear laughter; she is smiling; the soundscape is accompanied by drums (thanks to collaborator Greg Schutte) and soothing, stringed sounds while Ndosi's voice caresses and smiles as well. We are at the seashore, and the solo is lush, joyful, like the words of a current song by artist Amel Larrieux, quoted above—a song that also honors the fact that we are water, inside and out. The dancer's arms lift and her fingers suggest ideograms of water dripping down her body and scooped through her arms—recurring motifs in this work. She leaps softly, backbends, cavorts, gestures to the kids, and they respond. Then, as swiftly as the sea changes from playground to predator, the mood onstage undergoes a sea change, and the woman and kids race off. The ensemble returns, again representing collective conflict, or humanity in its demanding guise. In movement and words they intone a litany of complaints: "What we gonna do, how we gonna roll . . . why can't you pay attention to the water? The keeping it clean and the toilets . . . we can't pay attention . . . can't take the time to think about it, gotta make time to talk about it, talk about the water: corporations stealing, politicians selling the rights, fracking, earthquake, fire water, scarred lungs of the workers: gotta change the forecast; gotta do it together!"

Without being literal about it, a nonet of dancers embodies these fears, prophesized by Ndosi's Griot—panic, chaos, destruction.

Deeper into the piece Ananya becomes a dancing Kali—the goddess of empowerment, time and change, and also destruction—or this is how I see her. Dancing like a warrior, her huge eyes grow bigger as she stares out, flares her nostrils, bares her teeth. She dances an exorcism to cleanse humankind—or is it a curse to punish for misdeeds? Then, two curtains composed of seemingly hundreds of empty plastic water bottles, their labels removed, flank the stage. Beneath the curtains the dancers, dry-mouthed, collapse in slow motion. So Dasani, Evian, and Poland Spring waters could not save us. These curtains reminded me of the bottle trees, African in origin, that African Americans in the Deep South often made by hanging glass bottles on tree limbs in their gardens. Perhaps this is Ananya's ironic reference to that tradition: glass, a natural medium, hanging on nature's trees, protected us from evil spirits, in Africanist cosmology; inversely, man-made plastic bottles, littering the earth, cannot protect us from our own misappropriation of water.

We hear Ndosi scatting, crooning, humming offstage, accompanied by a trancelike slow beat on the drums. A sustained adagio octet is danced while the lighting design changes to deep indigo-ocean blue, and further deepens to a near-purple black. Out of the darkness Ndosi-Griot returns onstage, heralding a new mood of lightness. Here I am reminded of the different moods and faces of the Africanist orishas as they appear in a ceremony, with sometimes the same human being embodying different supernatural entities. Ndosi is sometimes Oshun, orisha of fresh waters; sometimes Oya, goddess of the wind; and then also Yemaya, deity of the ocean. In this celebratory mood it's as though a fresh wind has blown away the conflicts, and the dancers, too, are sounding joyful yelps as they move. They bow to the earth and pay reverence to the heavens, facing north, south, east, and west. A chant is started:

> Dance with us
> Gather your friends
> Become the water and
> Let it flow (with Ndosi chanting "cherish the water" as a refrain).

An aura of peace, pleasure, and ease pervades the stage space and spreads through the house; audience members accept the invitation to join the artists and dance with them onstage:

Soon
We'll dive through waltzing waves
And we'll be dancing too
Into my beautiful blue, open and true
Running deep, I'm running too
I'm water inside like my blue[3]

Mohona ends on a high octave. Consciousness and mindfulness have prevailed over chaos and conflict. There is hope in collective awareness! Blue waters, the (Ndosi) blues, blue colors as concept and hue dominated these estuaries of desire. (Note: the color blue, in chakra speak, is the color of spirit and clarity.) Artists and audience are enveloped in a mood of shared strength and affirmation, with water—and dance—celebrated and reaffirmed as elements fundamental to our humanity. What was said about why we humans care about literary characters I can also say about the importance of dance works of this caliber: "We use them to sort out basic moral problems. . . . We use them in place of statistics as tools."[4]

Recently someone sent me a YouTube video of a 109-year-old survivor of Theresienstadt, the Nazi concentration camp that was sort of a stage set constructed to prove that these prisons were actually cultural family getaways. This woman, Alice Herz, says it is music that kept her alive in and beyond the camps. Toward the end of this video she simply declares, emphatically, "Music is God!"[5] Coming full circle: though Ananya asserted she is not a "god" person, I can say that she makes me believe that dance is God. And like me—her "surrogate mom"—Ananya envisions the power of dance, as signifier and signified, to move mountains. Isn't that really what she's all about?

NOTES

1   "Bertolt Brecht quotes," Goodreads, accessed June 30, 2018, https://www
    .goodreads.com/author/quotes/26853.Bertolt_Brecht.
2   "Soon," first stanza from the album *Ice Cream Everyday*, Amel/Sky Larrieux
    (words); Laru Larrieux/Ibo Butler (sound), ©Blisslife Productions, 2013.
3   "Soon."
4   Blakey Vermeule, quoted in Heidi Julavits, "The Dark Side," *New York Times*,
    May 5, 2013, 20.
5   Victoria Fine, "She was 40 When the Nazis Took Her, Now She's Outlived Them
    and Has Something Incredible to Say," *Upworthy*, December 2, 2013, http://
    www.upworthy.com/she-was-40-when-the-nazis-took-her-now-shes-outlived
    -them-and-has-something-incredible-to-say.

21

FIRE FROM DRY GRASS

NIMO HUSSEIN FARAH

Nimo Hussein Farah was part of conversations during the creative process for *Tushaanal* (2011), and her images were exhibited in the lobby as per-performance context-setting visual design. She wrote this poem as a response to that process.

Should I blame the mothers,
or the villagers who did not sing?
Who did not light a bonfire from dry grass
or roast meat in my name?
They only sing songs when boys are born
and, like a straight arrow to an enemy's chest,
boys bring freedom.
To the people of my village, a boy completes a half-empty home
but a girl is pain, born from a man's crooked rib.
So I was welcomed with silence.

22

AFFIRMATION

ANANYA CHATTERJEA

Written by Chatterjea during the creative process for *Shyamali: Sprouting Words* (2017), this poem became part of the score for the final movement of the work. It was translated by dancers in various languages and recited by dancers in English and other languages. It was also recited live during parts of the concluding dance.

Standing in the scorching sun,
we kiss the earth,
hold each other sacred.
We refuse
the narrow lanes of hatred,
spineless fear,
violence of retribution.
The closing of my imagination
is outside of power's reach.
No, no, no, no, no.
In radical love,
I dissent.
I affirm.
Yes.

CONTRIBUTORS

SURAFEL WONDIMU ABEBE serves as an assistant professor of Performance Studies and Theory at the Africa Institute of Sharjah, where he completed the inaugural Okwui Enwezor postdoctoral fellowship in Visual Arts, Performance Studies and Critical Humanities. He is a research associate at VIAD, University of Johannesburg. Surafel served at Addis Ababa University for fifteen years, holding various positions at the Faculty of Humanities, English Department, Center for African Studies, and College of Performing and Visual Arts. He is also a performer, poet, and journalist.

SHERIE C. M. APUNGU is the proud daughter of Kenyan parents who encouraged her to invent an alternative world. In 2006, Ananya-di invited Sherie to train, and consequently taught her *how* to manifest alternative worlds. Sherie danced in five company productions and serves on the board for Ananya Dance Theatre. Since 2003, Sherie has contributed to or created processes that increase access to education and health services for underserved communities globally.

ANANYA CHATTERJEA's work as choreographer, dancer, and thinker brings together contemporary dance, social justice choreography, and a philosophy of inhabiting dance fully. She is artistic director of Ananya Dance Theatre, a Twin Cities–based professional dance company of BIPOC women, womxn, and femme artists, and cofounder of the Shawngrām Institute for Performance and Social Justice. Ananya has received a 2011 Guggenheim Choreography Fellowship, 2012 and 2021 McKnight Choreography Fellowship, 2015 Sage Outstanding Dance Educator Award, 2016 Joyce Foundation Award, 2018 Urban Bush Women Choreographic Fellowship, and 2019 Dance/USA Artist Fellowship. Her second book, *Heat and Alterity in Contemporary Dance: South-South Choreographies*, which reframes understandings of contemporary dance from the perspective of choreographers from South-South communities, was published in November 2020 by Palgrave MacMillan. She is professor of dance at the University of Minnesota, Twin Cities.

RENÉE COPELAND performed with Ananya Dance Theatre from 2010 to 2020, composing the original score for *Sutrajāl* (2019). Renée is cofounder of the performance art duo Hiponymous and a founding member of breakin'-based company BRKFST. She is a poet, a multi-instrumentalist, a singer-songwriter, and a McKnight Fellowship for Dance (2018) recipient. She reclaims and practices Sicilian folk art/magic.

THOMAS F. DEFRANTZ received the 2017 Outstanding Research in Dance award from the Dance Studies Association; directs SLIPPAGE: Performance, Culture, Technology, a research group that explores emerging technology in live performance applications; and contributed a voice-over for a permanent installation at the Smithsonian African American Museum. DeFrantz believes in our shared capacity to do better and to engage our creative spirit for a collective good that is antiracist, antihomophobic, proto-feminist, and queer affirming.

PATRICIA DEROCHER is a multimodal educator who left academia in 2019 to focus on more embodied forms of knowledge production. Trish's practice, Transformative Consciousness Coaching and Consulting, blends social justice philosophies, mindfulness, and somatic experiencing. Trish is currently working on establishing the Center for Transformative Consciousness in Vermont, a holistic wellness and educational center for activists, cultural workers, healers, changemakers, and innovators. Trish's book, *Transnational Testimonios: The Politics of Collective Knowledge Production*, was published in 2018.

JIGNA DESAI is professor in the Department of Gender, Women, and Sexuality Studies and the Asian American Studies Program at the University of Minnesota. She has written extensively on issues of race, gender, and sexuality in media and cultural production. She is the cofounder and codirector of Minnesota Youth Story Squad. She is dedicated to speculating on what a transformative and liberatory university might be.

BRENDA DIXON-GOTTSCHILD, PhD—professor emerita of dance studies at Temple University, author of four books and numerous articles on dance as a measure of culture and a barometer of social justice—writes, performs, and consults in the service of undoing racism.

NIMO HUSSEIN FARAH is an artist and activist who uses language to express things she finds too confusing. Her current undertaking is to develop her skills as an orator while blending Somali and English. Her poetry and short stories have been published in *Water-Stone Review*, the *Saint Paul Almanac*, and the *Loft Inroads* chapter book. As a storyteller she has shared her words at the Black Dog Café, the Loft, and Pillsbury House. She cofounded SALLI (Somali Arts Language and Leadership Institute). She is a 2014 Loft spoken word immersion fellow, a 2014 Bush fellow, a recipient of the Intermedia Arts VERVE grant, and a 2016 National Arts Strategies fellow.

RODERICK A. FERGUSON teaches at Yale University and is the author of *One-Dimensional Queer* (Polity, 2019), *We Demand: The University and Student Protests* (University of California Press, 2017), *The Reorder of Things: The University and Its Pedagogies of Minority Difference* (University of Minnesota Press, 2012), and *Aberrations in Black: Toward a Queer of Color Critique* (University of Minnesota Press, 2004).

SHANNON GIBNEY is a writer, educator, activist, and the author of *See No Color* (Carolrhoda Lab, 2015) and *Dream Country* (Dutton, 2018), young adult novels that won Minnesota Book Awards in 2016 and 2019. Gibney is faculty in English at Minneapolis College, where she teaches writing. A Bush artist and McKnight writing fellow, her new novel, *Botched*, explores themes of transracial adoption through speculative memoir (Dutton, 2022).

ZENZELE ISOKE is associate professor and chair of gender, women, and sexuality studies at the University of Minnesota. Drawing from the ideas of black decolonial thinkers, Isoke writes on the contemporary history of cities through the political struggles of self-identified black/queer women of the African diaspora. Writing across the fields of geography, political science, and urban anthropology, her scholarship spans several cities in the United States, the Middle East, and the Caribbean. Her book project, "Dissenting Lives: Black Femaleness, Racial Justice, Activist Praxis," uses decolonial poetics to theorize and explore black feminist politics through the mediums of collaborative art making, breath and meditation, and conventional grass-roots organizing in Minneapolis.

SIMI KANG is a queer, mixed Sikh American community collaborator, educator, artist, and scholar. Kang's work centers Southeast Asian American collaborative resistance as a site for imagining environmentally and economically just futures in Louisiana. In this work of collaborative resistance, Kang fights on behalf of resident expertise, ecosystem-level solidarity, and collective care. She is an assistant professor of Gender Studies at the University of Victoria, BC.

D. SOYINI MADISON is professor emeritus in the Department of Performance Studies at Northwestern University in Evanston, Illinois. Madison's scholarship and artistic practice focus on the intersections of labor activism, political economy of human rights, environmental justice, and indigenous performance tactics. Her book *Acts of Activism: Human Rights and Radical Performance* is based on local activists in Ghana, West Africa; recent books include *Critical Ethnography: Method, Ethics, and Performance* and *Performed Ethnography and Communication: Improvisation and Embodied Experience.*

DAVID MURA is a memoirist, novelist, poet, and literary critic. He has written the novel *Famous Suicides of the Japanese Empire* and two memoirs: *Turning Japanese: Memoirs of a Sansei*, a New York Times Notable Book of the Year, and *Where the Body Meets Memory: An Odyssey of Race, Sexuality, and Identity.* He's also written four books of poetry. His newest work is A *Stranger's Journey: Race, Identity and Narrative Craft in Writing.*

RICHA NAGAR's multilingual and antidisciplinary work blends scholarship, creative writing, theater, and activism to build alliances with people's struggles and to engage questions of ethics, responsibility, and justice. Her eight books include the trilogy *Playing with Fire: Feminist Thought and Activism through Seven Lives in India, Muddying the Waters: Coauthoring Feminisms across Scholarship and Activism*, and *Hungry Translations: Relearning the World through Radical Vulnerability.* She is a founding editor of *AGITATE! Unsettling Knowledges.*

MANKWE NDOSI is a culture worker, using creative practice to nurture community, ancestors, and the earth. She is part of a field of artists embedding creative practice into civic work. Her efforts have included interdisciplinary performance, arts-rooted community gatherings, active racial equity workshops with city housing inspectors, great black music series, and developing group healing workshops to support personal transformation from the inside out.

NAIMAH PETIGNY is a Black feminist scholar, dancer, and social justice educator. She grew up as a youth organizer in Western Massachusetts and danced in West African and Afro-Caribbean performance ensembles. Naimah graduated from Vassar College in 2014 and completed her PhD in gender, women, and sexuality studies at the University of Minnesota. Her scholarship centers expansive notions of blackness, embodiment, memory, and performance, and her dissertation, "The Hold Is Also an Embrace: Readings in Contemporary Black Feminist Performance," centers queer, contemporary Black feminist dance theater to rethink the relationship between performativity and Black liberation. She is currently assistant professor in literary arts and studies at the Rhode Island School of Design.

TONI SHAPIRO-PHIM, associate professor of creativity, the arts, and social transformation and assistant director of peacebuilding and the arts at Brandeis University, received a PhD in cultural anthropology from Cornell University. Her research, writing, teaching, and applied work focus on migration and displacement, war, genocide and gender violence, and the relationship between the arts and social justice concerns, with publications on arts and human rights, dance and transitional justice, community building, and antiviolence activism.

CHITRA VAIRAVAN is a contemporary dancer/choreographer of Tamil / South Indian–American descent. Her embodied practice and experimental process is rooted in deep listening, spatial observation, freedoms, poetry, vulnerability, and ancestral memory. Vairavan began her contemporary dance foundation as a founding member, rehearsal director, and principal with Ananya Dance Theatre over fourteen seasons. She continues to engage, explore, and create works as an artist and arts educator.

HUI NIU WILCOX is professor of sociology, women's studies, and critical studies of race/ethnicity at Saint Catherine University. Since 2004, Hui has been teaching at Saint Catherine University and dancing with Ananya Dance Theatre. Her research has focused on the sociology of dance, especially in connection to immigrant identities, race/ethnicity, multiculturalism, and transnational feminisms. Hui is currently studying the historical contexts and sociopolitical implications of dance in Ethiopia and its diaspora.

ALESSANDRA LEBEA WILLIAMS is a dancer-scholar and assistant professor of dance at Rutgers University–New Brunswick. She researches dance, Asian and African American culture, and gender and queer theory. She has been awarded fellowships such as the Inclusive Excellence Fellowship (University of Wisconsin–Whitewater, 2018–2019), Eugene V. Cota-Robles Fellowship (University of California, Los Angeles, 2010–14), and the Mellon Mays Undergraduate Fellowship (Macalester College, 2005–7). As an artist in Ananya Dance Theatre, Williams has performed nationally and internationally in eight of the company's productions: *Sutrajāl* (2019), *Shaatranga* (2018), *Shyamali* (2017), *Horidraa* (2016), *Roktim* (2015), *Moreechika* (2012), *Ashesh Barsha* (2009), and *Pipaashaa* (2007).

INDEX

A

Alliances: Ananya Dance Theatre (ADT), 26, 27; artists, 217; asymmetrical, 5; building, 3; friendships and, 201; justice movements, 65; neoliberal, 133, 159; paradoxical, 129; South, 138

allies, 66, 196, 237

Amenshewa, Askale, 132

Americanness, 68, 105, 160

Amkpa, Awam, 31

Ananya Dance Theatre (ADT): *Aahvaan: Invoking the Cities,* 173–74, 175, 177; activism, 26, 64, 65, 106, 115, 124, 145, 212; aesthetics, 170; African American experience, 95; artists of color, 33–34, 69, 121, 169, 217, 218; ArtsLab, 37; BIPOC solidarity, 151; Black and brown histories, 98; Black and brown oppressions, 92; Black resistance politics, 105; Black women's collective history, 117; Blackness, 105, 108–9, 110, 112, 113–14, 117, 122–23; body memory, 121; Carlos, 75, 80, 83, 84, 85, 86; Chatterjea, 204–5, 206, 208, 215; coalitions among BIPOC communities, 16; collaborative nature, 61, 75, 80, 106; collective, 147; communal resistance, 187; community building, 241; community of singularities, 228; creative processes, 4, 15, 16, 115, 146, 187; creative resistance, 232; Crossing Boundaries (CB) and, 128, 129–30, 132–33, 138, 140, 159; cultural insurgency, 106–7; Daak, 221; dance forms, 209; dance methodologies, 107; dance moves, 120; dancers, 38, 40, 56, 64, 91, 114; decolonization, 69; East African communities and, 131–32; Ethiopian National Theatre, 134, 139, 166; evolution of, 23, 26, 52; feminism, 211–12; feminist aesthetics, 64; field trip, 216; first work, 27–28; food sovereignty, 145, 150–51; fostering connections, 234; generating hope, 17; global gender struggle, 104; healing, 58, 63; history, 25; identity, 59–60, 61; Indian dance, 205; introduction, 3; *Kshoy!/Decay!,* 104; love, 63, 75; mapping out struggles, 210; mission, 3; *Mohona: Estuaries of Desire,* 246; movement, 38, 61, 64, 106–8, 115, 116, 117, 148; multiyear

projects, 31; *Neel: Blutopias of Radical Dreaming,* 52; Odissi footwork, 116, 185; Ordway Theatre, 175–76; organizational strategies, 4; philosophy of, 52; political identities, 207; politics, 62, 63, 105, 161, 170, 229; practices, 16–17, 105, 107, 108, 174, 214; praxis, 145, 146, 148, 150, 155, 211; project, 229, 230; rage, 63; *Roktim: Nurture Incarnadine,* 128, 133, 134, 135, 138, 150–55, 156–57, 163; safe space, 57; safety of artists, 41; *Shyamali: Sprouting Words,* 185; social justice, 23, 29, 37, 38, 52, 106, 214, 217; socially accountable artistic practice, 36; spiritual activists, 58; staged stories of humanity, 135–36; starting out, 250; struggles of, 23; systemic violence, 57–58; tenth anniversary, 7, 52; transnational feminist storytelling, 107, 132, 156; Twin Cities, 3, 105–6, 107–8, 109, 122, 147, 168, 170; vigil, 67; Wilcox, 56, 60, 61, 63, 69, 218; Williams, 170–72; Yellow Movement (YM) and, 136–37, 139; yogic movements, 118–19; Yorchhā, 115, 118. *See also* ADT performances

ancestors, 65, 106, 117, 146, 200

ancestral, 10, 104, 119, 243

anti-Blackness, 107, 111, 140

anticapitalist, 211

antihomophobic cultural production, 28

antiracism, 28, 59, 66, 76, 96, 166, 187, 211

antisexism, 28

Anzaldúa, Gloria, 58

appropriations, 15, 36, 251

Apungu, Sherie C. M., 77, 85–87, 88–89, 173*fig.,* 202–3

Arbery, Ahmaud, 76

The Archive and the Repertoire: Performing Cultural Memory in the Americas, 9

Arreola, Dora, 28

The Art of War, 175

artistic excellence, 3, 23, 52, 170, 177

arts activism, 170, 177

Ashesh Barsha: Unending Monsoon, 30, 76, 90, 251

Asia, 29, 117, 173, 190, 195

Asian Americans: alienation, 65; artists, 16, 170; Asian American studies, 161; bodies, 159; descriptors, 59; identity,

violence (*continued*)
    survivors, 137; systemic, 11, 31, 57–58,
    82, 215, 221, 251; unspeakable acts of, 218
visibility, 214
vulnerability, 241, 242, 243

W

war, 85, 91, 102, 141n5, 143n26, 166, 194,
    218–19
water: *Aahvaan: Invoking the Cities,* 173;
    bottles, 254; capitalism, 31; ceremony,
    248; contemporary issues, 119; dioxins
    in, 122; *Duurbaar: Journeys into Hori-
    zon,* 29, 63, 248–50; emotional life of,
    251; hauling, 108; insecurities, 145; jus-
    tice, 66, 67; labor of women, 171; meta-
    phor, 63, 228, 248; *Mohona: Estuaries
    of Desire,* 63, 76, 179–81, 248, 250; para-
    dox, 63–64; pollution, 76; potable, 11;
    protectors, 10, 145; resources, 93, 149;
    river, 111–12; song, 68; stolen, 113; wish-
    ing well, 174
Wells-Barnett, Ida B., 101n58
white supremacy, 76, 105, 122, 124, 131, 165, 189
whiteness: American, 160; byproducts of,
    124; Eurocentric conversations, 189;
    irrelevance, 49; Minnesota, 47; mulit-
    culturalism, 120; relationships to, 59;
    structures of, 14; surrounded by, 192;
    value of, 52
wholeness, 32, 56, 58, 67
Wilcox, Hui Niu: Alexander and, 58, 60,
    61–62, 68; Ananya Dance Theatre
    (ADT), 7, 56–57, 60, 61, 63, 69, 218;
    China, 59, 160; daughters, 63, 67, 92;
    Ethiopia, 159, 161–67; feminist frame-
    work, 92; healing, 58; hyperfemininity,
    74; *Mohona: Estuaries of Desire,* 251*fig.*;
    Moreechika: Season of Mirage, 77, 78,
    90, 173*fig.*; *Neel: Blutopias of Radical
    Dreaming,* 14; paradigm shift, 218;
    performances, 91; puppetry and, 89,
    90; Saint Catherine University, 59, 60;
    Shyamali: Sprouting Words, 206*fig.*,
    230*fig.*; social justice, 56; sociology, 56,
    59, 68; solo, 253; stereotypes, 160–61;
    Sutrajāl: Revelations of Gossamer,
    107*fig.*; "the Empress of Fortune and
    Whimsy," 174

Williams: African Americans, 170, 171;
    Alessandra Lebea, Carlos and, 75–78,
    89–90; Ananya Dance Theatre (ADT),
    170–72; Carlos and, 89–90; Gibney
    and, 171; Macalester College, 171; Min-
    neapolis, 170; *Pipaashaa: Extreme
    Thirst,* 60, 76, 90; puppetry, 86*fig.*,
    173*fig.*; *Shyamali: Sprouting Words,*
    206*fig.*, 230*fig.*; *Sutrajāl: Revelations
    of Gossamer,* 186*fig.*
Wilson, August, 169, 176
Woldeamanuale, Negest L., 49*fig.*
women and femmes: agency for, 34;
    alliance-building, 9; Ananya Dance
    Theatre (ADT), 3, 23, 76, 147; artistic
    practices, 78; audiences, 38, 39; descrip-
    tors, 18n1, 34; disappearance of, 30;
    displacement, 88; empowerment, 31;
    ensemble dancing, 16; exploitation, 92;
    garments, 93; global issues, 4; histo-
    ries, 17, 38, 39–40; Indian dance forms,
    76, 77; multiple communities of, 6;
    multiple oppressions, 76; resistance
    movements, 97; social justice, 39;
    space for, 27, 28; stories of, 13, 31, 33;
    struggles against systemic violence,
    11; transformative power, 17; work of,
    6, 8, 10, 32, 37
women of color: Ananya Dance Theatre
    (ADT), 69, 121, 137, 138, 217–18; bodies,
    128, 132, 134, 159; call for action, 57;
    contemporary moment for, 216; dance
    group, 47; descriptor, 18n1; experiences
    as, 232; feminism, 196, 204–5, 207, 208,
    209, 210–12; histories, 117; history of,
    56; indigenous racisms, 60; inequities,
    214; laboring subjects, 153; lives of, 54;
    marginality, 131, 136; movement build-
    ing, 53; queer, 6; spaces for, 201; stories,
    76, 116; taking up space, 119; trauma,
    119; traumatic experiences, 57
Women's Environmental Institute, 29, 172,
    251
women's studies, 62
"Work Women Do," 32
working-class, 6, 11, 59, 133
workshops, 28, 38, 60, 61, 64–65, 66, 145, 161
Worku, Azeb, 127
Worku, Meaza, 127